BIBLE AND NOVEL

Bible and Novel

Narrative Authority and the Death of God

NORMAN VANCE

UNIVERSITY PRESS

Great Clarendon Street, Oxford, OX2 6DP,
United Kingdom

Oxford University Press is a department of the University of Oxford.
It furthers the University's objective of excellence in research, scholarship,
and education by publishing worldwide. Oxford is a registered trade mark of
Oxford University press in the UK and in certain other countries

© Norman Vance 2013

The moral rights of the author have been asserted

First Edition published in 2013

Impression: 1

All rights reserved. No part of this publication may be reproduced, stored in
a retrieval system, or transmitted, in any form or by any means, without the
prior permission in writing of Oxford University Press, or as expressly permitted
by law, by licence or under terms agreed with the appropriate reprographics
rights organization. Enquiries concerning reproduction outside the scope of the
above should be sent to the Rights Department, Oxford University Press, at the
address above

You must not circulate this work in any other form
and you must impose this same condition on any acquirer

British Library Cataloguing in Publication Data

Data available

ISBN 978-0-19-968057-3

Printed and bound by
CPI Group (UK) Ltd, Croydon, CR0 4YY

Contents

Preface	vi
Acknowledgements	xi
1. God and the Bible, Secularisms and Novels	1
2. The Authority of the Bible	30
3. The Crisis of Biblical Authority	59
4. George Eliot's Secular Scriptures	92
5. Thomas Hardy: The Church or Christianity	114
6. Mary Ward and the Problems of History	135
7. Rider Haggard: Adventures with the Numinous	161
8. Conclusion: Authority, the Novel, and God	190
Bibliography	200
Index	227

Preface

We have always told stories about ourselves to ourselves. We inherit various narratives about life and culture, whether Bible stories, novels, histories, or master-narratives such as the idea of progress or the onset of modernity. These tend to be commended to us on the authority of parents and mentors, or tradition or fashion. They are much studied by theologians, literary critics, historians, and social scientists, to all of whom the present book is addressed. But in his counter-biblical *Back to Methuselah* (1921) the sceptical George Bernard Shaw makes one of his characters from the future ask why people 'persist in making up silly stories about the world and trying to act as if they were true'.[1] Almost inevitably, as we grow older we start to wonder about some of the familiar stories: broadening perspectives can lead to questions and sometimes to downright repudiation. That process of interrogation may be itself the basis of a new narrative, or it may lead to critical re-examination and new understanding of an apparently familiar narrative.

Adults have (usually) grown out of belief in Santa Claus, or fairies, and that aspect of the maturing process provided pioneer sociologists such as Max Weber with a model for one of the key narratives of emergent modernity that we have inherited, what has been variously described as 'the disenchantment of the world' (Weber's own phrase),[2] or 'secularization', or the growing acceptance of the 'death of God'. There is another broadly similar narrative, cherished by generations of literary critics, about the rise of the novel as the successful struggle of the unillusioned real against the enchantments and delusions of fantasy and romance, not to mention the supernatural. It has even been claimed, in the words of the Hungarian critic Georg Lukács, that 'the novel is the epic of a world that has been abandoned by God'.[3] The two narratives have often seemed to

---

[1] Bernard Shaw, *Back to Methuselah: A Metabiological Pentateuch* (London: Constable, 1925), Part 4, Act 1, p. 159.

[2] Max Weber, 'Science as a Vocation' [1919], in H. H. Gerth and C. Wright Mills, eds, *From Max Weber: Essays in Sociology* (London: Routledge, 1948), p. 155.

[3] Georg Lukács, *The Theory of the Novel* (1916), trans. Anna Bostock (London: Merlin Press, 1971), p. 88.

Preface vii

support each other, particularly in nineteenth-century England, where they were presided over by apparently post-Christian, self-consciously realist novelists such as George Eliot and Thomas Hardy. But our world has grown older, and our perspectives have altered, since the time when in the pride of their self-conscious modernity people started to tell the stories of the disenchantment of the world and the rise of the novel. Can we still believe these now-traditional stories? How do we read them now? Postmodernists or even post-secularists, or whatever we are now, we have embarked on a new round of interrogation and revision. Among social scientists and literary critics alike there are various stirrings of disenchantment with disenchantment, and new intuitions that despite the apparent triumphs of the secular we may still need the category of the religious and some kind of religious narrative if we are to understand and explain our present and indeed our past.[4] Reconsidering and reimagining rather than simply repudiating the Bible may be a symptom or aspect of the same concerns, and it may be that the process started earlier than we think. Timothy Larsen's recent study *A People of One Book: The Bible and the Victorians* has produced evidence that even Victorian atheists and agnostics read their Bibles and were closer to biblical idiom than has usually been acknowledged.[5] This book is offered as a contribution to the continuing process of rereading, interrogation and revision, encouraged by the emergence, or perhaps more accurately the re-emergence, of what is now identified as post-secular awareness. So far the category of the 'post-secular', like the category of the 'postmodern' out of which in a sense it has evolved with the underacknowledged support of the social theorist Jürgen Habermas,[6] has been invoked mainly to signal gaps and perceived inadequacies in existing descriptions of our social and cultural condition. There is uncertainty about whether 'post-secular' should be taken to mean that we are moving on and away from secular society,

---

[4] See, for example, Steven D. Smith, *The Disenchantment of Secular Discourse* (Cambridge, Mass.: Harvard University Press, 2010); Terry Eagleton, *Reason, Faith, and Revolution: Reflections on the God Debate* (New Haven: Yale University Press, 2009); Bill Brown, 'The Dark Wood of Postmodernity (Space, Faith, Allegory)', *PMLA* 120 (May 2005), 734–50.

[5] Timothy Larsen, *A People of One Book: The Bible and the Victorians* (Oxford: Oxford University Press, 2011).

[6] See Jürgen Habermas et al., *An Awareness of What is Missing: Faith and Reason in A Post-Secular Age* (Cambridge: Polity Press, 2010).

viii   *Preface*

that we can witness a significant change in the circumstances or context in which life is now lived—an alleged change that has been disputed[7]—or whether it indicates mainly a refinement of our conceptual vocabulary, a more sophisticated and nuanced language of description that goes beyond the simplifications and false certainties associated with the alleged but increasingly uncertain triumph of the secular. This second, more modest, possibility could help us engage more effectively not just with the contemporary world but with earlier mental and moral worlds we may have overmodernized or oversecularized and may not have fully understood. Literary commentators, tiring of the postmodern, have begun to invoke the postsecular in discussions of contemporary fiction on both sides of the Atlantic to describe engagements with or intimations of the numinous or of disconcerting otherness.[8] But for the moment they have mostly been less willing to apply the 'post-secular turn' to earlier quasi-secular writing or to entertain the possibility that, even when scientific and secular modernity seemed to be triumphantly in the ascendant in the later nineteenth century, some novels could provide ways of seeing beyond the narrowly secular and of reimagining the religious.

This book offers post-secular readings of some nineteenth- and early twentieth-century English novelists as a way of rereading the familiar but possibly flawed and inadequate narratives of secularization, the apparent eclipse of biblical authority, and the rise of the novel, suggesting they might not tell the whole story or tell it in ways that are still helpful to us. Are secular novels simply chronicles of the world without God or can they still be religious by other means? Can they anticipate some of the insights of some contemporary theologians by reimagining and reformulating rather than abandoning essentially religious and biblical themes and insights?

A key aspect of the narrative of secularization in Britain is the subnarrative of the waning authority of the Bible, an ironic coda to the earlier Protestant triumphalist narrative celebrating scriptural

---

[7] See Arie L. Molendijk et al., eds, *Exploring the Postsecular: The Religious, the Political and the Urban* (Leiden, Brill, 2010), esp. James A. Beckford, 'The Uses of Religion in Public Institutions', pp. 382–98.

[8] John A. McClure, *Partial Faiths: Postsecular Fiction in the Age of Pynchon and Morrison* (Athens, Georgia: University of Georgia Press, 2007); Jo Carruthers and Andrew Tate, eds, *Spiritual Identities: Literature and the Post-Secular Imagination* (Bern: Peter Lang, 2010).

Preface

authority freed at last from the dead hand of ecclesiastical tradition. But the familiar, oversimplified, much-mythologized narratives of the rise and the fall of scriptural authority, more closely entangled with each other than is usually realized, need to be revisited and read more warily, which is attempted in chapters two and three of the present study. The evidence of various different kinds of authority attributed to the Bible and of different ways of reading and rereading it leads into consideration of the novel as—sometimes—another way of reading God and the Bible. The second part of the book rereads selected English novelists, all of conventionally Anglican religious nurture (whatever happened later), as they tell new stories that appropriate and reimagine aspects of biblical narrative.

Among the novelists, George Eliot is given pride of place in Chapter 4, both as a pioneer 'post-Christian' novelist (or so the story goes) and as a scholarly critic and translator who had already reflected on the reflections of others on meaning and authority in the scriptures (not an obvious concern of contemporaries such as Dickens), before turning to write her own narratives. It is easy to read her novels—which engage with the growing good of the world rather than the kingdom of God—as secular scriptures, or replacement bibles. But these novels, and those of the more acerbic and overtly iconoclastic Thomas Hardy a little later, can also be read as radically Christian rather than post-Christian texts, religiously grounded 'experiments in life' (as Eliot tentatively called them) observed under rapidly changing moral and historical conditions.[9] Even if the novel is indeed the epic of a world abandoned by God, which is open to dispute, it can still inherit and develop the biblical habit of storytelling with a purpose along with the epic and biblical responsibility to engage with and embody a particular history. *Robert Elsmere*, and Mary Ward's other less familiar novels, can be read as stories with a grand purpose, attempted imaginative histories sensitive to the historical contexts and concerns of scriptural narrative, incorporating the recent history of moral and religious thought, complicated and enriched rather than crushed by challenges to orthodoxy. The further complication of other faiths and cultures and unfamiliar religious traditions, encountered by nineteenth-century Christian missionaries

---

[9] Eliot to Dr J. F. Payne, 25 January 1876, *The George Eliot Letters*, ed. G. S. Haight, 9 vols (Oxford: Clarendon, 1954–78), VI, 216–17.

and by secular anthropologists, provided Rider Haggard with exotic subject matter for his enduringly popular religiously inflected fictions and provided his readers with unexpected stimulus and opportunity to reimagine the religious sublime presented in and developed from biblical narrative.

Acknowledgements

This study and its author have benefited greatly from conversations drawing on the generosity and learning of many friends, colleagues, and students at the University of Sussex and elsewhere, notably Peter Abbs, Gavin Ashenden, John Barton, Adriana Bontea, Andrew Chitty, Saul Dubow, Henri Durel, Robert Fraser, Knud Haakonssen, Mary Hammond, Andrew Holmes, Margarita Kohlenbach, Vicky Lebeau, David Livingstone, Richard Murphy, Bob Owens, Gillian Piggott, Vincent Quinn, Nicholas Royle, Louise Schweitzer, Lindsay Smith, Daniel Steuer, Naomi Tadmor, Jenny Bourne Taylor, Fiona Turner, Martin Van Gelderen, Aakanksha Virkar-Yates, Keith Whitelam, Julian Wolfreys, and Brian Young. To these I would add John Burrow, Mary Dove, John Lowerson, Stephen Medcalf, and my parents Myrtle and William Vance, who all provided support, stimulus, and good counsel but did not live to see this work complete. As always, my greatest debt is to my wife, Brenda.

I am grateful for opportunities to try out some of the material of this book in guest lectures or papers at various conferences and other gatherings, in Bedford, Florence, Lewes, London, Loughborough, Lyons, the University of Sussex, and Worthing. Earlier versions of parts of some chapters were published in my contributions to Andrew Hass, David Jasper, and Elisabeth Jay, et al., eds, *The Oxford Handbook of English Literature and Theology* (Oxford: Oxford University Press, 2007) and W. R. Owens and Stuart Sim (eds.), *Reception, Appropriation, Recollection: Bunyan's* Pilgrim's Progress (Bern: Peter Lang, 2007).

1

God and the Bible, Secularisms and Novels

'Gott selbst ist todt' (God Himself is dead)
(G. W. F. Hegel, 1802)

'Dieu est mort! Le ciel est vide... Pleurez! Enfants, vous n'avez
plus de père!' (God is dead, heaven is empty—weep children,
you no longer have a father.)

(Gérard de Nerval, 1844)[1]

If God was dead there would indeed be tears. If what was dead was
not God but some familiar understandings of God and of the Bible
there might still be tears, but there might also be reimaginings, new
stories developing new understanding. There were. Some of them
took the form of novels.

In France and Germany, by the 1840s rationalism, revolutionary
excitement, and romantic despair had stimulated radical speculation
and critical biblical scholarship to the point of unsettling traditional
religious belief. It was, as usual, less dramatic in England. Even so,
doubts were stirring. In 1846 George Eliot was completing her translation from the German of David Strauss's harshly demythologizing
Life of Jesus. But she was sick at heart, 'Strauss-sick'.[2] Too much was
being destroyed. Her continuing attachment to the human Christ in
the now-challenged gospel narrative complicated the consciously

---

[1] G. W. F. Hegel, *Faith and Knowledge* (1802), trans. Walter Cerf and H. S. Harris
(Albany: State University of New York Press, 1977), p. 190, referring to the effect of
negative philosophical constructions of infinity; Gérard de Nerval, epigraph to 'Le
Christ aux Oliviers' (1844), *Oeuvres complètes*, ed. Jean Guillaume and Charles
Pichois, 3 vols (Paris: Gallimard, 1989), III, p. 439.

[2] Gordon S. Haight, *George Eliot: A Biography* (Oxford: Clarendon Press, 1968),
pp. 58–9, quoting a letter of February 1846.

2   *God and the Bible, Secularisms and Novels*

secular humanism of the novels she went on to write. Other novels and novelists registered and acted on some of the same complicated feelings, even when they were committed, in varying degrees, to a largely post-Christian or at least post-ecclesiastical modernity.

Eliot had lost confidence not just in scripture as conventionally understood but in any providential direction in human affairs. For her, as for other writers and thinkers of her time, this called for some kind of replacement or restatement, some new, more secular, narrative of ultimate purpose and incremental human improvement, outlining and sustaining progress not necessarily towards the City of God but towards the possible perfection of the city of man. Could versions of this reimagined narrative be plotted in and through the novel? Could novels take on something of the authority once vested in the scriptures? How much could be transferred from the old to the new? Were secular hopes the end of religion, or the new religion? These questions can be explored not just in the writings of George Eliot but in Thomas Hardy, Mary Ward, and Rider Haggard, all bestselling novelists, all disposed to explore ultimate questions in their own way.

Social and moral as well as religious issues were at stake. Bold spirits began to ask whether—if God was dead—everything was permitted. This fundamental question was rather anxiously debated in 1877 in the leading periodical *The Nineteenth Century* under the heading 'The Influence on Morality of a Decline in Religious Belief'. The issue was European rather than just English: it is squarely confronted as a speculation attributed to the intellectual Ivan Karamazov in Dostoevsky's last great novel *The Brothers Karamazov*, published in 1880 and available soon after in French translation. Friedrich Nietzsche proclaimed his own version of the 'death of God' in 1882.[3] He rather resented English half-measures, but backhandedly acknowledged the new moral and cultural importance of novelists and of the novel form when he castigated the 'moralising little women *à la* Eliot' who had got rid of the Christian God but still clung to a residually Christian morality and so annoyingly softened and obscured the bleak and brilliant clarity of his vision of a transvalued and transformed modern world.[4]

---

[3] See Sir James Stephen et al., 'The influence upon morality of a decline in religious belief', *The Nineteenth Century* 1 (April, May, 1877), 331–58, 531–46. Nietzsche's first use of the phrase 'death of God' was in 1882 in *The Gay Science*, Book 3, section 108, trans. Josefine Naukhoff (Cambridge: Cambridge University Press, 2001), p. 109.

[4] Friedrich Nietzsche, *Twilight of the Idols* (1889), trans. Duncan Large (Oxford: Oxford University Press, 1998), p. 45.

God and the Bible, Secularisms and Novels   3

As Nietzsche had realized, the English novel had now come of age as a morally serious art form: Eliot and other thoughtful novelists were continuing the process of redeeming fiction from perceived cultural marginality ('only a novel') and accusations of triviality or worse, and helping to secure its importance in moral discourse. Despite an official rhetoric of repudiation, aspects of the sometimes frivolous or fantastic romance form were often adapted for this purpose. But a fierce new intellectual honesty empowered a retreat from much of the false sentiment of merely escapist romance, and the increasingly challenged confidence associated with biblical literalism and narratives of the miraculous, to develop through the dynamics of plot and character more nuanced perceptions of the complex processes of human interaction and historical change, and those elusive intimations of the transcendent that the twentieth century would eventually describe as 'the numinous'.

AFTER THE BIBLE

In the new age of Darwinian biology, and the progressive social science of George Eliot's mentor Herbert Spencer, identifying any kind of change or development, even developments in thinking about God, tended to evoke analogies from the life sciences and attract the language of 'evolution'.[5] The more thoughtful novelists could be seen as engaging formally and thematically with the possibilities of moral, social, and spiritual evolution. Gillian Beer has explored some of the implications of this in her excellent study *Darwin's Plots*.[6] Yet it has not always been sufficiently remarked that such 'evolutionary' plots appropriate some of the authority and sense of direction once attributed to the Bible and to biblical narrative, whether encountered directly or in mediated form. Stories of this kind participate in, and complicate, the progressive secular narrative, which in effect appropriated and reformulated the eschatological grand narrative of

---

[5] See, for example, Grant Allen, *The Evolution of the Idea of God* (London: Grant Richards, 1897), and, more generally, John Burrow, *Evolution and Society* (Cambridge: Cambridge University Press, 1966).

[6] Gillian Beer, *Darwin's Plots: Evolutionary Narrative in Darwin, George Eliot and Nineteenth-century Fiction* (London: Routledge, 1983).

4 God and the Bible, Secularisms and Novels

collective 'salvation history' (what German theologians describe as *heilsgeschichte*) culminating in the new heaven and the new earth described in the book of Revelation. This narrative pattern, deduced from but not fully explicit in scripture, had been tidied up and formalized for the benefit of the Church in the early fifth century in St Augustine's *City of God*. The novelists and other writers could also appropriate and transform biblical narratives of individual quest or trial such as the stories of Abraham and Job or the lyrical desolations and exaltation of the psalmist. Augustine's autobiographical *Confessions*, saturated in the scriptures, provided an influential link between biblical and fictional narrative by supplying an exemplary personal narrative history of the restless pilgrim soul finding ultimate rest in God. There were, of course, many subsequent versions and appropriations of essentially biblical narrative materials, notably (for English readers) Bunyan's *The Pilgrim's Progress* and Milton's *Paradise Lost*, enduringly popular works, both of which attracted imaginative illustrators such as the early Victorian John Martin (1789–1854). The theme of secular pilgrimage in Victorian fiction has been critically addressed by Barry Qualls,[7] but that is only one aspect of the narrative transformation of biblical material in nineteenth-century novels.

Augustine's linear view of history, refuting pagan theories of eternal recurrence without beginning or end, looked forward to and encompassed the 'last things' (*ta eschata* in biblical Greek), animated by faith and hope and the vision of the Kingdom of God. 'Eschatology' and the Christian hope had been part of the upbringing of influential thinkers such as Hegel and it has indeed been suggested that religion was the underlying condition of possibility for Hegel's historical thought.[8] The German philosopher Karl Löwith, writing in 1949, argued more generally that modern historical consciousness—including the various philosophies of history developed by Hegel, Comte, Marx, and others—could in a sense be seen as secularized eschatology.[9] The idea was pursued a few years later in the German political scientist Eric Voegelin's ambitious and idiosyncratic theory of 'Gnostic' eschatology. It was fairly generally accepted that the

[7] Barry Qualls, *The Secular Pilgrims of Victorian Fiction* (Cambridge: Cambridge University Press, 1982).

[8] Emil L. Fackenheim, *The Religious Dimension in Hegel's Thought* (Bloomington and London: Indiana University Press, 1967), pp. 22–3.

[9] Karl Löwith, *Meaning in History* [1949] (Chicago: University of Chicago Press, 1957).

God and the Bible, Secularisms and Novels 5

unrealized millenarian expectations in the early Church of Christ's second coming had been defused in St Augustine's *City of God*, where they are accommodated into a theology of Christ's abiding presence in the Church, which was even now the kingdom of Christ.[10] Voegelin suggested that, even so, millenarian expectations had never really gone away, and described at some length the millenarian thought of the twelfth-century mystic Joachim of Fiore. He claimed that impatient millenarian expectation tended to surface with potentially disastrous effect as radical alienation from the present order of the world and determination to transform it in the here and now. This immanentist eschatology represented a kind of deluded self-divinization, he maintained, expressed as activist commitment to the immediate redemption of man and society, and its most sinister modern forms were Marxism and Nazism.

Voegelin's hostile, indeed incipiently paranoid, account of modern immanentist eschatology, popular with the American Right, takes a promising idea several stages too far. It has more to say about Cold War mentalities than about secular modernity. In the 1960s even Löwith's less extreme theory of secularized eschatology was systematically challenged by another German philosopher, Hans Blumenberg.[11] Yet contemporary scholars are still fascinated by what they see as 'political religion' or transfigured religious ideas and traditions at work in the emerging narratives of political struggle and incipient nationalisms of the modern world. The religious ideas did not even have to be Christian: as early as 1856, as the historian Michael Burleigh has recently noted, Alexis de Tocqueville saw in the French Revolution an immensely influential quasi-Islamic religious revolution striving not just for the reform of France but the regeneration of the human race.[12]

---

[10] See Augustine, *City of God* 20.9, trans. Henry Bettenson (Harmondsworth, 1984).

[11] Eric Voegelin, *The New Science of Politics* (Chicago: University of Chicago Press, 1952); Hans Blumenberg, *The Legitimacy of the Modern Age* (1966), trans. Robert M. Wallace (Cambridge, MA: MIT Press, 1983).

[12] Alexis de Tocqueville, *L'Ancien Régime et la révolution* (1856), quoted by Michael Burleigh, *Earthly Powers: Religion and Politics in Europe from the Enlightenment to the Great War* (London: Harper Perennial, 2006), p. 3. See also Burleigh's *Sacred Causes: Religion and Politics from the European Dictators to Al Qaeda* (London: Harper Perennial, 2007).

6   *God and the Bible, Secularisms and Novels*

Political or secular 'religion' could still sustain the dreams and visions of agnostic or speculative novelists of religious nurture. Their acts of subscription to and participation in some form of post-biblical grand narrative, some version of 'salvation history', could be seen to anticipate, embody or modify the new claims of the secularist social scientists from Herbert Spencer to Max Weber, their approximate contemporaries. George Eliot was the pioneer and the key figure in this development: her seemingly post-Christian fictions represented an intellectual-historical milestone, regretted by the faithful but enthusiastically endorsed by secular humanists, particularly in university English departments.

But times have changed. Secularization has proved to be neither as inevitable nor as productive of certain good as had been expected. The optimistic secular project of 'the growing good of the world', as George Eliot called it,[13] has in many parts of the world remained an aspiration rather than a deliverable programme, ironically making it more like a religion than not. It has in its turn been radically challenged in the present era of postmodernism, in which Jean-François Lyotard and others enjoin incredulity towards grand narrative and challenge the self-confidence of self-conscious progressive 'modernity'. Questions have been raised about the extent to which modernity itself can still be reliably identified as the demystified product of rational and secular processes.[14] In social and political thought, intellectual climate change has ensured that the traditions of inexorable progress stemming from Comte and Hegel—varieties and compounds of French positivism, German Idealism, and Marxism—are no longer such vigorous growths. The once-new faith and confidence of Victorian and post-Victorian sociology, including the quasi-scientific narrative of secularization itself, perceived as an integral and inevitable dimension of advancing modernity, have crumbled a little under the assault of today's newer agnosticisms. In *We Have Never Been Modern* (1991; English translation 1993), the French philosopher and anthropologist of science Bruno Latour draws attention to the extent to which social and cultural networks

---

[13] George Eliot, *Middlemarch* [1871–2], ed. David Carroll, World's Classics (Oxford: Oxford University Press, 1997), 'Finale', p. 822.

[14] Jean-François Lyotard, *The Postmodern Condition: A Report on Knowledge* (1979), trans. Geoff Bennington and Brian Massumi (Manchester: Manchester University Press, 1984). See also Michael Saler, 'Modernity and Enchantment: A Historiographical Review', *American Historical Review* 111 (June 2006), 692–716.

God and the Bible, Secularisms and Novels 7

and contexts shape and relativize seemingly absolute and transhistorical scientific and social-scientific doctrines. The ostensibly value-free 'scientific' claims of sociology, stemming from the rigorously scientific aspirations of nineteenth-century German research culture, have been called into question, not least by the theologian John Milbank, one of the champions of a new 'radical orthodoxy', who claims that sociology itself has a deep structure of ideology embedded in its very foundations.[15] But sceptical interrogations in our own time can at least help to focus attention on the object of interrogation. As the idea of the 'post-secular' begins to gain intellectual currency this is a timely moment to reconsider and reread the complexities of yet another world we have already lost: the brash, newly 'secular' if not necessarily irreligious world, recently deprived of the unquestioned presence and authority of God and the Bible, as it was reflected, constructed, and explored by some leading Victorian novelists.

SECULARISMS

Secularism and secularization—watchwords of nineteenth-century freethinkers and twentieth-century sociologists, rallying cries of emerging modernity—were always rather unwieldy notions, and progressive revisions and complications of theories of secularization have made things worse. Terms such as 'secularization' are still widely current in various different contexts, not necessarily even remotely connected with each other. There is still an implicit assumption that the different kinds of alleged 'secularization' are all parts of one stupendous whole, belonging with an unassailable master narrative. But this begs too many questions. The language of secularization tends to have different kinds of currency among historians, social scientists and theologians. One starting point might be the definition proposed by the sociologist Bryan Wilson, who sees secularization as 'a process whereby religious thinking, practice and institutions lose

---

[15] Bruno Latour, *We Have Never Been Modern*, trans. Catherine Porter (Harlow: Longman, 1993); John Milbank, *Theology and Social Theory: Beyond Secular Reason* (1990), 2nd ed. (Oxford: Blackwell, 2006).

8   *God and the Bible, Secularisms and Novels*

social significance'.[16] But the messy plurality and fluid and volatile nature of 'thinking, practice and institutions', and the different ways in which they relate to each other over time, give some indication of the problems.

One of the most stimulating forays into this difficult territory is the historian Owen Chadwick's *Secularization of the European Mind in the Nineteenth Century* (1975). But why just the nineteenth century? Why not start with the Enlightenment? Chadwick accommodates the point by noting that Hume and Voltaire had played their part in an earlier age, and he could easily have added Spinoza or Hobbes or Bayle. While Chadwick distinguishes between enlightenment for the few and secularization for the many,[17] implying that social process follows some way behind intellectual change, his magnificently artificial construction of 'the European Mind' still begs questions of definition and overhomogenizes, implicitly blurring possible distinctions between individual and collective mentalities, likely to change at different rates. One of the troubles is that social scientists and social historians of the secular tend to operate statistically, reviewing figures of declining church attendance and so on, but historians of ideas and mentalities usually operate textually, appraising and collating individual statements and reflections that may sit at some distance from social practice. It is becoming more and more difficult to accept 'secularization' and 'the secular' as coherent and useful categories. Ian Hunter's fine essay in intellectual history *The Secularisation of the Confessional State* (2007) has really nothing to do with either the death of God or the decline in the social significance of religion as identified by sociological analysis: it is a study of the political thought of the seventeenth-century German academic jurist Christian Thomasius, who argued that the state and the prince should not be saddled with upholding and enforcing any particular form of religious belief. Hunter suggests that this secularizing aspiration is actually religious in origin, stemming from the pietist retreat from sterile polemical dogmatism and inappropriate rule making in religious matters. By the end of the eighteenth century it was clear that Thomasius had won the argument, at least in Germany. But this

---

[16] Bryan Wilson, *Religion in Secular Society: A Sociological Comment* (London: C.A. Watts, 1966), p. xiv.

[17] Owen Chadwick, *The Secularization of the European Mind in the Nineteenth Century* (Cambridge, 1975), p. 5.

God and the Bible, Secularisms and Novels   9

had taken a century, thus demonstrating the disjunction, at best a time lag, between any kind of new thinking and significantly changed social and institutional practice. Historians of earlier periods have tried to harness the term 'secularization' in order to identify a distinctive pattern of change in the period under review, like Chadwick acknowledging but also sidestepping the theoretical difficulties and instabilities that the concept presents. The trouble is that the secularizing process, like the rise of the middle classes, can be almost endlessly backdated. The high watermark of a society in which religion had maximal social significance, the point from which the stages of the secularization process can be traced, is as liable to infinite regress as other vanished golden ages and lost paradises, all the way back to the Garden of Eden. The term 'secularization' is implicitly holistic, relating to the whole of society, and it is also implicitly teleological, implying a process that leads to an achieved steady state, but all too often 'secularization' in historical usage seems to relate to parts rather than wholes and to relatively short-term and reversible developments. The effect is that the general process is apparently prolonged world without end and the steady state is forever just over the horizon. To take just one example, it has been claimed that 'secularization' of charity was already happening in England in the 1530s, at the time of the dissolution of the monasteries.[18] If so, what was there left to secularize more than three centuries later? Yet as late as 1851 the term 'secularism' was coined by the militantly post-Christian G. J. Holyoake, recognized as a leading 'secularist' (a term also dating from 1851),[19] to indicate support for a still incomplete process, a cause that still needed to be fought for. Writing in 1906 the American scholar Henry Plum cheerfully asserted that the Teutonic Knights, founded as a military-monastic order in 1190, were 'secularized' at the time of the Reformation.[20] This was perfectly true, but it was only for a time. Historians are prone to intervene and pronounce prematurely, before events have run their course (if they ever do), and Plum was

---

[18] The issue is debated in chapter 4 of J. Thomas Kelly, *Thorns on the Tudor Rose: Monks, Rogues, Vagabonds, and Sturdy Beggars* (Jackson: University of Mississippi Press, 1977).

[19] *Oxford English Dictionary* under 'secularism', 'secularist'.

[20] Harry Grant Plum, *The Teutonic Order and its Secularization: A Study in the Protestant Revolt* (University of Iowa Studies in Sociology vol. 3, no. 2) (Iowa City, 1906).

10   *God and the Bible, Secularisms and Novels*

not to know that after many further vicissitudes, and two world wars, the order would continue into the twenty-first century in Austria and Germany, once again under largely religious auspices.

Some of the problems associated with the category of the 'secular' are illustrated in passing in *The Stripping of the Altars* (1992), Eamon Duffy's masterly investigation of fifteenth- and sixteenth-century traditional religious practice in Britain. Duffy notes that wills of the period indicate benefactions to support various socially and humanly worthy ends, which might seem to be in effect secular but, so far from claiming them as evidence of incipient secularization, he quite rightly points out that they are acts of charity in the New Testament sense, outward practical expressions, in the world of men and women, of inner religious commitment.[21]

John Sommerville's study *The Secularization of Early Modern England* (1992) bears an artfully arresting title: for most of us, early modern English society is not obviously 'secular' and may indeed even represent some kind of high watermark against which the subsequent ebbing of religion as socially significant can be measured. The explanatory subtitle 'From Religious Culture to Religious Faith' introduces a subtle and intriguing though perhaps historically rather debatable refinement into the bland category of 'secularization'. Picking up on the subtheory of 'privatization', which sociologists have used to refine secularization theory, Sommerville proposes the privatization of religion, and by implication a consequent loss of the social significance of religion, as a necessary consequence of a degree of institutional secularization. But this does not fully consider the extent to which deepening or more extensive personal devotion may still depend on some form of perceived social and institutional support, however contested or attenuated, extending throughout and indeed beyond the nation.[22] This kind of support is usually called the Church.

Writing about English society in the half-century after the Restoration, Blair Worden has thoughtfully explored the 'question of secularization'. He discusses interesting evidence of changes in language,

---

[21] Eamon Duffy, *The Stripping of the Altars: Traditional Religion in England 1400–1580* (London and New Haven: Yale University Press, 1992), p. 368.

[22] C. John Sommerville, *The Secularization of Early Modern England: From Religious Culture to Religious Faith* (Oxford: Oxford University Press, 1992).

God and the Bible, Secularisms and Novels   11

attitude and institutions.[23] But as he notes himself, some of the changes were reversed just a little later with the rise of Methodism and evangelicalism, and a return to what evangelicals tended to call 'seriousness'. It has been demonstrated that the language of political thought of the same period does indeed show signs of increasing secularization.[24] The evidence is certainly there, but is it evidence of a temporary fashion or of an irreversible process? Once again the question arises, if the process was irreversible and under way in the seventeenth century, why was a militant secularist agenda still being promoted by Victorian radicals more than two hundred years later? Taken in isolation, the change in political language can prove little, and it is not necessarily significant in the longer term, but there is often an implicit assumption on the part of those identifying such patterns that this kind of change is inevitable and inexorable, the direction in which things obviously ought to move and to continue moving. This assumption can be traced back to Enlightenment attitudes.

During the Enlightenment of the eighteenth century, the 'Siècle des lumières', the metaphor of light was obviously central. For some of the *philosophes*, at least, it was taken for granted that institutional religion was a superstitious darkness to be dispelled by the clear light of reason. In the 'Preliminary Discourse' to the *Encyclopédie* (1751) Jean Le Rond d'Alembert deplored what he saw as the silencing of reason under the theological despotism and prejudice of earlier ages, including by implication early modern England in the reign of Queen Elizabeth I (1558–1603). He described the proto-enlightenment figure Francis Bacon (1561–1626) as 'born in the depths of the most profound night' to work in the shadows preparing the light that would eventually illuminate the world.[25] This dramatic narrative of the inevitable triumph of secular reason provided a model and stimulus for nineteenth- and twentieth-century theories of secularization. In Voltaire and Marx, Auguste Comte, and Herbert Spencer, the

---

[23] Blair Worden, 'The Question of Secularization', in John Houston and Steve Pincus, eds, *A Nation Transformed: England after the Restoration* (Cambridge: Cambridge University Press, 2001), pp. 20–40.

[24] Steve Pincus, *Protestantism and Patriotism. Ideologies and the Making of English Foreign Policy 1650–1668* (Cambridge: Cambridge University Press, 1996), p. 447.

[25] Jean Le Rond d'Alembert, *Preliminary Discourse to the Encyclopedia of Diderot*, trans. Richard N. Schwab (Chicago: University of Chicago Press, 1995), pp. 73–4.

12   *God and the Bible, Secularisms and Novels*

eventual eclipse of religion was an article of faith masquerading as a rational certainty.

It would be unfair to saddle later social theorists with such wholesale convictions, and, as the American sociologist Nicholas Demarath has pointed out, the much-maligned 'secularization thesis' of the sociologists is all too easily demolished if it is presented in melodramatic terms as an inevitable transition from all to nothing, from a mythical world where religion dominated every aspect of life to an equally mythical world in which religion has completely disappeared.[26] 'Secularization' has earned a permanent place in the vocabulary and conceptual arsenal of sociology. Even so, secularization theory still bears traces of its dogmatically prescriptive Enlightenment origins, buttressed by Marxian militancy and rationalist triumphalism, and it still lies open to constant modification and revision in the light of new developments and unruly empirical data.[27]

In the pioneering work of Max Weber, Enlightenment conviction modulates into romantic reverie without losing its rationalist edge. Romantic poetry is at least partly predicated on a sense of loss, which is articulated by imaginative identification and re-creation of that which has been lost. One of the functions of ancient myth is perhaps to testify to an already vanished or vanishing sense of the numinous, a world of legitimized fancy and the imagination, and Schiller's celebrated poem 'The Gods of Greece' ('Die Götter Griechenlands') (1788), revisits and re-creates the imagined world of classical mythology when nature itself was instinct with divinity ('Die engotterte natur'), only to regret that it has now receded into the domain of poetry.[28] Weber's reiterated view of secularization as the 'disenchantment of the world' ('Entzauberung der Welt')[29] follows Schiller in its elegiac nostalgia while insisting that, on rational ground, it was bound to happen.

---

[26] Nicholas Demarath, 'Secularization Extended: From Religious "Myth" to Cultural Commonplace', in Richard K. Fenn, ed., *The Blackwell Companion to Sociology of Religion* (Oxford: Blackwell, 2001), p. 212.

[27] See in particular the geographical range and theoretical caution of David Martin, *On Secularization. Towards a Revised General Theory* (Aldershot: Ashgate, 2005).

[28] Friedrich Schiller, 'Die Götter Griechenlands' in *Sämtliche Werke* I (Munich: Carl Hauser Verlag, 1958), pp. 169–73.

[29] Max Weber, *The Protestant Ethic and the Spirit of Capitalism* [1904–5], trans. Talcott Parsons (London: Routledge, 1992), p. 105; Max Weber, 'Science as a Vocation' [1919], in H. H. Gerth and C. Wright Mills, eds, *From Max Weber: Essays in Sociology* (London: Routledge, 1948), p. 155.

God and the Bible, Secularisms and Novels   13

For Weber, if not necessarily for the historians and theologians, Protestantism as it had developed in Germany and in Britain could be seen as an increasingly secular religion in which strenuous if lonely economic individualism was a consequence of a now purely personal faith, relying on grace alone and abandoning all belief in magical, sacramental and institutional means of securing salvation. For other sociologists, however, notably Emile Durkheim[30] (who had worked on Australian aboriginal religion), religion and the religious world, properly understood, had never been inherently mysterious or enchanted: religion was in effect social construction serving social functions. What was inexorably changing with advancing modernity was perhaps not so much religion as the understanding of it, arguably an improvement rather than a loss. But reducing religion to the explicable could help to reduce religion. As Bryan Wilson has observed, claiming to understand religious motivations and the social functions of religion, while not directly disposed to evoke hostility towards religion, was nevertheless cumulatively effective in challenging its purely supernatural credentials and its credibility, and in licensing disbelief.[31]

Sociologists by definition operate in terms of the quantifiable, so statistical evidence of declining church attendance (particularly in Britain), and refinements of secularization theory, have pursued each other for several generations through textbooks and journal articles. One of the most recent interventions in the debate, by Callum Brown, claims that secularization in Britain has happened so fast over the last forty years, out of step with economic and social modernization, that it shows that secularization theory is wrong.[32] Other challenges to the theory have tended to draw attention to new religious movements outside traditional institutional Christianity, or rapid growth in religious observance in other areas of the world, which fundamentally challenge assumptions of inexorable decline in the social significance of religion as an aspect of developing modernity. Theories of modernity may be wrong as well. It is only quite recently that it has been suggested that what is really at issue and merits

---

[30] Emile Durkheim, *The Elementary Forms of the Religious Life*, trans. Carol Cosman (Oxford: Oxford University Press, 2001).
[31] Wilson, *Religion in Secular Society*, pp. 52–3.
[32] Callum G. Brown, *The Death of Christian Britain: Understanding Secularisation 1800–2000* (London: Routledge, 2001).

14   *God and the Bible, Secularisms and Novels*

attention in the so-called 'secularization debate' may be the nature and quality of religious experience and its effects in social thought and action, as opposed to statistically verifiable evidence of participation in traditional institutional religion. Institutions are not everything, and declining church attendance, it has been observed, need not necessarily be incompatible with a continuing sense of religious identity in the nation.[33] The closing of churches and the death of God as traditionally conceived might signal change rather than decay, religious paradigm shift rather than collapse. For the purposes of the present study, this possibility needs to be explored in relation to the Victorian fictions in which conventional religion apparently dwindled or died but where, as it will be argued, it was actually reconfigured and continued by other means.

Back in the churches and universities, theological discourse has been engaging in its own ways with secularism and 'secularization'. At least three positions can be distinguished: the conservative pessimist position, which accepts that secularization is happening and deplores it, and deplores liberal attempts within the churches to accommodate it; the more or less conservative optimist position, which denies that secularization is either inevitable or irreversible; the radical optimist position, which looks beyond the churches and their traditions and sees in the development of secular society evidence of a paradigm shift that calls for fundamentally new theological orientations.

The pessimists are variously represented by Edward Norman, who thinks the Church has gone wrong through jumping on secular bandwagons and failing to mind its own business, mainly souls and sins,[34] and the theologians of 'radical orthodoxy' such as John Milbank. Attempted theological rapprochement with secular society, as represented by the American theologian Harvey Cox's once-celebrated *Secular City* (1965), is now (rather unfairly) condemned as hopelessly dated, a misconceived sell-out to a questionable theory of social development.[35] Conservative optimists also repudiate Harvey Cox and insist that atheism rather than religion is on the wane. They

---

[33] Jeremy Morris, 'The Strange Death of Christian Britain: Another Look at the Secularization debate', *Historical Journal* 46 (2003), 963–76.

[34] Edward Norman, *Secularisation* (London: Continuum, 2002).

[35] John Milbank, Catherine Pickstock, and Graham Ward, eds, *Radical Orthodoxy: A New Theology* (London: Routledge, 1999). For a partial defence or rehabilitation of Harvey Cox, see T. J. Gorringe, *A Theology of the Built Environment* (Cambridge: Cambridge University Press, 2002).

God and the Bible, Secularisms and Novels   15

point to new forms of religious expression outside the established churches and to religious resurgence in the former Soviet Union and elsewhere. Whether one accepts the conservative optimist position or not there is certainly evidence in various parts of the world, notably South Korea and Sri Lanka, that religion, specifically the Christian religion, is still very far from losing social significance.[36] The philosopher Gordon Graham has responded to growing awareness of the continuing presence and power of religion outside Western Europe by suggesting that perhaps 'the idea of secularization, and the related debate about the consequences of secularism, may be a relatively local, and even minor, affair, confined to two centuries of European history'.[37]

Among the more notorious radical optimists of the 1960s were not just Harvey Cox but Paul van Buren and John Robinson, author of *Honest to God* (1963). A starting point for all of them was Dietrich Bonhoeffer's wartime prison meditations about the meaning and status of Christianity in a harshly modern world virtually without a sense of God.[38] Bonhoeffer also lies behind more recent work such as Jürgen Moltmann's *God for a Secular Society* (1997). Moltmann meets the secularizers on their own ground of social significance and the public domain by arguing for the continuing public and political relevance of theology, anticipating or perhaps inaugurating the 'post-secular turn' by reinstating God in the project of modernity (the original German title is *Gott im Projekt der modernen Welt*). Others, particularly in America, have risked or enjoyed notoriety and accusations of heresy by taking Nietzsche's 'Death of God' as a starting point, an indication of a cultural condition and an intellectual paradigm shift that theology must accommodate, and have explored

---

[36] For optimists, see for example the Roman Catholic sociologist Andrew M. Greeley, *The Persistence of Religion* (London: SCM Press, 1973) and the Protestant historian Alister McGrath, *The Twilight of Atheism: The Rise and Fall of Disbelief in the Modern World* (London: Rider, 2004). For South Korea, see Andrew E. Kim, 'History of Christianity in Korea: From its Troubled Beginning to its Contemporary Success', <http://www.kimsoft.com/1997/xhist.htm> (accessed 10 July 2006); for Sri Lanka, see R. L. Stirrat, *Power and Religiosity in a Post-Colonial Setting: Sinhala Catholics in Contemporary Sri Lanka* (Cambridge: Cambridge University Press, 1992).

[37] Gordon Graham, *The Re-enchantment of the World: Art versus Religion* (Oxford: Oxford University Press, 2007), p. 186.

[38] Dietrich Bonhoeffer, *Letters and Papers from Prison* (Glasgow: Collins/Fontana, 1959), esp. pp. 91–3, letter of 30 April 1944, reflecting on the meaning of Christianity in a society now virtually without religion.

16 *God and the Bible, Secularisms and Novels*

the possibilities of a 'Death of God' theology in which 'secularity' is seen as a Christian obligation, 'a renewal, a reaffirmation, of the biblical doctrine about the nature of this world'.[39] For them at least, Victorian doubters and agnostic or spiritually restless novelists such as George Eliot and Dostoevsky can be seen as a solution, or at least a new point of departure, rather than as a problem or a symptom of infectious error.

Some of these theologians, and some sociologists and historians, have noticed that the secular and the religious, like the world and the Church, need not and indeed should not be treated as inevitable opposites. Religious rhetoric has sometimes exalted contempt for the world, as a way of commending spiritual discipline and the asceticism of the monastic life. Perhaps the most extreme version of this is Bernard of Cluny's twelfth-century poetic diatribe *De Contemptu Mundi*. Selections were translated into English verse by John Mason Neale, providing Victorian congregations with several rather dismal popular hymns such as 'The world is very evil' (*Hora Novissima*) and 'Brief life is here our portion' (*Hic breve vivitur*). But to the religious mind the world as we have it, however mishandled by man, was created by God, a given that is fundamental to the biblical record and the reason why the Bible begins with the creation narrative. So the secular world is, or ought to be, also and always of profound religious significance, the arena in which, and in terms of which, the workings of God and of religious faith can be made manifest in this life.

It is ironic that the English words 'secular' and 'secularism', so defiantly championed by anti-religious Victorian freethinkers such as Charles Bradlaugh and George Holyoake, have a partly religious history that can be traced back to the New Testament itself. In the medieval church, secular priests, as opposed to members of religious orders, were not priests who had abandoned the things of God for the things of the world but priests who were doing the work of God in the world. 'Secular' is connected with the Latin noun *saeculum* used in the Vulgate to translate the New Testament Greek term *aion*. The same term is used in the 'Septuagint', the Greek version of the Old Testament, to translate the Hebrew '*olam*': all three terms can indicate

---

[39] Gilbert Gabriel Vahanian, *The Death of God* (New York: George Braziller, 1961), p. 61.

God and the Bible, Secularisms and Novels   17

a space of time, an indefinitely long period, or an age.[40] But other meanings developed. From the sense of 'age' there arose a more specialized sense, found in Matthew 12:32, for example, where it is translated as 'this world' in the King James version, of 'pertaining to the present age', the world as we have it as opposed to the world to come. In Hebrews 1:2 and 11:3 the plural *saecula* (reproducing the plural form of the original Greek, *aionas*), translated as 'worlds' in the King James version, indicates the universe, the divinely created material world considered under the aspect of time. The time-bound world, the epoch of human history, had religious significance for the faithful. This was the world that Christ was born into, and the world of time represented the space and opportunity in this life for doing God's work, the site of encounter with the transcendent and the infinite. Liturgical formulae such as *in saecula saeculorum* in Romans 16:27 and Revelation 1:6 ('for ever', or 'unto the ages of ages'), literally translating the original Greek (*eis tous aionas ton aionon*), linked the term for the present age with the description of God's eternity.

For all their diversity, the sometimes fumbling negotiations and invocations of the secular and secularization in the discussions of the theologians, historians, and sociologists—and the neglected, originally religious, context and significance of the term 'secular'—should alert us to a kind of incoherence and instability and call into question any assured grand narrative of universal and irreversible religious decline. They draw attention to latently religious possibilities and implications in secular discourse, enabling post-secular readings of 'secular' or 'post-Christian' fiction.

NOVELS

How exactly does all this link up with the novel? Max Weber's bold characterization of the Protestant ethic, and his narrative of the growth of this-worldly or secular mentalities under its auspices, gave Ian Watt encouragement half a century ago to identify the rise of the English novel as an essentially Protestant development, and to

---

[40] See Charlton D. Lewis and Charles Short, *A Latin Dictionary* (Oxford, Clarendon Press, 1969), under *saeculum* II.C; G. Abbott-Smith, *A Manual Greek Lexicon of the New Testament* (Edinburgh: T & T Clark, 1999), under *aion*.

18 *God and the Bible, Secularisms and Novels*

present Daniel Defoe's fictional versions of the operation of secular economic individualism as a natural starting point.[41] For a time, Watt's seminal study seemed to be the received wisdom on the subject, but the topic has been much debated. Successive literary histories have sought to revise, feminize, amplify, and backdate the rise of the novel in various ways.[42] Considering the history of the English novel in conjunction with the history of the changing status of the English Bible modifies the picture yet again, giving much more prominence to John Bunyan and *The Pilgrim's Progress* (1678), for example, and much less to Defoe.

The very Englishness of Watt's seminal account of the English novel is one of its limitations. For Watt, as for a number of early English novelists and moralists, the novel is or ought to be an essentially sober affair. Its identity and its claims on our attention, its claim to cultural and indeed moral seriousness and respectability, are usually presented as depending on what is rather loosely called 'realism'. Characteristically this is supposed to involve being firmly rooted in probabilities and material realities, the essentially middle-class everyday world of Defoe and Richardson rather than Don Quixote's fantastic daydreams. It is predicated on contrast with extravagant far-fetched romances and wild stories of foreign (often French) origin. In 1783 James Beattie, Professor of Moral Philosophy at the University of Aberdeen, warned that, 'Romances are a danger-ous recreation . . . and tend to corrupt the heart and stimulate the passions. A habit of reading them breeds a dislike to history . . . with-draws the attention from nature, and truth; and fills the mind with extravagant thoughts, and too often with criminal propensities.'[43]

At first glance, the apparent repudiation and exclusion of romance seems unproblematic and entirely sensible, particularly when it is contrasted with nature and reason and what we might call common

---

[41] Ian Watt, *The Rise of the Novel* (London: Chatto & Windus, 1957).

[42] See for example Michael McKeon, *The Origins of the English Novel: 1600–1714* (Baltimore: Johns Hopkins University Press, 1987); Geoffrey Day, *From Fiction to the Novel* (London: Routledge, 1987); Margaret A. Doody, *The True Story of the Novel* (New Jersey: Rutgers University Press, 1996); and the present writer's essay 'Protest-ant Form and Catholic Fiction?', in Jacqueline Belanger, ed., *The Irish Novel in the Nineteenth Century* (Dublin: Four Courts Press, 2005), pp. 139–49.

[43] James Beattie, 'On Fable and Romance', in *Dissertations Moral and Critical* (1783), reprinted in Ioan Williams, ed., *Novel and Romance 1700–1800: A Documentary Record* (London: Routledge, 1970), p. 327.

God and the Bible, Secularisms and Novels   19

sense. The eighteenth-century English novel would certainly not have benefited from slavish imitation of interminable aristocratic French romances such as Madeleine de Scudéry's *Artamène, ou le grand Cyrus* (1649–53, English translation 1653–5, reprinted 1691). *Don Quixote* (1605–15) had already satirized the preposterous chivalric romances of old Spain, and in *The Female Quixote; or the Adventures of Arabella* (1752) Charlotte Lennox detailed the absurdities and entirely imaginary perils entailed by Arabella's delusion that her world was a world of heroic romance, of narratives such as *Artamène*, read in 'very bad Translations'.[44] One of the chapters is rather drily entitled 'Containing an Incident full as probable as any in *Scudéry's Romances*' (Book 6, chapter 7). Fanny Burney claims that her first novel *Evelina* (1778) avoids 'the fantastic regions of Romance, where Fiction is coloured by all the gay tints of luxurious Imagination, where Reason is an outcast, and where the sublimity of *the Marvellous* rejects all aid from sober Probability'.[45] In Clara Reeve's dialogue *The Progress of Romance* (1785) Euphrasia insists that, in contrast to the novel, the romance 'describes what never happened nor is likely to happen'.[46] In similar vein, in the preface to *Memoirs of Emma Courtney* (1796), Mary Hays repudiates the improbable, specifically the 'fantastic models' of characterization 'in which nature and passion are melted away'.[47]

On this showing, the fantastic and the improbable have no part in the novel. The form is apparently firmly tied to the daylight world of the 'probable', almost as a necessary condition for being taken seriously. Jane Austen's *Northanger Abbey* (1818), with the examples of Fanny Burney and Maria Edgeworth very much in mind, seeks to vindicate the still-disputed moral seriousness of the novel form by using it to pursue afresh the project of Lennox's *The Female Quixote*, repudiating disordered fantasy and nightmare and far-fetched Gothic romance as acceptable or plausible constructions of life. For this purpose the novel form is defended as a lively and well-written repository of intelligent common sense:

---

[44] Charlotte Lennox, *The Female Quixote* World's Classics (Oxford: Oxford University Press, 1998), book 1, chapter 1, p. 7.

[45] Fanny Burney, *Evelina* (Oxford: Oxford University Press, 1968), p. 8.

[46] Clara Reeve, *The Progress of Romance through Times, Countries, and Manners*, 2 vols [1785] (New York: Garland Publishing, 1970), I, p. 111.

[47] Mary Hays, *Memoirs of Emma Courtney*, World's Classics (Oxford: Oxford University Press, 1996), p. 4.

20 *God and the Bible, Secularisms and Novels*

'And what are you reading, Miss—?'
'Oh! It is only a novel!' replies the young lady: while she lays down her book with affected indifference, or momentary shame.—'It is only Cecilia, or Camilla, or Belinda'; or, in short, only some work in which the most thorough knowledge of human nature, the happiest delineation of its varieties, the liveliest effusions of wit and humour are conveyed to the world in the best chosen language.[48]

There was no real place in the novel thus described for the wild excesses of romance, such as the nightmares of the Gothic tradition—and sober Victorian novelists took note. Writing to George Eliot in 1863, Anthony Trollope described his work in terms that he knew Eliot would find sympathetic:

> You know that my novels are not sensational. In *Rachel Ray* I have attempted to confine myself absolutely to the commonest details of commonplace life among the most ordinary people, allowing myself no incident that would be even remarkable in every day life. I have shorn fiction of all romance.[49]

But not all romances were bad. Repudiations of romance seemed by extension to involve repudiating the dreams, visions, and vividly heightened experiences that were important to poets and biblical writers as devices for going beyond daylight probabilities, ways of providing access to the sublime or the numinous. Such matters seemed by default to be the exclusive province of romance, as described by Northrop Frye, with its capacity for replacing 'the world of ordinary experience by a dream world, in which the narrative movement keeps rising into wish fulfillment or sinking into anxiety and nightmare'.[50] Officially at least, the novel form in England, pointedly distinguished from romance, seemed to be firmly committed to realism, confined to the 'real' world of everyday experience.

But as Margaret Doody has pointed out:

> The cult of Realism affected critical practice and literary history far more than it did the creative practice of novel-writing... the *novelists* of the nineteenth century (as distinct from the critics) were in touch with

---

[48] Jane Austen, *Northanger Abbey,* World's Classics (Oxford: Oxford University Press, 2003), chapter 5, p. 24.

[49] Trollope to George Eliot, 18 October 1863, *The Letters of Anthony Trollope,* ed. N. John Hall, 2 vols (Stanford: Stanford University Press, 1983), I, p. 238.

[50] Northrop Frye, *The Secular Scripture: A Study of the Structure of Romance* (Cambridge, MA: Harvard University Press, 1976), p. 53.

God and the Bible, Secularisms and Novels   21

the entire tradition of fiction, and their deeper roots tapped into the great stream, even if that was running underground.[51]

This great stream, enriched by foreign and exotic tributaries, included the wayward romance, which was far too useful and attractive to be permanently excluded. Handy as a demonized Other, seldom defined or exemplified, romance is both elusive and indomitable in the history of the English novel. Many early novels, particularly the novels of sentiment, are in fact tacitly complicit with the emotional and imaginative excess associated with officially despised 'romance'. The perilous and extreme imagined situations ridiculed and repudiated in Charlotte Lennox's *The Female Quixote* are somehow not really very different in kind from the tragic and extreme misadventures of Richardson's suffering heroine Clarissa. As John Mullan puts it, 'It is not possible finally to separate romance from that which claims to be other than romance, the disreputable from the instructive text.'[52] The terms 'romance' and 'novel' are in fact often used interchangeably in the eighteenth century and subsequently, not as a result of sloppiness but because the categories overlap.

If one takes the official repudiation of romance at face value, the romantic novel of the nineteenth century as developed by Bulwer Lytton, much admired by Rider Haggard, or Charlotte Brontë, much admired by Mary Ward, not to mention Scott, much admired by everyone, is almost a contradiction in terms. Thomas Carlyle's bizarre and fantastic but influential fictional narrative of spiritual crisis, *Sartor Resartus* (1833), would hardly count as a novel at all, and indeed successive editions of the *Oxford Companion to English Literature* have carefully avoided calling it one. But fictional prose narratives of emotional extremity and anguished inner awareness— by the nineteenth century usually identified unequivocally as novels—did not come from nowhere. The suggestion of something alien and foreign, implied in terms such as 'Gothic', cannot be altogether sustained, and indeed David Punter has indicated domestic sources for Gothic fiction in the Elizabethan and Jacobean drama.[53]

---

[51] Margaret A. Doody, *The True Story of the Novel* (New Jersey: Rutgers University Press, 1996), p. 296.

[52] McKeon, *Origins of the English Novel*; John Mullan, *Sentiment and Sociability: The Language of Feeling in the Eighteenth Century* (Oxford: Clarendon, 1988), p. 102.

[53] David Punter, *The Literature of Terror: A History of Gothic Fictions from 1765 to the Present Day* (London: Longman, 1980).

22　　*God and the Bible, Secularisms and Novels*

Rousseau was an important and frequently acknowledged influence on novels of perfervid feeling, but Rousseau's *Julie, ou la Nouvelle Héloïse*, 'full of nature and extravagance' according to Beattie,[54] had adapted its epistolary form from Richardson's *Clarissa*. Fictional extravagance could also draw on German romantic influences, particularly important for Bulwer Lytton, novelist, romantic idealist, and translator of Schiller, and for those other distinguished translators from the German: George Eliot and Thomas Carlyle.

Indebted to German Romanticism, and in particular to Goethe and the romantic narratives of 'Jean Paul', that is, Johann Paul Richter, Carlyle's *Sartor* shares Jean Paul's commitment to representing the imagination and the inner life through which religious awareness and its absence or loss can be explored. Carlyle's early translations of two of Jean Paul's shorter works, *The Life of Quintus Fixlein* (1796) and *Schmelzle's Journey to Flaetz* 1809), both published in 1827, had already indicated his allegiance. A century before Nietzsche and Dostoevsky, Jean Paul used his own flexible and compendious version of the novel form to explore such themes as the moral and psychological significance of perceived divine absence, the death of God. Subject to vivid dreams himself, including a dream of his own death, and deeply affected by the death of the closest friend of his youth in 1786, by 1789 Richter had already written a fictionalized dream-narrative in which the great tragic humanist Shakespeare preaches from the grave that there is no God. Shakespeare's Prospero in *The Tempest* taught Richter that life itself might be a dream ('We are such stuff/As Dreams are made of'), fitfully disclosing fragments of the truth and reality lying somewhere beyond it, and this was a lesson Jean Paul passed on with interest to Carlyle and other romantic dreamers. The other English influence on Richter's apparently very German text is Edward Young's *Night Thoughts on Life, Death and Immortality* (1742–5), which he read in J. A. Ebert's German translation (1770).[55]

Jean Paul's free-standing nightmare vision of the death of God, subsequently adapted so that it is proclaimed by Christ himself, was incorporated into the opening of his novel *Siebenkäs* (1796–7). In subsequent editions it was moved to the middle of the novel so that it

---

[54] Beattie in Williams, ed., *Novel and Romance 1700–1800*, p. 325.
[55] Discussed in J. W. Smeed, *Jean Paul's 'Dreams'* (London: Oxford University Press, 1966), pp. 14–24.

God and the Bible, Secularisms and Novels 23

had some bearing on the developing narrative. In the later editions, the immediate emotional context is despair arising from blighted hope: Siebenkäs had planned a pleasant walk on a magnificent starlit night with his wife, but this degenerated into a jealous wrangle in the churchyard, which was then rather artificially resolved or rather suspended by a peacemaker. This is then followed by the narrator's dream of being inside a church and hearing the address of the dead Christ to the resurrected dead, announcing his bleak discovery that there is no God.

The sequence ends with an awakening that implies a return to the healing possibility of belief after all, 'my soul wept for joy that it could still worship God'. But the imaginative possibility of a godless universe had been vividly entertained, and it found its way into the poetry of Gérard de Nerval (quoted as an epigraph to this chapter) and into English fiction. Carlyle included a translation of 'The Dream of the Dead Christ' in his article on Jean Paul in 1830.[56] *Siebenkäs*, now largely forgotten, had some impact in England as well as France and Germany. Fanciful or not, it was read by that arch-realist George Eliot.[57] It was translated twice, once in 1845 by E. H. Noel and again in 1877 by Alexander Ewing. The 'Dream' narrative influenced the annihilating sense of spiritual desolation, the 'Everlasting No', experienced by the protagonist of Carlyle's *Sartor*, and it may also lie behind Bulwer Lytton's short story 'A Dream of the Dead', an enigmatic vision of eternity published in *Blackwood's Edinburgh Magazine* in September 1859. The possibility of the death of God, or at least of the falsity of traditional dogma and religious imagining, haunted the agnostics of English fiction from J. A. Froude's protagonist Markham Sutherland in *The Nemesis of Faith* (1849) to Mary Ward's still-theistic *Robert Elsmere* (1888). Richter's 'Dream of the Dead Christ', perhaps mediated by extensive quotation in French translation in Madame de Staël's *De l'Allemagne* (1810), also helped to condition the desolations of French poets such as Alfred de Vigny and Leconte de Lisle, not to mention Gérard de Nerval, which in their turn fed the modish gloom of the English *fin de siècle*.[58]

---

[56] Thomas Carlyle, 'Jean Paul Richter', *Foreign Review and Continental Miscellany* 5 (1830), 1–52: the translation is on pp. 48–51.
[57] Rosemary Ashton, *George Eliot: A Life* (London, 1996), p. 60.
[58] Madame de Staël, *De l'Allemagne* [1810], part 2, 28; J. W. Smeed, *Jean Paul's 'Dreams'*, pp. 82–4.

24   *God and the Bible, Secularisms and Novels*

French as well as German Romanticism could bring the extravagances of romantic and poetic exaltation and despair, and indeed ways of conveying religious awareness, to the sober English novel. We know that Charlotte Brontë's French studies in Brussels included romantic writers such as Lamartine and Victor Hugo and, perhaps most important, Chateaubriand, whose life and thought also provided an important stimulus to Mary Ward's novel *Eleanor*. Charlotte Brontë, under the direction of her gifted tutor Constantin Heger, transcribed well-chosen descriptive passages including several from Chateaubriand's *Atala* and *Génie du Christianisme*, a liberating exercise that helped her in her subsequent fiction to articulate vivid imaginative experience.[59] If some mid-Victorian writers remained wary of the romance, others, such as the American Nathaniel Hawthorne, deliberately embraced it. So did Bulwer Lytton, much admired by Rider Haggard. In *A Strange Story* (1862) Lytton deliberately constructs what he describes as a romance, rather than a realist novel, to take his protagonist, a medical doctor, beyond the limitations of his rationalism and scientific materialism so that he can understand something of the nature of the soul and the inexhaustible wonders of God. By the end of the nineteenth century, as Patricia Beer has observed, the romance had more or less come into its own once again as an ally rather than an adversary of the novel, not just as apparent in science fiction but as a device for transfiguring the ordinary in the stories of H. G. Wells and Arnold Bennett.[60]

Officially repudiating romance was not in any case enough on its own to establish the cultural credentials and the aesthetic and moral dignity of the novel form. Austen's famous defence of the novel in *Northanger Abbey* was written about 1803, when theology, philosophy and poetry, and history and biography, still tended to be the officially preferred sources of high seriousness and knowledge about human nature. Unqualified acceptance of the novel as a form that could incorporate and distil the best of what was offered in these older literary forms came only gradually, helped on its way by Sir Walter Scott's well-documented historical romances, which could be represented or excused as participating in the dignity of history. Novels were also tolerated and partly redeemed when they could be seen to

---

[59] Enid L. Duthie, *The Foreign Vision of Charlotte Brontë* (London: Macmillan, 1975), pp. 192–3.

[60] Gillian Beer, *The Romance* (London: Methuen, 1970), pp. 69–79.

God and the Bible, Secularisms and Novels   25

engage vigorously with contemporary social issues. But even a century after Austen, Edwardian ladies were not expected to read novels in the morning, since that needed to be reserved for more serious pursuits such as interviewing the housekeeper. George Eliot's attack in 1856 on 'Silly Novels by Lady Novelists' was prompted in part by a sense that respect for the form still needed to be earned and some of the feebler and more pretentious lady novelists were doing nothing to help.[61]

Popular discontents and the 'hungry' 1840s had stimulated social-problem novels by Dickens, Disraeli, Elizabeth Gaskell and Charles Kingsley. By mid-century, Kingsley and Newman, at odds about almost everything else, had both made use of the novel form to popularize controversial religious issues. But this was all in the face of stubborn if residual religious unease about novels and the potentially wayward secular imagination, which if given the opportunity was disposed to dwell on dangerous matters such as sexuality, moral and imaginative disorder, and defiant individual choice. Evangelicals retained some of their suspicion of the novel for a long time.[62] In 1859, the year George Eliot published *Adam Bede*, the success of a great evangelical crusade in Ireland was gauged by the fact that a local bookseller reported he had not sold a single novel for three weeks.[63] In 1860 the young Edmund Gosse was understandably puzzled when his father, a member of the Plymouth Brethren sect, sternly banned him from reading Scott's novels, citing them to be false and disturbing pictures of life, but unaccountably tolerated Dickens.[64] As late as 1864 Trollope was fuming against a general attack by the Archbishop of York on the immorality of fiction.[65] Religious hostility to novels was not confined to evangelical Protestants. The Papal Index of Prohibited Books, published until 1966, had banned Richardson's novel *Pamela* in 1744, Rousseau's *Emile* in 1763, Sterne's *Sentimental*

---

[61] George Eliot, 'Silly Novels by Lady Novelists', *Westminster Review* 66 (October 1856), 442–61.

[62] For a carefully nuanced view of evangelical modes of engagement with 'secular' culture, see Doreen Rosman, *Evangelicals and Culture* (London: Croom Helm, 1983).

[63] James Johnston, *An Impartial History of the Revival Movement* (Belfast, 1860), p. xv; see also Norman Vance, *Irish Literature, a Social History* (Oxford: Blackwell, 1990), pp. 129–31.

[64] Edmund Gosse, *Father and Son: A Study of Two Temperaments* (London: Heinemann, 1907), chapter 10.

[65] Trollope, *Letters* I, pp. 285–6.

26   *God and the Bible, Secularisms and Novels*

Journey in 1819, and, in the course of the nineteenth century, work by Balzac, Victor Hugo, Flaubert, and Zola. In 1864 alone Flaubert's *Madame Bovary* and Hugo's *Les Misérables* were placed on the Index, along with Renan's *Vie de Jésus*.[66] It seems likely that most of the English novels of the period escaped not because they were more respected and respectable than their French counterparts but because there were relatively few English Catholics whose souls might be at risk from reading them.

Secular philanthropists and utilitarian city fathers could be just as uneasy about fiction. Recent research on library history has indicated that even into the twentieth century there were grave doubts as to whether endowed or public libraries were justified in stocking fiction, rather than 'proper' books.[67] The liberal and radical deists who founded the Belfast Linen Hall Library in the eighteenth century stipulated that no novels should be purchased, and the library faithfully stuck to the principle until late-Victorian borrowers almost stopped using it altogether because fiction was available elsewhere.[68] The rather dry-as-dust Victorian social scientist Herbert Spencer thought that the London Library should not waste its subscription income on buying novels, except of course for those of his protégé George Eliot, who was herself something of a social scientist in her fiction.[69]

It was partly because of Eliot that it finally came to be widely accepted that the novel could, after all, be a serious mode of discourse. Serious people had read and even reviewed novels in the past. Richard Whately, later Oxford Professor of Political Economy and Archbishop of Dublin, had written enthusiastically (if anonymously) about Jane Austen in the *Quarterly Review* in 1815 and again in 1821. But there was a certain defiance about these essays: he accepted in 1815 that novel-reading might be attended by a certain furtive if not exactly guilty delight, in biblical terms, 'A novel . . . is frequently

---

[66] See *Index librorum prohibitorum*, available online at <http://www.beaconfor freedom.org/about_database/index_librorum.html> (accessed 12 August 2009).

[67] Mary Hammond, '"The Great Fiction Bore": Free Libraries and the Construction of a Reading Public in England 1880–1914', *Libraries and Culture* 37:2 (Spring 2002), 83–108.

[68] John Killen, *A History of the Linen Hall Library 1788–1988* (Belfast: Linen Hall Library, 1990).

[69] Suzanne Graver, *George Eliot and Community* (Berkeley: University of California Press, 1984), p. 12.

God and the Bible, Secularisms and Novels   27

"bread eaten in secret"'. By 1821 he rather tentatively claimed that 'The times seem to be past when an apology was requisite from reviewers for condescending to notice a novel.'[70] By the 1880s the devout and serious Mr Gladstone himself was writing earnestly in the periodical press about Mary Ward's novel *Robert Elsmere*. Where earlier generations of evangelicals had been suspicious of most novels as worldly distractions from the spiritual life, the prominent Methodist T. G. Selby wrote perceptively in *The Theology of Modern Fiction* (1896) about Eliot and Hardy. Leslie Stephen, born into an evangelical family, pioneer intellectual historian and agnostic philosopher, author of *History of English Thought in the Eighteenth Century* (1876) and *The Science of Ethics* (1882), took serious novels seriously when he was editor of the *Cornhill Magazine* in the 1870s, gave shrewd editorial advice about fiction to the young Thomas Hardy, and published a short book about George Eliot (1902). Overseas writers took to commenting on the nineteenth-century English novel in relation to the moral and religious history of the country. Mary Ward's *Robert Elsmere* prompted lectures and pamphlets in Australia and the United States as well as in Britain. The American Irvingite divine Samuel J. Anderson took time to discuss George Eliot in his *Christianity and Anti-Christianity in their Final Conflict* (1898). The French scholar of English Literature Louis Cazamian published his pioneering academic study of Victorian social-problem fiction *Le Roman social en Angleterre* in 1903.

Like the middle classes who chiefly read novels, the novel itself has always been rising, but from the 1870s and 1880s it finally achieved the kind of cultural and indeed moral authority dreamed of by Jane Austen. By 1890 Eliot's *Daniel Deronda* and Mary Ward's *Robert Elsmere* had been joined on the fiction shelf by Dostoevsky's *Brothers Karamazov* (in French translation), and the life or death of God and issues of messianic destiny were engaging novel readers as well as theologians. The best fictional narratives could now share or even usurp the respect once accorded exclusively to biblical narrative.

Particularly from the time of the sixteenth-century European Reformation the vernacular Bible had done much to stimulate the development of the written vernacular language and to promote

---

[70] Richard Whately, '*Emma*', *Quarterly Review* 14 (October 1815), 188 (alluding to Proverbs 9:17); '*Northanger Abbey* and *Persuasion*', *Quarterly Review* 24 (January 1821), 352.

28 *God and the Bible, Secularisms and Novels*

literacy, in Britain as in Germany, helping to create the conditions and the popular readership that subsequently sustained the novel form. Now, with what Hans Frei has called 'the eclipse of biblical narrative',[71] the novel itself began to take over and to provide new narratives, which sometimes aspired to be reimagined versions of scripture. The grand themes of God, Man, Nature, and History were still there, in a sense, in varying degrees, but the language and the treatments were different. Not only were the new narratives fresher and more readable (most of the time): they sidestepped the problem of trying to distinguish between literal and moral or religious truth, which complicated modern readings of biblical narrative, since nobody had ever expected fictional narrative to be literally true even if it could convey important truths and insights. The day of the novelist as 'truth-teller', to use the critic Laurence Lerner's phrase, had definitely arrived.[72] It helped that the novel form, predicated on the delineation of individual character and the self as moral agent, increasingly committed to exploring the inner life and the nature of the imagination, could build on a long history of dramatized subjectivity that can be traced back through Augustine's *Confessions* to the Bible itself, to the desolation and exaltation of the psalmist or the sufferings of Job. As the Canadian philosopher Charles Taylor has argued, modern identity itself can be seen as a consequence of Judaeo-Christian theism.[73] Another link between self-consciously secular narrative and the transcendent is represented by the endlessly theorized imaginative possibilities of the sublime. This ancient notion, linked by Longinus in the first century to the Genesis creation account, reactivated by Boileau's influential translation of Longinus (1674), was reapplied to biblical materials in Robert Lowth's eighteenth-century lectures on Hebrew poetry. It was discussed by Addison, Burke, and Kant, given visual expression by romantic painters of the 'apocalyptic sublime', and has enjoyed a postmodern renaissance in the work of Jean-François Lyotard and Slavoj Žižek in a way that suggests the notions of transcendence to which it relates have continuing cultural

---

[71] Hans Frei, *The Eclipse of Biblical Narrative: A Study in Eighteenth and Nineteenth Century Hermeneutics* (New Haven and London: Yale University Press, 1974).

[72] Laurence Lerner, *The Truth-tellers: Jane Austen, George Eliot, D. H. Lawrence* (London: Chatto, 1967); see also John Gibson, *Fiction and the Weave of Life* (Oxford: Oxford University Press, 2007).

[73] See Charles Taylor, *Sources of the Self: The Making of the Modern Identity* (Cambridge: Cambridge University Press, 1989).

God and the Bible, Secularisms and Novels 29

currency.[74] The novel form also depends on the endlessly adaptable theme of pilgrim quest, which can be traced back through Bunyan's *The Pilgrim's Progress* to Abraham in the Old Testament.[75] The theme of social deliverance and the more or less messianic hero and deliverer, aspiring saviour of his people, picked up in Walter Benjamin's concept of 'weak messianism', has biblical resonances that are strengthened when one realizes that the term 'charismatic', often used to describe the gifted leader in fact and fiction, was itself adapted from the New Testament term for spiritual gifts by Max Weber and others.[76]

The categories of the sublime, the pilgrimage, and 'messianism' can help us to reread secular Victorian fictions as modern narrative reimaginings of scriptural themes. But first it will be necessary to revisit the traditional Protestant narrative of the apparent triumph of biblical authority and the equally familiar narrative of the apparent collapse of biblical authority. Neither tells the whole story, which is also the story of neglected continuities between the Bible and the English novel. Reimagining the religious truth of biblical narrative, or imaginative rereading of scripture, continued in but certainly did not begin with the Victorian novel. Nor is it as apparent as may have been thought that there ever really was an innocent paradise to be lost (or a fools' paradise), in which no one doubted that the scriptures were authoritative sources of scientific and historical as well as religious teaching, and the sacred book was at the heart of everyone's faith.

---

[74] For aspects of the sublime, see Philip Shaw, *The Sublime* (London: Routledge, 2006); Peter de Bolla, *The Discourse of the Sublime: Readings in History, Aesthetics and the Subject* (Oxford: Blackwell, 1989); Morton Paley, *The Apocalyptic Sublime* (New Haven and London: Yale University Press, 1986).

[75] For the currency of the pilgrim idea, see Barry Qualls, *The Secular Pilgrims of Victorian Fiction*; also W. R. Owens and Stuart Sim, eds, *Reception, Appropriation, Recollection: Bunyan's* Pilgrim's Progress (Bern: Peter Lang, 2007).

[76] For weak messianism, see Walter Benjamin, 'Theses on the Philosophy of History' (1940), II, VI, *Illuminations*, trans. Harry Zohn (London: Fontana/Collins, 1973), pp. 255–7. For *charisma* as 'spiritual gift', see Romans 1:11, 12:6, etc., and Max Weber, *The Theory of Social and Economic Organization*, trans. A. M. Henderson and Talcott Parsons (London: William Hodge, 1947), esp. chapter 3.

2

The Authority of the Bible

Nineteenth-century Britain witnessed numerous religious controversies relating to doctrine and Church order, but these were as nothing by comparison with the perceived crisis of biblical authority in the face of modern knowledge, particularly in relation to miracles and Creation. Questioning anything that the Bible said was too easily construed as questioning the whole basis of the Christian faith. And yet the Bible had not even been mentioned in some of the oldest agreed statements of the faith of the Church such as the Apostles' Creed and the earliest version of the Nicene Creed, both dating from early in the fourth century.

Questions and anxieties increased with the growth of secular knowledge. By the middle of the nineteenth century, Enlightenment and rationalist scepticism, particularly about miracle-narratives, was reinforced by a more rigorously critical historiography and a more confidently materialist understanding of nature and human physiology. Even before the publication of Charles Darwin's famous *On the Origin of Species* in 1859, advances in geology and palaeontology called into question any literal understanding of the Genesis creation account. The adverse effects of *On the Origin of Species* on religious belief have been exaggerated, and there were Christian Darwinians such as Charles Kingsley, but some dedicated men of science such as the abrasive Irish physicist John Tyndall, Professor of Natural Philosophy at the Royal Institution from 1853, had begun to give the impression that the only truths worthy of the name were scientific. The apparent link between the new science and scepticism in religious matters was vigorously developed by 'Darwin's bulldog' T. H. Huxley, usually credited with inventing the term 'agnostic' to describe his own position. Huxley read Mary Ward's sceptical *Robert Elsmere* with interest; his wide circle of acquaintance included not just

The Authority of the Bible 31

Ward but other novelists such as George Eliot and Thomas Hardy, all responsive to the scientific and intellectual advances of their time. For them, as for many of their contemporaries, neither scripture nor religion more generally could ever be quite the same again, though it needs to be emphasized that scripture and religion could engage the creative imagination all the more because of the questions being asked.

The story of the apparently rapidly declining fortunes of the Bible in Victorian Britain has often been told, usually in brashly oversimplified and indeed mythologized form as a straightforward narrative of decline and fall, mists of mystification and superstition finally dispelled by the dry light of reason and modern knowledge. But in order to understand fictional reimaginings of scripture this narrative needs to be revised. It should be seen as a more nuanced record of varied and changing habits of Bible reading and reflection on what the Bible was really for. This was a complex process in which creative reimaginings of biblical themes by novelists of religious nurture played an important part. The novels discussed in subsequent chapters can be seen both as imaginative transformations of scripture and contributions to this developing history of reading. They variously initiate and respond to new kinds of biblical understanding, and breathe new life into older modes of non-literal reading and commentary that emphasized poetry, metaphor, allegory, and parable. The apparent crisis of scriptural authority that stimulated or precipitated these kinds of reading belongs in a much broader historical context of identity politics, tendentious appropriation and misappropriation, misunderstanding, and misreading. This context includes the story of how the Bible came to be invested with so much authority in the first place, itself usually oversimplified and mythologized as the founding narrative of Protestantism.

Nineteenth-century Britain was culturally as well as religiously identified as Protestant, despite the problem of Catholic Ireland and despite Catholic enclaves in England and Scotland. Protestantism had its aggressive side, nurtured on Gothic tales of oppressed or oppressive monks and nuns, popular legends of Catholic conspirators such as Guy Fawkes, and heroic and perhaps divinely assisted victory against Catholic Spain at the time of the Spanish Armada. The Bible, identified as a key symbol of Protestantism and somehow the basis of Britain's success in the world, was traditionally accepted as important, even by those who never read it. A popular engraving of

32 *The Authority of the Bible*

T. J. Barker's portrait of Queen Victoria (*c.*1862) (now in the National Portrait Gallery), showing her presenting a kneeling African prince with a Bible, was captioned 'The Secret of England's Greatness'. In the sixteenth century, according to the traditional rather oversimplified narrative, the continental reformers had rejected the authority and many of the practices of the Roman Catholic Church as unscriptural, signalling the breach with Rome by vesting authority in matters of faith in the Bible rather than the traditions of the Church. The Church of England formally adopted this position in 1562 in the sixth of the Thirty-Nine Articles, 'Of the Sufficiency of the Holy Scriptures for Salvation'. The authority of scripture, independent of the Church and its traditions, was reiterated, in more severely exclusive terms, in the fourth article of the *Westminster Confession of Faith* (1647), originally intended as the basis of the national religion to replace the Articles and used and respected in Britain and America ever since by many Nonconformists and Presbyterians:

> The authority of the holy Scripture, for which it ought to be believed and obeyed, dependeth not upon the testimony of any man or church, but wholly upon God (who is truth itself), the Author thereof; and therefore it is to be received because it is the Word of God.

In 1860 the American Presbyterian Anna Bartlett Warner distilled this principle into the opening lines of a popular children's hymn: 'Jesus loves me—this I know,/For the Bible tells me so'.[1]

Such dogmatic assurance, never unchallenged despite popular belief to the contrary, may have been a great comfort to the faithful, but by the later nineteenth century it was wearing thin. People were becoming wary of what the Bible told them, at least about some things. Biblical miracles had been under more or less sustained attack in some quarters since Hume included a sceptical 'Essay upon Miracles' in his *Philosophical Essays Concerning Human Understanding* (1748), later retitled *An Enquiry Concerning Human Understanding*. A special chapter was devoted to miracles in T. H. Huxley's sympathetic study of Hume (1879), published in the popular English Men of Letters series. Were the scriptures really authoritative and literally

---

[1] Text of the Westminster Confession from Philip Schaff, ed., *The Creeds of Christendom*, 6th ed. (1931), 3 vols. (repr. Grand Rapids, MI: Baker Books, 2007), III, p. 676. Anna Bartlett Warner's hymn was written for her sister Susan Warner's pious novel *Say and Seal* (London: Richard Bentley, 1860) in which it is sung to a dying child.

The Authority of the Bible 33

true, miracles, creation narrative and all? Or did advances in the natural sciences, historical knowledge, and the (mainly German) critical scholarship espoused by liberal churchmen and secular sages now threaten to relegate them for ever to the status of romantic myth or pious fiction? The issue was hardly a new one, and it was much older than German critical scholarship, but it had become sharper and more urgent with the growth of a popular readership interested in science and speculation as well as religion.

Among traditionalist British Protestants there was the additional fear that the cherished sovereignty of scripture was now under attack from Catholic as well as liberal opinion, within as well as outside the Church of England. Traditional Anglican teaching, represented by the sixth of the Thirty-Nine Articles, had been elaborated in learned and time-honoured commentaries on the Articles such as that of Gilbert Burnet, Bishop of Salisbury (1699, new edition 1837). But it was audaciously challenged in the 1830s by the leader of the Oxford Movement, John Henry Newman, committed to developing a more Catholic understanding of the Church of England, but not yet a Roman Catholic. In his *Lectures on the Prophetical Office of the Church* (1837) he had flown in the face of popular Protestant opinion on the supremacy of scripture in matters of faith, claiming it was presumptuous for individuals to expect to find Christian faith and knowledge simply by reading the Bible for themselves, without external guidance of the kind represented by the traditions of the Church. In a further set of lectures on *Holy Scripture in its Relation to the Catholic Creed* (1838), published as Tract 85 of the controversial series of Tracts for the Times, he identified rather than resolved difficulties in proving the doctrines of the Church directly from scripture. It was, arguably, a dangerous all-or-nothing tactic: for Newman the traditional, Catholic, teaching of the Church was essential to make sense of scripture, but highlighting problems with scripture on its own as a source of authority to promote controversial and widely resisted teaching about the authority of Church tradition ran the risk of leaving people with nothing at all to rely on, distrusting scripture and tradition alike. Matters came to a head in Newman's notorious and ingenious Tract 90 of 1841, which was widely condemned. This attempted to read the Articles in a Catholic sense, or at least to demonstrate that they did not explicitly exclude Catholic teaching, and to argue in particular that article six need not formally commit Anglicans to the cherished Reformation principle of *sola*

34   *The Authority of the Bible*

scriptura, scripture on its own as the supreme authority in matters of faith.

Diehard Protestant opinion was outraged. The sovereignty of scripture among Anglicans was briskly reaffirmed in polemical works such as J. L. Jackson's *The Character of Scriptural Inspiration: The Authority of Holy Scripture with the Church of England* (1842), which vigorously attacked Newman and the other 'Tractarians'. But this traditional position, particularly in its more narrowly literalist versions, became more and more vulnerable to attack in succeeding decades, as science and critical and historical scholarship made further advances. The leading secularist G. W. Foote, editor of the *Freethinker*, who tried to enlist Thomas Hardy as a fellow freethinker, published his dismissive study *Bible Romances* in 1882.[2] 'Romances' was a carefully calculated sneer, meant to indicate material that was one stage worse than pure fiction, as it suggested the far-fetched unbelievable narratives against which the more sober and realistic novel form had defined itself in the previous century. But as already discussed in Chapter 1, the realm of romance was also the world of the imagination, giving access to the possibilities of transcendence, which was increasingly respected after the example of Wordsworth and the other romantic poets. Foote had no religious imagination, or any other kind, and had not realized, or chose to ignore, the extent to which popular romance and the realist novel had already converged to colonize and develop the imaginative terrain and the religious agendas of biblical narrative in the perennial quest for truth and understanding.

In February 1889 T. H. Huxley resumed his habit of poking scientific holes in scripture, or at least scripture understood literally, in a sceptical magazine article on the miraculous gospel narrative of the Gadarene swine. The Bible needed a new champion. Mr Gladstone, famously devout, was now the Grand Old Man of British politics and the greatest parliamentary orator of the age, as well as the most prominent critic of *Robert Elsmere* in 1888. He was enlisted to write for the defence, and against Huxley, in the religious magazine *Good Words*, and his articles were collected under the resonant title *The Impregnable Rock of Holy Scripture* (1890). It soon became clear that the issue was not really about truth but about dogma. Two rival

---

[2] G. W. Foote, *Bible Romances* (London: Freethought Publishing Co., 1882) (a fourth edition was published in 1922).

The Authority of the Bible 35

faiths were at stake. The religious conservatives, who sought reassurance from Mr Gladstone that Foote and Huxley and the German critics were mistaken or harmless, or preferably both, needed the Bible to be as true and as uncomplicatedly authoritative as ever, while the secularists and agnostics looked to Huxley, and to Foote's patronizing and dismissive riposte to Gladstone, for additional confirmation of their negative conviction that the Bible was merely a literary curiosity of no special authority.[3]

As so often happens, heated controversy had muddled the terms of the debate, confusing different kinds of truth and different kinds of authority, and setting up an artificial polarity: either the Bible was literally true or it was completely untrue. No scope was allowed for intermediate possibilities, or awkward questions such as that of Bacon's jesting Pilate, 'What is truth?' But what kinds of truth might one reasonably look for in scripture? What kind of authority might it have? How should people read the Genesis creation narrative or Old Testament historical narratives or the partly miraculous gospel narratives in the era of Darwinian science and critical history? Was it now time to reconfigure and reimagine religious truth, perhaps with the aid of different narratives such as those supplied by the novelists?

The self-confident rationalist legacy of the Enlightenment was still continuing to sponsor progressive and iconoclastic grand narratives such as W. E. H. Lecky's *Rise of Rationalism in Europe* (1865), describing thick darkness overcome, the ruthless dispelling of the dreams and fantasies of earlier ages in the cold clear daylight of reason and incipient modernity, not to mention the unillusioned realism supposedly characteristic of Victorian fiction. Was the Bible simply a compendium of pre-modern delusion? Was there anything of value left in it for rational and liberal Christians to hang on to? Were the scriptures and the authority traditionally vested in them simply relics of an earlier and less enlightened epoch? British secularists, following the example of French positivists and radical German Hegelians and socialists, were sure that the scriptures had had their day. The attractively simple narrative of darkness gradually dispelled

---

[3] T. H. Huxley, 'Agnosticism' (1889), reprinted in *Essays upon Some Controverted Questions* (London: Macmillan, 1892); for Huxley and Gladstone, see Adrian Desmond, *Huxley: Evolution's High Priest* (London: Michael Joseph, 1997), pp. 155–200; G. W. Foote, *The Grand Old Book: A Reply to the Right Hon. W. E. Gladstone's 'The Impregnable Rock of Holy Scripture'* (London: Progressive Publishing Co., 1891).

36 *The Authority of the Bible*

and steadily enhanced understanding was attractive not just to rationalists but to liberal and progressive churchmen, open to new approaches to the scriptures, and to progressive novelists. But it was stubbornly resisted by diehard religious conservatives who sensed that it was in tension with the transhistorical truth-claims of biblical teaching as traditionally understood, particularly the unchanging status claimed in the scriptures for the ever-living Christ, the same yesterday, today, and for ever (Hebrews 13:8). Was reading scripture in search of unqualified and absolute truth itself an aspect of the dead past, now consigned to the dust heap of history? Was the apparent decline of traditional scriptural authority simply an aspect and a function of the allegedly inevitable disenchantment of the world, the secularization process, to be understood as a manifestation of modernity? Or was the cultural narrative more complicated than that? Could there be modern but still religious readings of the scriptures? Might it be the case, with the scriptures as with religious awareness more generally, that a self-consciously scientific and progressive age was providing fresh perspectives, witnessing change rather than decay?

The long history of debate about the status and authority of scripture was once again brought to public notice by the outcry that greeted the donnishly liberal attitudes to scripture in *Essays and Reviews* (1860), the authors of which were identified as the 'seven against Christ' in unkind allusion to Aeschylus' play *The Seven Against Thebes*. It was renewed by the disconcertingly unfamiliar phrasing of some passages in the Revised Version of the English Bible in 1881–5, attributable both to improved linguistic knowledge and a more reliable, more 'scientific' Greek text for the New Testament based on carefully comparing and classifying the numerous surviving manuscripts.

It is perhaps clearer to us now than it was then that what was at issue in the nineteenth century was not so much the fate of the Bible as particular ways of reading it. Narrowly literal readings had become more vulnerable than ever. And yet the Bible had not always been read like this. The new geology of the nineteenth century, and the vast abysses of geological time it revealed, challenged literal reading of the detail of the Genesis creation narrative, and made it clear that the earth's origins lay much further back in time than the traditional date of 4004 BCE. But narrowly literal reading of the scriptures had never been universal, even in antiquity, and the apparently time-honoured

The Authority of the Bible 37

traditional date was itself only about two hundred years old. There had been many other approximations but this particular estimate stemmed from the seventeenth-century chronological researches and close readings of James Ussher, Archbishop of Armagh, whose conjectural dates proposed in his *Annales Veteris Testamenti* (1650) were inserted in the margins of the Authorized Version on the authority of William Lloyd, Bishop of Worcester, from about 1701 onwards. Victorian Bibles sometimes modified or supplemented Ussher's dates, within the same overall time-scheme, in the light of later chronological research such as the Irish polymath William Hales' laborious *New Analysis of Chronology* (1809–12).

Ussher's various chronological studies, extending over 2,000 published pages, drawing on all that was then known about the whole range of ancient history and incorporating dates such as the death of Nebuchadnezzar established from non-Biblical sources, assumed the possibility of a detailed mathematical precision for which the data and the techniques had not been available in earlier ages. The study of biblical chronology seems to have begun early in the third century with the lost *Chronographiai* of Julius Africanus (*c*.170–240), a probable source for the *Chronicoi Canones* or 'Chronological Canons' of Eusebius, Bishop of Caesarea, which were in their turn incorporated into his *Ecclesiastical History* at the beginning of the fourth century.[4] But by the seventeenth century vastly more information was available.

Ussher represented the high point of a recent but solid tradition of European Renaissance scholarship, which included other landmarks such as J. J. Scaliger's *De Emendatio Temporis* (1583). There were many other Renaissance chronologists, but the mathematical certainty and precision they all sought eluded them in one particular at least. Estimates for the creation ranged from 3928 (John Lightfoot) to 4103 (Brian Walton), and before them Jewish teachers had fixed on 3760, the date still used today as the basis of the Jewish calendar. 'You will find it easier to make the wolf agree with the lamb than to make all chronologers agree about the age of the world', claimed the

---

[4] James Ussher, *Annales Veteris et Novi Testamenti* (1650–54), and *The Annals of the World* (1658), discussed by James Barr, 'Why the World was Created in 4004 BC: Archbishop Ussher and Biblical Chronology', *Bulletin of the John Rylands Library* 67 (Spring 1985), 575–608. See also Jack Finegan, *Handbook of Biblical Chronology* (Princeton: Princeton University Press, 1964).

38   *The Authority of the Bible*

Heidelberg mathematician Jacobus Curio in 1557.[5] The lack of consensus indicated that on the available evidence no precise dating was possible, though this seems to have generated no traumatic anxieties at the time: the matter was apparently regarded as scientifically interesting rather than of particular religious importance.

The thirst for ever more precise knowledge was typical of early modern Europe. This was an era of epic voyages of discovery: Portuguese, Spanish, Dutch, and English. The European discovery of the Americas presented both opportunities and problems, including the difficulty of deriving the populations of both the Old World and the New World from Adam and Eve. Ussher's contemporary Pererius (Isaac de la Peyrère), a French Calvinist lawyer, diplomat, and armchair geographer, began to speculate heretically about pre-Adamite man and multiple human origins.[6] Cartographers were busy redrawing maps and filling up outlines and blank spaces in the light of fresh knowledge, hoping to fit together into a coherent whole both the diverse fragments of the known world and the jumble of more or less mysterious names, hints, and details that had come down from ancient sources, including the scriptures.

Eusebius of Caesarea had been a pioneer in trying to make sense of the places as well as the dates of the Bible, drawing for geographical information on earlier Greek sources such as Josephus' *Jewish Antiquities.* His *Onomasticon,* in Jerome's Latin translation, was widely available in the Christianized West and represented a starting point for the European—and Eurocentric—process of extending and organizing geographical knowledge. Ussher himself published *Geographical and Historical Disquisition Touching...Asia* (1641) and Ussher's contemporary and scholarly correspondent Samuel Bochart, Protestant pastor of Caen, compiled massive interim reports on sacred geography since the scattering of the nations after Babel, beginning with *Phaleg, seu de Dispersione Gentium et Terrarum* (1646). This aspect of the process of making modern sense of ancient

---

[5] For Lightfoot and other Renaissance chronologists, see C. A. Patrides, 'Renaissance Estimates of the Year of Creation', *Huntington Library Quarterly* 26 (1963), 315–22; Jacobus Curio, *Chronologicarum Rerum Liber* II (Basle, 1557), is quoted in Philip C. Almond, *Adam and Eve in Seventeenth-Century Thought* (Cambridge: Cambridge University Press, 1999), p. 83.

[6] For Pererius and Pre-Adamitism, see David N. Livingstone, *Adam's Ancestors: Race, Religion and the Politics of Human Origins* (Baltimore: Johns Hopkins University Press, 2008).

The Authority of the Bible 39

records, myths, legends, and vague reports continued—with increasing success and increasing help from archaeological evidence—into the nineteenth century, into the world of Rider Haggard and the European exploration of black Africa and other even more remote regions such as central Asia.

Ussher's geographical and chronological interests both stemmed from the would-be scientific tidy-mindedness of his age. His ambition was not just to date the creation but to construct a coherent and comprehensive chronological scheme, reducing the whole of human history, including scripture history, to some kind of rational order. The aspiration shared by Renaissance mapmakers and chronologists was signalled in the title, borrowed from an ancient Hebrew chronicle, which the Cambridge scholar Hugh Broughton gave to his chronological treatise, *A Seder Olam, that Is: Order of the World* (1594). What needs to be kept in mind is that while the cartographers, geographers, and chronologists drew freely on pre-scientific biblical materials designed for other purposes, alongside other ancient sources, there was little that was inherently religious (or anti-religious) about their published work: mistakes were made, constantly, but this did not greatly matter as religion itself was not at stake. The biblically imagined world they sought to reduce to different kinds of order was richer, more enigmatic, and more durable than their descriptions of it. It continued to signify, religiously and imaginatively, independently of them.

The chronologists' tendency to posit a remote but still comfortably imaginable beginning not too far from 4000 BCE can be traced back to a Talmudic tradition attributed to Tanna of the House of Elijah (Abodah Zarah 9a), which had been picked up by Protestant reformers such as Philipp Melanchthon, that the earth would endure for a total of six thousand years. The six millennia poetically corresponded to the six days in which it had been created (since it was claimed in Ps.90:4 that a thousand years in the sight of the Lord were but as yesterday when it is past, and as a watch in the night). It was also claimed that the Messiah would come two-thirds of the way through the course of world history, after 4,000 years, which would give Christians at least a date for the creation of around 4,000 years before Christ. But this tradition, abstracted from rather than directly indicated in scripture, represented a religiously imaginative rather than a precisely mathematical understanding of time, even though it provided the Renaissance chronologists with a framework for very

40 *The Authority of the Bible*

precise calculations based on comparing biblical and non-biblical kingship records and historical annals, and factoring in verifiable astronomical data that served as markers.

If biblical chronologists were trying to make sense of time within a traditional framework, Bible-reading astronomers were trying to make sense of space. The wonderfully dramatic biblical story of the sun standing still over the earth at Gibeon, so that Israel would have extra daylight in which to defeat its enemies (Joshua 10:12–13), presented similar challenges to the new Renaissance appetite for quasi-mathematical certainty and was still being debated by German critics such as G. L. Bauer two centuries later. How could such a thing happen? The astronomer Galileo, aware with Copernicus that it was the earth that moved round the sun rather than the other way round, and eager to demonstrate that modern science did not undermine the integrity of scripture, published a *Letter to the Grand Duchess Christina* (1615) in which he ingeniously interpreted the passage to make it accord with the new heliocentrism, only to get into trouble for even raising a matter that had not previously caused much anxiety or concern. Bauer, more plausibly, suggested that this was an ancient poetic fragment taken over, and taken literally, by a later historical writer. Poetic reading of scripture was not a new-fangled German idea but well established: even before Galileo and Copernicus, Dean Colet of St Paul's (1466?–1519) had written that the opening chapters of Genesis contained poetic rather than scientific truth.[7] Victorian anxieties or misgivings about the authority of Genesis, and of scriptural narrative more generally, represented a challenge not so much to the Bible as to unsustainable—and relatively recent—attempts to read symbolic and imaginative religious narrative scientifically and literally instead of religiously.

It might have seemed new and daring for Hume in the eighteenth century, or Huxley in the nineteenth, to raise difficulties about biblical miracles and challenge the scientific accuracy and value of biblical narrative, but it was not. Spinoza had devoted the sixth chapter of his *Tractatus Theologico-Politicus* (1670) to dismissing miracle as absurd,

---

[7] See T. M. Rudavsky, 'Galileo and Spinoza: Heroes, Heretics and Hermeneutics', *Journal of the History of Ideas* 62 (Oct. 2001), 611–31; for Bauer's *Hebräische Mythologie* (1802), see J. W. Rogerson, *Myth in Old Testament Interpretation* (Berlin and New York: Walter de Gruyter, 1974), pp. 8–9; for Colet, see J. K. S. Reid, *The Authority of Scripture: A Study of the Reformation and Pre-Reformation Understanding of the Bible* (London: Methuen, 1957), p. 24.

The Authority of the Bible   41

and had claimed that biblical narrative was more concerned with appealing to the religious imagination than with objective accuracy. Victorian doubters and scoffers had forgotten, or did not know, that it had been realized long ago that the Bible was not, and was never meant to be, a scientific book. Galen, the great Greek physician of the second century of the common era, had disagreed with Genesis, which he had probably encountered in Greek translation. He complained that by the standards of modern Greek science 'Moses', traditionally credited with authorship of the first five books of the Bible, had not produced a philosophical or scientific account of the beginning of things when he described the creation of the world in six days. Everything was attributed directly to the creative word of God, without any reference to the secondary causes through which things actually happen. Galen had noticed what many Victorians failed to notice, that the Genesis creation account was theological rather than scientific.[8]

Galen was a Gentile, or outsider, with no particular commitment to Jewish religious tradition or the theology of Genesis. But even among the committed, the rabbis who taught the Hebrew scriptures at this time and the early church fathers, it was possible to read scripture attentively and reverently without straining credulity or stumbling over details through expecting the texts to be always literally true, or to provide total and sufficient explanations. Explanatory oral matter was often incorporated in the Targums, the interpretative Aramaic translations of the Hebrew scriptures, and there was a rabbinic tradition of *mashal* or parable to elucidate particular passages, precisely because it was felt further explanation was sometimes needed. Long before the Victorian novel, biblical narrative was being reimagined and new stories were being used to explain old ones. Jerome, the greatest biblical scholar of the early church, loved the scriptures but freely admitted there were difficulties and obscurities, particularly in prophetic texts such as Ezekiel and in the opening chapters of Genesis. He noted that by tradition the Jews did not study such awkward passages until they were thirty years old. In fact detailed public discussion of the perplexing six-day creation account and other problem passages such as the mysterious vision of the chariot

---

[8] See R. Walzer, *Galen on Jews and Christians* (London, 1949), which prints, translates, and discusses the six references to Jewish or Christian ideas that have survived in Greek or Arabic texts of Galen.

42   *The Authority of the Bible*

in the opening chapter of Ezekiel, was officially discouraged in the second-century Mishnah and again in the sixth-century Babylonian Talmud: much of the material was held to be an esoteric mystery, a source of wonder, and the literal sense of the details did not necessarily matter very much.[9] In any case, details could be treated imaginatively and poetically when it suited. The Bible spoke of days, but what was a day? Rabbis quoted in the Talmud found it perfectly legitimate to recall the psalmist's claim that 'a thousand years in thy sight are but as yesterday when it is past' (Psalm 90:4) and to deem a day in the creation narrative to be a vividly poetic way of indicating a thousand years, a figure that was itself obviously rhetorical rather than mathematically precise.[10]

If early Jewish commentary was not particularly familiar to most Victorian churchmen, the same could hardly be said of the church fathers. They were frequently cited by the earliest apologists for the Church of England such as Thomas Cranmer and John Jewel to emphasize continuity with the early Church despite the breach with Rome, and they enjoyed a new lease of life when Newman's *Church of the Fathers* (1840), his polemically motivated translation of selections from Athanasius (1842), and Tractarian and post-Tractarian patristic scholarship more generally, gave rise to new editions and new English translations. Early Victorian translators were often associated with Newman and the *Library of the Fathers of the Holy Catholic Church*, which he founded in 1838, along with Keble and Pusey, but the next generation, including the contributors to the translations of Ante-Nicene, Nicene, and Post-Nicene Fathers published by T. & T. Clark in Edinburgh, were contemporaries of the later Victorian novelists such as Mary Ward. Like Ward, many were also associated with the magisterial *Dictionary of Christian Biography* (1877–87), edited by Sir William Smith and Henry Wace. One of the many scholarly contributors was Rev. W. H. Fremantle, eventually Dean of Ripon,

---

[9] Jerome, Letter 53 to Paulinus, on the study of scripture, in J. P. Migne, ed., *Patrologia Latina* (PL) 22.547, and Jerome, *Letters and Select Works*, trans. W. H. Fremantle, Nicene and Post-Nicene Fathers (Grand Rapids, MI: W. B. Eerdmans, 1996), p. 101; *Mishnah*, Hagigah 2.1; *Talmud* Hagigah 11b. All references to the Mishnah are to the Herbert Danby translation (London: Oxford University Press, 1933); all references to the Talmud are to the English translation of the Babylonian Talmud, ed. Isidore Epstein, 18 vols (London: Soncino Press, 1962).

[10] Sanhedrin 97a; Rosh Hashanah 31a.

The Authority of the Bible   43

the translator of Jerome and author of *The Gospel of the Secular Life* (1882); Fremantle was a pioneer of the 'secular' social gospel reflected in *Robert Elsmere* a few years later.

Early and respected Christian commentators such as Origen in the third century, and Gregory of Nyssa in the fourth, could be seen to have ranged well beyond the literal sense of scripture, particularly the terse formal austerity of the creation narrative in Genesis, to tease out or impose meaning, system, and coherence in the light of established teaching of the Church and the Greek philosophy of their time. Origen showed a frankness and an imaginative freedom of interpretation that might have got him into serious trouble in the Victorian Church. Material preserved in the *Philocalia*, an early selection of his writings, reveals that he had noted commands in the Law of Moses that he felt were either unreasonable or, if taken literally, impossible. He had also identified what seemed to him obviously unhistorical elements in both Old and New Testament narratives, incidents that never happened though they were a figurative means of revealing certain mysteries. With considerable originality, and minimal scriptural warrant, he reimagined the Genesis creation story, transforming it into a lofty cosmic myth. He proposed a two-stage model of creation, first a spiritual creation of a finite number of 'noetic' beings or disembodied rational essences, co-eternal with God, simultaneously created through the divine Logos or Word before time, and then, after these of their own will had fallen away from God, a corporeal creation binding souls to bodies in the material world as we know it.[11]

Gregory, much influenced by Origen, was another who saw the Genesis creation account not as history but as storytelling, a way of placing doctrines before the faithful in the form of narrative. He complemented his brother Basil's extended meditations on the six-day work of creation by devoting a treatise specifically to the creation of man, claiming, again without specific scriptural authority, that for this last and summative work of creation God carefully prepared

---

[11] Origen, *Philocalia,* trans. George Lewis Edinburgh: T.&T. Clark, 1911), 1.16–20 'Of the Inspiration of the Divine Scripture'; *De Principiis* 1.8.1, 2.2, 2.6.3, 2.9, in J. P. Migne, ed., *Patrologia Graeca* (PG) 11.176, pp. 186–7, 211, 225–33, and *Writings,* 2 vols, trans. Frederick Crombie, Ante-Nicene Christian Library (Edinburgh: T. & T. Clark, 1869–72), I, pp. 65, 77–9, 109, 126–36, discussed by J. N. D. Kelly, *Early Christian Doctrines,* 5th ed. (London: Continuum, 2006), pp. 180–1.

44   *The Authority of the Bible*

matter beforehand and incorporated the possibilities of earlier forms of life.[12]

Augustine, the great expositor of the scriptures, found it necessary to go beyond them even in a commentary on the literal text of Genesis. Influenced by Plato's view that time itself was created with the world—and alert to the epistemological gulf between divine (and angelic) and human consciousness, eternity, and time—he suggested, like Origen before him, that the entire work of creation might actually have been pre-temporal and simultaneous through the Eternal Word of God: he argued ingeniously that the formal narrative division into six days, separating creation into distinct phases, represented a kind of translation into the human world of space and time, necessary to convey the wonder and multiplicity of the creation to time-bound believers.[13]

In later times believers have often been given less scope by preachers and teachers to range beyond the spare detail of the biblical text. Scripture has been required to make sense of itself on its own. The all-sufficient truth and authority claimed for the Bible have characteristically been 'proved' by supplying proof-texts from scripture itself, meticulously detailing chapter and verse. A rather over-worked favourite, invoked by preachers from St John Chrysostom to the present, is the claim of 2 Timothy 3:16 that 'All scripture is given by inspiration of God, and is profitable for doctrine, for reproof, for correction, for instruction in righteousness.' But the now rather archaic method of argument from proof-texts bristles with difficulties. Because it is self-referential it cannot convince, unless one is already convinced that the Bible is authoritative. It can also distort original meanings by indiscriminately assembling snippets of scripture wrenched from different contexts. New Testament proof-texts for the authority of scripture as a whole are particularly problematic because, as the biblical scholar James Barr has pointed out, at the time of writing the content of the Bible as we know it had not yet been settled, a process completed only towards the end of the second century. So even New Testament references to 'Scripture' or 'the

---

[12] Gregory of Nyssa, *Oratio Catechetica* 5 (PG 45.21–4); *De Opifico Hominis* 3.2 (PG 44.136).

[13] Augustine, *De Genesi ad Litteram*, 4.33, 34 (PL 34.317–9); Plato, *Timaeus*, 37d, e.

The Authority of the Bible 45

Word of God' cannot refer to the Bible as we now have it.[14] In any case, that particular argumentative mode of reading the Bible, piling up precise references to chapter and verse to prove a point or justify a doctrine, was a comparatively late development in the history of Christianity, only really possible after clear agreement had been reached on how the text should be divided into chapters and verses. There were various different divisions in antiquity, mainly to produce manageable portions of text for reading aloud, but the modern chapter divisions are said to have been inserted in the (Latin) Bible between 1206 and 1228 by Stephen Langton, Archbishop of Canterbury. Numbered verse divisions came even later: verse numbers were used for the Hebrew Bible from the mid-fifteenth century and were taken over into early printed editions such as Robert Estienne's French (1553) and Latin (1555) Bibles, while New Testament verse numbers first appear in 1551, in Estienne's Greek and Latin edition of the New Testament prepared in Geneva. The first English Bible to provide chapter and verse divisions as we know them was the Geneva Bible of 1560.[15]

The attribution of supreme authority to a printed or written text is obviously a function of a culture in which writing is well established and valued, but the texts of scripture, both Old Testament and New Testament, as we now have them, owe much to earlier oral tradition. Written versions of originally oral material, often treated with particular reverence in effectively non-literate societies, have their own authority because they fix the tradition and ensure continuity, but the transition from oral to written forms can give rise to tensions and exclusions and to pedantic narrowness, or at least allegations of it. The custodians of the tradition are no longer the faith community as a whole but a subset of it, a literate elite with an authority that can be contested. The Torah, the Written Law of the Hebrew scriptures, was interpreted and elaborated through traditions of teaching, the Oral Law, which was itself collected and written down by Judah haNasi (Judah the Prince) as the Mishnah in the second century of the common era. Oral commentary on the materials of the Mishnah,

---

[14] James Barr, *Holy Scripture: Canon, Authority, Criticism* (Oxford: Clarendon Press, 1983), p. 20.

[15] David Daniell, *The Bible in English* (New Haven and London: Yale University Press, 2003), p. 5; Owen Chadwick, *The Early Reformation on the Continent* (Oxford: Oxford University Press, 2001), pp. 6–7, 14, 36.

46 *The Authority of the Bible*

extending the tradition, was in its turn recorded in the Babylonian and Palestinian Talmuds. But as the Oral Law was evolving, the Sadducees, a priestly sect who feature in the New Testament record, came into conflict with the Pharisees by rejecting the Oral Law and accepting only the authority of the written Torah.

As William Schniedewind has demonstrated, this kind of tension between oral and written can be traced in the development of the Bible itself, not just in the evolution of the Hebrew scriptures but in the formation of the New Testament.[16] Nineteenth-century critical scholarship, more familiar with written than with oral culture, tended to underestimate the role and significance of oral tradition. Elaborate if sometimes contested documentary hypotheses to explain different strands and layers of biblical material, brought to a high degree of precision and sophistication by K. H. Graf (1815–69) and Julius Wellhausen (1844–1918), say at least as much about the mindset of nineteenth-century bookmen as they do about the Bible, and more modern scholarship has modified the documentary theories to take account of the fact that before the materials were committed to writing they would have been preserved, shaped, and developed within the oral traditions of believing and worshipping communities. Jesus himself, a teacher who left no book of his own, is recalled and recorded as demonstrating a capacity to see beyond the written scriptures. The Sadducees, hereditary priests of the Temple, rejected the idea of resurrection, upheld by their rivals the Pharisees, on the grounds it was not found in the Hebrew scriptures. When the Sadducees tried to involve Jesus in this controversy and catch him out, he rebuked them, and their narrowly dogmatic insistence on the written text alone, by saying, 'Ye do err, not knowing the scriptures, nor the power of God' (Matthew 22:29). The implication is that really knowing the Hebrew scriptures, grasping the true meaning of the Law or Torah, depends not just on technical understanding of the written documents but on a living encounter with the spirit that lies behind them. The point was not to belittle the written law, which Jesus could invoke himself on occasion, or the Hebrew scriptures, which he read aloud in the synagogue in Nazareth, according to Luke 4:16–18, but to suggest that the written word needed to be understood in the context of religious teaching empowered by religious experience.

---

[16] William M. Schniedewind, *How the Bible Became a Book* (Cambridge: Cambridge University Press, 2004).

The Authority of the Bible 47

The potential for tension between the preached and the written word, tradition and scripture, was there even before organized Christianity. In modern times the cultural authority of written texts derives largely from the standing of the author: even the most minor works of James Joyce, like those of his distinguished biographer Richard Ellmann, command attention because the named author is famous and widely respected. But it was different in Old Testament times. There is no word in biblical Hebrew that exactly corresponds to 'author' in the modern sense. The nearest term is *sofer*. The word for a written record is *sefer* and the related *sofer* denotes the person who does the writing, not an originator or creative writer but an enumerator, tally-clerk or scribe, a record-keeper who simply makes a note of what he is told, whether numbers or narrative. The authority of the written text derived not from a named author but from the collective memory that lay behind the text, the community that had hitherto preserved the materials and traditions by oral transmission.

Unfortunately the scribes could assume airs and authority over against the communities they were supposed to serve. In a largely non-literate society, scribes were associated with administrative functions either at court or in the temple, complicit with ruling elites, keeping records as part of a system of regulation. In the Old Testament world, in the seventh century before the common era, there seem to have been murmurings against the exclusive authority of the scribes, who took it upon themselves to preserve and control the written tradition, and a reaction in favour of the oral tradition of the community and its continuing life through the spoken word of teachers and prophets. A difficult passage in Jeremiah seems to indicate prophetic impatience with scribes and with a people who might have the written text of the law but have still gone astray:

> How do ye say, we are wise, and the law of the Lord is with us? Lo, certainly in vain made he it; the pen of the scribes is in vain [or, (Revised Standard Version) the false pen of the scribes has made it into a lie]. The wise men are ashamed, they are dismayed and taken: lo, they have rejected the word of the Lord; and what wisdom is in them?[17]

---

[17] Jeremiah 8:8–9; unless otherwise indicated biblical quotations are from the 1611 King James or 'Authorized' Version; Schniedewind, *How the Bible Became a Book*, p. 116.

48   *The Authority of the Bible*

The key contrast is between the (written) 'law of the Lord' and the spoken prophetic 'word of the Lord' to which the scribes are deaf, foolishly deluded into thinking that possession of the written law on its own gives all necessary wisdom.[18] This interestingly prefigures the issue in later Judaism and within the Christian Church of whether the authority of written scriptures was really all-sufficient, independent of oral traditions of preaching and teaching. It was a moot point even in the early days of the Church, and one of the crucial issues at the time of the Reformation.

The problem of scriptural authority could be illustrated by the much-debated doctrine of the Trinity: this emerged gradually in the teaching and traditions of the Church and could be deduced from and supported by scripture, but it was not explicitly expounded or developed there. There was in fact no New Testament Greek word that could be translated as 'Trinity'. The terms employed by explicitly Trinitarian theologians, the Latin 'Trinitas', used by Tertullian (*Against Praxeas* 2), and the Greek *trias*, used by Theophilus of Antioch, seem to date from the end of the second century or the beginning of the third. Furthermore, if authority was vested in the scriptures there was still the problem of identifying which writings counted as 'scripture'.

There was eventually more or less general agreement about which early Christian writings were authoritative or 'canonical' scriptures, although there were continuing misgivings in the Eastern Church about Revelation and it was omitted from the early Syriac and Armenian versions of the New Testament. The New Testament scriptures gradually acquired the same privileged and authoritative status as the Old Testament in Judaism. But this was a comparatively late development: the first Christians heard rather than read about the message of the gospel. They were not biblical Protestants *avant la lettre* despite the familiar Protestant narrative to the contrary. James Barr observes that 'We . . . have to recognise that the idea of a Christian faith governed by Christian written holy scriptures was not an essential part of the foundation plan of Christianity.'[19] He goes on to point out that the earliest letters of Paul show no awareness that Christianity depended on written scriptures. Reference to the letters

---

[18] Discussed in John Bright, *Jeremiah* (The Anchor Bible) (Garden City, NY: Doubleday, 1965), p. 63f.

[19] Barr, *Holy Scripture*, p. 12.

The Authority of the Bible   49

of Paul is respectfully made in 2 Peter 3:15–16, associating them with other scriptures, but this is mainly to note that they contain difficulties and that, like the 'other scriptures', they are liable to be misread by the 'unlearned and unstable', 'unto their own destruction'.

Evidence of the danger as well as the authority of scripture abounds in the early Church. Some of the earliest Christian attempts to invoke the authority of scripture seem to have been heretical, or at least idiosyncratic, rather than orthodox. Somewhere around 140, the much-maligned Marcion, founder of a breakaway Christian community in Rome, insisted on a Gospel of Love, which was scriptural but selectively so. It wholly excluded the Law, rejecting the Old Testament completely, and appealed only to the authority of ten of St Paul's letters and an unorthodox edited version of St Luke's Gospel. It is in fact not until after the time of Irenaeus, at the beginning of the third century, that there is fairly general acceptance of the fully scriptural nature of all the writings we now think of as the New Testament.[20]

Despite the discouraging example of Marcion, which showed where scripture-based teaching could go wrong, the Church came to see that it needed scripture as a basis for teaching and a test of orthodoxy. In the writings of the Apostolic Fathers at the end of the first and the earlier part of the second centuries there are some early citations of short passages from what we now call the New Testament, although recent scholarship suggests that these writers may not have used the gospels directly, or as we have them, possibly depending instead on a harmonized version of the gospel narrative, and that they also seem to have felt able to use what were subsequently deemed apocryphal or non-authoritative sources for the words of Jesus.[21] An ancient Greek homily, dating from the second century, traditionally misdescribed as the Second Epistle of St Clement to the Corinthians, is perhaps the earliest surviving work to extend the word 'scripture' (*graphe*), previously used of the Hebrew Bible, to the New Testament. After quoting the Greek text of Isaiah 54:1, 'Rejoice, thou barren that bearest not', and applying it to the early condition of the Christian Church, the anonymous author proceeds to quote 'another scripture',

---

[20] J. N. D. Kelly, *Early Christian Doctrines*, p. 56.
[21] See Helmut Koester, 'Gospels and Gospel Traditions', in Andrew F. Gregory and Christopher M. Tuckett, eds, *Trajectories through the New Testament and the Apostolic Fathers* (Oxford: Oxford University Press, 2005), pp. 40–4; Andrew F. Gregory and Christopher M. Tuckett, eds, *The Reception of the New Testament in the Apostolic Fathers* (Oxford: Oxford University Press, 2005), pp. 53, 157, 277.

50   *The Authority of the Bible*

implying material of comparable authority, which turns out to be Matthew 9: 13, 'I am not come to call the righteous, but sinners [to repentance].'[22] This was a pastorally invaluable text, presumably much used in preaching, which was also invoked in the early Alexandrian work known as the Epistle of Barnabas.[23] In one of the early second-century Epistles of St Ignatius of Antioch, convincingly vindicated as authentic by Archbishop Ussher, New Testament 'gospel' and Old Testament 'prophets' were cited in the same sentence as being of seemingly equal importance.[24]

Before long the polemical treatises of the church fathers abounded in brief statements, almost slogans, the patristic equivalent of sound bites, which emphasized the value of the scriptures in a manner that would prove very useful to subsequent defenders of the Bible. Jerome's Prologue to his commentary on Isaiah summed up his own discussion in five words: *ignoratio Scripturarum, ignoratio Christi est*, 'ignorance of the scriptures is ignorance of Christ'. By the end of the second century Irenaeus firmly maintained that 'the Scriptures are indeed perfect, since they were spoken by the Word of God and His Spirit'. They were nothing less than 'the ground and pillar of our faith'.[25] Clement of Alexandria devoted a chapter of his *Stromata* (or 'Miscellanies') to the contention that scripture is the criterion by which truth and heresy are distinguished. Scripture could rescue men from the deceptions of heresy, he insisted, because it embodied the teaching of the Lord through the prophets, the gospel, and the blessed apostles, leading its readers from the beginning of knowledge to the end.[26] Early in the third century Hippolytus confidently claimed that, 'There is, brethren, one God, the knowledge of whom we gain from the holy scriptures and from no other source... Whatever things, then, the holy Scriptures declare, at these let us look; and whatsoever things they teach, these let us learn....'[27] In the fourth

---

[22] See 2 Clement 2, Greek text and translation in J. B. Lightfoot and J. R. Harmer, eds, *The Apostolic Fathers* (London: Macmillan, 1898), pp. 43–4, 86–7.

[23] Epistle of Barnabas 5, Lightfoot and Harmer, *The Apostolic Fathers*, pp. 248, 273.

[24] Epistle of Ignatius to the Smyrnaeans 5, 7, Lightfoot and Harmer, *The Apostolic Fathers*, pp. 128, 129, 157, 158.

[25] Jerome, *Prolog. ad Isaiam* (PL 24.17) and *Letters and Select Works*; Irenaeus, *Against Heresies* 2.28, 3.1 (PG 7.804–5, 844), trans. Alexander Roberts and James Donaldson (Edinburgh, T. and T. Clark, 1868), pp. 220, 258.

[26] Clement of Alexandria, *Stromata* 7.16 (PG 9.532).

[27] Hippolytus, *Against the Heresy of Noetus* 9 (PG 10, 315–8), in *Writings* II (Dogmatical and Heretical), trans. S. D. F. Salmond (Edinburgh: T. and T. Clark, 1869), p. 60.

The Authority of the Bible 51

century Athanasius affirmed that, 'The holy and divinely-inspired Scriptures are sufficient for the enunciation of the truth.'[28]

But the status and use of scripture in early Christianity is more complicated and ambivalent than these quotations might suggest. If the scriptures could teach, they also needed to be taught, and taught in the right way, however that might be determined. Jerome, the great biblical scholar and translator, urged study of the scriptures on his correspondent Paulinus, but also pointed out that there were substantial difficulties and mysteries to be explained, so expert guidance was needed. People might think they could interpret the scriptures for themselves and teach them before they had properly learned them, he warned, but, uninstructed, they would tear them apart, distort the meaning, and force their own constructions upon them.[29]

In the right hands and correctly interpreted, the scriptures could be used, as appropriate, to safeguard the faith, quell unruly elements, and silence or at least discountenance heretics. The Gnostics laid claim to sometimes bizarre ancient traditions, but their teaching could be dismissed as inconsistent with scripture. On the other hand, as Jerome had indicated, the meaning of the scriptures was not always quite as plain and unmistakeable as Protestant preachers and polemical church fathers might suggest. Key passages could be read the wrong way. It could be dangerous to depend too much on the scriptures in isolation from authoritative teaching of the faith, or the right sort of ancient tradition, which was exactly what the heretics tended to do. The church historian Eusebius warned against reading the scriptures recklessly and rejecting traditional principles, knowing nothing of Christ.[30] Tertullian, who was deemed to have slipped into heresy himself in his later years, was in his orthodox heyday so incensed with heretical uses and abuses of scripture that he felt heretics should not be allowed to argue from scripture. Since it was never possible to convince the heretics that they had misunderstood or misapplied the scriptures, it was best to exclude scripture from the debate altogether. Instead of true Christian faith stemming from the scriptures properly understood, he seemed to suggest that the proper understanding of the scriptures stemmed from Christian faith and the

---

[28] Athanasius, *Oratio contra Gentes* 1 (PG 35.4) (my translation).
[29] Jerome, Letter 54 (PL 22.544) and *Letters and Select Works*.
[30] Eusebius, *Church History* 5.28 (PG 20.516).

The Authority of the Bible

traditions of the church.[31] St Augustine, a great commentator on scripture though he was, went even further in suggesting that he would not believe the text of the gospel unless the authority of the Catholic Church impelled him to do so.[32]

This illustrates the sometimes unstable and contingent relation between scripture and Church tradition, an ancient issue revisited rather than discovered by Victorian liberalism. The context of this passage is that Augustine needs to defend church authority against widespread Manichaean heresy rather than to defend scripture, as such, at this particular moment. Once under the influence of the Manichees himself, Augustine is anxious to refute the claim of Mani (Manichaeus) to be an apostle of Christ, and so rejects Mani's own appeals to the gospel when that is inconsistent with the teaching of the Church. There is an element of rhetorical exaggeration to make a point. Point-scoring is part of the point: patristic writings are nearly always controversial and rhetorical, at least to some extent. Augustine and his orthodox predecessors wrote not just to affirm and explain the faith but to snipe at the heretics, Manichaeans, Marcionites, and Valentinians. Some of the early church fathers, notably Clement, Tertullian, and Irenaeus, who all seemed to support the primacy of scripture in a soundly proto-Protestant manner, could also be quoted in support of the traditionally Catholic idea of a (more or less) independently important oral tradition, consistent with but (probably) separate from scripture, handed down in the Church from apostolic times. If scripture could be misused or misunderstood by heretics, what further authority apart from scripture itself could be invoked by the Church to preserve the integrity of the faith? There needed to be a rule of faith, core teaching that could be used as a principle of doctrinal regulation. For Clement of Alexandria this rule of faith was older than any of the heresies.[33] He identified it as a secret, unwritten tradition of teaching, although he seemed to imply that this was ultimately derived from scripture.[34] Tertullian, however, ranked the unwritten rule of faith transmitted from the apostles to be above the scriptures, since the scriptures could be so easily abused by

---

[31] Tertullian, *On Prescription against Heretics* 15–18 (PL 2.28–31).

[32] Augustine, *Contra Epistolam Manichaei quam vocant fundamenti* 5 (PL 42.176).

[33] Clement, *Stromata* 7.17 (PG 9.545–554).

[34] Clement, *Stromata* 5.10 (PG 9.93–102). See R. P. C. Hanson, *Origen's Doctrine of Tradition* (London: SPCK, 1954), p. 189.

The Authority of the Bible 53

heretics.[35] Irenaeus was himself only at two removes from the apostles since, as he tells us, he had as a boy seen Polycarp, Bishop of Smyrna, who had known and had instruction from the apostles and many who had seen the Lord. In consequence he laid considerable stress on the cumulative, though not particularly secret, authority of the apostles and their successors, the bishops of the church, independent of the scriptures.[36]

By the time we get to Origen in the third century, however, that oral tradition may have become attenuated. Perhaps, as R. P. C. Hanson has suggested, it had effectively come to an end as a source of authority in the Church.[37] Origen believed that the scriptures were verbally inspired, but there was no narrow literalism about his conviction, which delivered him from some of the worst embarrassments and absurdities of later biblical literalists. In a sense, he anticipates Victorian developments by reading the Bible not for the letter but the underlying spirit of Christian teaching—as George Eliot, Thomas Hardy, and Mary Ward all tried to do. Origen was exasperated by what he saw as the unrewarding obsession with the letter of the text in much rabbinic exegesis and ranged freely, at times perhaps recklessly, beyond the literal sense to propose allegorical or spiritual meanings consistent with the general teaching of the Church as it had evolved, constantly invoking St Paul's dictum that the letter killeth but the Spirit giveth life (2 Corinthians 3:6).[38] There was, after all, New Testament precedent for allegorical reading: in I Corinthians 9:8–14, for instance, Paul had rather imaginatively applied the Old Testament injunction not to muzzle an ox treading grain (Deuteronomy 25:4) to the apostles' right to material support, and Paul had actually used the word 'allegorized' (*allegoroumena*) to describe his reading of the two sons of Abraham in terms of the old Israel and the Church (Galatians 4:24). Origen and his successors were confident that, even if the literal meaning of any given passage was a little strange, holy

---

[35] Tertullian, *On Prescription against Heretics* 19–22 (PL 2.31–5), *Writings* pp. 251–3.

[36] Irenaeus, *Against Heresies* 3.3 (PG 7.848–53), pp. 260–4.

[37] R. P. C. Hanson, *Origen's Doctrine of Tradition*, p. 191.

[38] R. P. C. Hanson, *Allegory and Event. A Study of the Sources and Significance of Origen's Interpretation of Scripture* (London: SCM Press, 1959), pp. 12, 187, 305. For discussions of 'letter' and 'spirit', see Origen, *De Principiis* 1.1.2 (PG 11.122), *Writings* I, pp. 9–10; *Contra Celsum* 7.20 (PG 11.1449), *Writings* II, p. 443; *In Matthaeum*, discussing Matthew 19:12 (PG 13.1256).

54 *The Authority of the Bible*

scripture was valuable by definition, so the text might still be religiously useful if interpreted allegorically. The different levels of meaning that could be supplied by this method were formalized by later commentators such as John Cassian, writing in the fifth century, into a fourfold scheme embracing the historical or literal, the allegorical (particularly useful for reading the Old Testament in relation to the Christian Church), the tropological or moral, and the anagogical or mystical, relating to the ultimate goal of the Christian life.[39]

There was a risk, not always avoided, of getting carried away and disregarding the literal or surface meaning altogether. The parable of the Good Samaritan (Luke 10:30–37) provides one example: it was, and is, a good story as it stands, but in the hands of Augustine and others almost every detail could be and was seized upon for possible allegorical significance. The luckless traveller who fell among thieves between Jerusalem and Jericho and was left half dead was the human race; being left half dead (or half alive, *semivivus*, in the Latin of the Vulgate) indicated the imperfect spiritual state of sinful man, and the inn to which he was brought to be looked after was clearly the Church.[40] But even though Augustine had used and valued allegorical methods himself, the later Augustine at least found it increasingly necessary to insist that figurative interpretation should not preclude attentiveness to the literal meaning of the text.

The warning was necessary because there were considerable advantages to purely allegorical reading. The 'Song of Songs' in particular, beautiful and strange, could be mined for symbolic meanings beneath its surface eroticism, always something of an embarrassment to austere commentators. Jewish exegesis in the Talmud had suggested that the lover and the beloved in the Song represented an allegory of God's dealings with the congregation of Israel. Origen had suggested it was an epithalamium, or marriage song, and began his commentary by talking about love, which he felt was the main theme, but he soon moved on to discussing it in terms of the love of the soul, or the Church, for the Word of God. Origen, Bede, Gregory the Great, Anselm, and Alcuin all contributed to a Christian tradition

---

[39] John Cassian, 'De Spirituali Scientia', *Collationes* 14.8 (PL 49.963–4). All four levels of interpretation are applied to the word 'Jerusalem', literally the city of the Jews, allegorically the Church, tropologically or morally the soul of man, and anagogically the City of God.

[40] Augustine, *Quaestiones Evangelii* 2.19 (PL 35.1340).

The Authority of the Bible   55

of allegorizing commentary represented in the *Glossa Ordinaria*, a medieval compilation of glosses on the detail of the text.[41] As Ann Matter has observed, allegorical reading permitted considerable flexibility of interpretation and by the twelfth century a shift of emphasis can be noted from reading the Song as primarily about the relations between Christ and his Church to seeing it as concerned with the love between God and the individual soul, originally regarded as a secondary meaning. This allegorical reading persisted into the nineteenth century to help sustain Hopkins' poem 'The Wreck of the Deutschland'.[42]

The 'Song of Songs' is of course a special case, but the allegorizing method could be applied even to relatively straightforward narrative episodes, and it could be reflected in the liturgy and in religious art as well as in direct biblical commentary. There are traces of this even in Protestant preaching and eighteenth- and nineteenth-century Protestant hymnody, as G. P. Landow has demonstrated. The Exodus narrative of emergence from slavery in Egypt and desert wandering (a model for arduous personal quest for novelists such as Rider Haggard) provides a case in point. A. M. Toplady's celebrated hymn 'Rock of Ages' (1776) is about personal devotion but it also allegorizes the moment when Moses struck the rock in Horeb and water gushed forth for the thirsty children of Israel (Exodus 17:6) by linking it with the crucifixion. Paul, representing the Israelites in the wilderness as a model for the situation of contemporary Christian believers, had already described the water as 'spiritual drink' and insisted 'that Rock was Christ'. The smitten rock was a traditional type of Christian baptism in religious art, and as early as the seventh century Isidore of Seville, carefully studied by the youthful Mary Ward in the course of her research on early Spain, had insisted on the link between the smitten rock (*petra virga percussa*) and the pierced side of Christ on the cross (*percussus in cruce Christus*). The ninth-century Carolingian commentator Ratramnus and others had taken this further, seeing the

---

[41] Origen, *The Song of Songs: Commentary and Homilies*, trans. R. P. Lawson (New York: Newman Press, 1956), pp. 21, 23; see *Glossa Ordinaria Pars 22 in Canticum Canticorum*, ed. Mary Dove, Corpus Christianorum, Continuatio Mediaevalis CLXX (Tournai: Brepols, 1997).

[42] E. Ann Matter, *Voice of My Beloved: the Song of Songs in Western Medieval Christianity* (Philadelphia: University of Pennsylvania Press, 1990), pp. 88–111. For Origen and Hopkins, see Aakanksha Virkar-Yates, 'Baptism and Ascent in the Poetry of Gerard Manley Hopkins', unpublished D.Phil. thesis, University of Sussex, 2009.

56 *The Authority of the Bible*

manna and the water from the smitten rock in the wilderness as a prefiguring of the mystery of the body and blood of Christ celebrated by the Church in the Eucharist.[43]

In another allegorical development of the Exodus narrative, the deliverance of the children of Israel from Egyptian bondage was joyfully celebrated in Psalm 114, beginning (in the Latin of the Vulgate) *In exitu Israel...*, 'When Israel went out of Egypt...', and the anagogical or mystical interpretation given to this was that it also celebrated Christian death, with the prospect of heaven, as a deliverance from bondage. From the sixth century in the Western Church that particular psalm had been included in the last offices for the dying and in the burial service. Dante alluded to this in the second canto of the *Purgatorio* in the *Divine Comedy*, just after the emergence from the abode of the dead in the *Inferno*, by representing it as being sung aboard the ship of souls approaching the purgatorial mountain.[44]

Dante's cosmic vision in the *Commedia* was perhaps the most ambitious and effective imaginative elaboration of the teaching of the scriptures and the Church that has ever been penned. But there was growing unease, particularly after the Reformation, with imaginative elaboration and allegorical interpretation of scripture that could be seen as the work of man rather than of God. Protestant orthodoxy on the primacy of scripture could perhaps have considered itself as on safer ground by appealing to John Wycliffe (*c.*1330–84), the 'morning star of the Reformation', as the aggressively Protestant ex-Carmelite Friar John Bale called him in 1548.[45] Religious and literary interest in Wycliffe persisted to the nineteenth century and beyond: a substantial selection of his English works was edited in 1869–71 by Thomas Arnold the younger, father of Mrs Humphry Ward, who like his daughter had a strong personal investment in questions of problematic religious authority and identity. Wycliffe is

---

[43] Isidore, *Quaestiones in Vetus Testamentum: In Exodum* 24.1 (PL 83.299); Ratramnus, *De Corpore et Sanguine Domini* 22 (PL 121.137); G. P. Landow, *Victorian Types, Victorian Shadows: Biblical Typology in Victorian Literature, Art and Thought* (Boston, MA: Routledge, 1980), pp. 66–94.

[44] Dante, *Purgatorio* 2.46.

[45] John Bale, *Illustrium maioris Britanniae scriptorum [. . .] Summarium* (Ipswich, 1548), f.154ᵛ, cited in David Daniell, *The Bible in English* (New Haven: Yale University Press, 2003), p. 70. 'Wyclif' is used here only when citing scholarly publications or bodies which use that form of the name.

The Authority of the Bible 57

associated with the pioneering translation of the whole Bible into English, although it seems he had no direct involvement in the Wycliffite version, based on the Latin Vulgate rather than the original Greek and Hebrew, which was undertaken by his disciples c.1380–92. He had, however, written a polemical treatise on the truth of scripture, *De veritate sacrae scripturae* (1377–8).[46] But this is a more complex, and a more medieval and philosophical, document than one might expect, and the familiar Protestant narrative of Wycliffe as morning star of the Reformation is an oversimplification. Wycliffe invokes, and heeds, patristic as well as scriptural authority, particularly Augustine, assuring readers that apparent contradictions in scripture have been resolved by the fathers.[47] He shows willingness to accommodate the four levels of meaning developed in patristic and medieval exegesis, and like other medieval commentators (and like Augustine before them) he is happy to regard the 'literal' sense as including figurative references, particularly references to Christ.[48]

There is a politics of authority, as well as a concern for theology and epistemology, behind Wycliffe's championing of scripture. For Wycliffe, scripture clearly opposes the widespread abuses and aberrations sanctioned by Church authority, identifiable with the papacy. He notes that, while the Pope is quick to claim scriptural warrant for the authority and power he exercises, all power is actually from God. He insists that it is as important to scrutinize self-serving papal attempts to limit scriptural study to what is institutionally convenient as it is to interrogate false prophets or wolves in sheep's clothing. Scripture, he maintained, is always superior to the merely human traditions represented by papal decrees.[49]

This emphasis was reflected in the preaching of the 'Lollards'. Lollard sermons, following Wycliffe's teaching and example, were strongly biblical, based on complete passages of scripture rather than an isolated text, but the exposition was often actually quite traditional. The preachers, while claiming they were expounding the

---

[46] John Wyclif, *De veritate sacrae scripturae* (1377–8), Latin text ed. Rudolf Buddensieg, 3 vols (London: Wyclif Society, 1905); selections in Ian Christopher Levy, ed. and trans., *On the Truth of Holy Scripture* (Kalamazoo, Michigan: Medieval Institute Publications, Western Michigan University, 2001). References are to Part 1 of the Latin text, in vol. 1 of the Wyclif Society edition.

[47] Wyclif, *De veritate* chapter 5, p. 98; chapter 9, p. 192.

[48] Wyclif, *De veritate* chapter 6, pp. 119–22; chapter 4, p. 92.

[49] Wyclif, *De veritate* chapter 11, pp. 262–5; chapter 15, p. 395.

58   *The Authority of the Bible*

'literal sense' of the scriptures, extended 'literal' to mean what they felt the author—that is, God—had intended, not necessarily just the surface meaning, so as with Wycliffe allegorical interpretation was not ruled out.

It was not Wycliffe's privileging of scripture as such but the anti-papal attitude of *De veritate sacrae scripturae* and other polemical works, and his rejection of the Eucharistic doctrine of transubstantiation, that ensured that after his death his legacy and the work of the 'Lollards' more or less loosely associated with his work would remain controversial. Eventually more than 200 Wyclifite propositions were formally condemned at the Council of Constance in 1415. The English Carmelite Thomas Netter (*c.*1375–1430), one of the most effective critics of Wycliffe and the Lollards in the early fifteenth century, attacked Wycliffe's low view of the Church rather than his high view of scripture. Netter anticipates Newman and the Tractarians: he was perhaps the first of many Catholic apologists to claim that it was logically inconsistent for advocates of scriptural authority to exalt the canonical scriptures but to deny the authority of the Church: he argued that recognition of what was canonical scripture, and therefore authoritative, had itself been an authoritative act of the Church, upheld by tradition, so scriptural authority and Church authority could not easily be separated.[50] But this did not altogether address the attractiveness of appealing to scripture as a way of demonstrating perceived abuses and misused authority within the Church, a habit that eventually issued in the European Reformation. Nor did it entirely dispose of the reported words of Jesus himself, inviting interested individuals to 'Search the scriptures' (John 5:39) for confirmation of his divine mission rather than look to more institutional forms of authority.

---

[50] Anne Hudson, *The Premature Reformation: Wycliffite Texts and Lollard History* (Oxford: Clarendon Press, 1988), pp. 270–1; 50, 230.

3

The Crisis of Biblical Authority

The Wycliffite challenge to papal authority discussed in the previous chapter made it clear that the issue of scriptural authority was and would continue to be political as well as religious. It was linked, as so many novels would be, with moral questions of personal autonomy, the inner life, and the individual conscience. In a sense it could be seen to mark the beginning of a more personal and individualistic approach to religion, which eventually found its apparently more or less secular counterpart in fictional narratives of personal pilgrimage. But it is hard to be sure how much direct influence Wycliffe and his followers had on the later fortunes of the Bible and the embattled attitudes of Victorian Britain. In this, as in other matters, the popular Protestant narrative of the triumph of the English Bible almost certainly overstates the continuities in an attempt to fortify what Gladstone belligerently called the 'impregnable rock of holy scripture' against the challenges of modern scepticism. Hussite interest in Wycliffe's teaching ensured that copies of his works were preserved in Bohemia even though they had been destroyed elsewhere, but the Hussites, like the Lollards, partly anticipated rather than directly influenced the continental reformation of the sixteenth century. Phrases in the Wycliffite Bible, which circulated very widely in manuscript, may well have lingered in the memory of preachers and subsequent translators. Some seem to anticipate the English of Tyndale's sixteenth-century translations and the enduringly popular King James Version of 1611, so direct influence is certainly possible. But there could be an element of coincidence in this: to take one example, the familiar phrase 'the salt of the earth' (Matthew 5:13), which appears in both the Wycliffite Bible and the King James version, is the natural, obvious, and literal rendering of two words in the Latin Vulgate (*sal terrae*), which themselves literally translate from the

60 *The Crisis of Biblical Authority*

original Greek (*to halas tes ges*), so it is hardly surprising that this phrase is found in almost all the English versions, whether they derive from the Vulgate or directly from the original Greek text.[1]

The English Bibles of the sixteenth and seventeenth centuries were produced in a different historical context from the Wycliffite Bible. The issue of authority was now not just between papal decrees and the text of scripture but between Popes and secular Christian princes, involving questions of regional and national religious identity. The most important model for the vernacular Bible was probably Luther's German version of 1522 rather than the Wycliffite translation, and it was Lutheran and then Calvinist teaching rather than memories of Wycliffe that encouraged Bible reading and preaching directly based on the scriptures in English.

Nineteenth-century constructions of Reformation thought, often dogmatic and oversimplified, placed enormous emphasis on the supreme authority of scripture and the unscriptural iniquities of Rome and of pre-Reformation traditions, strategically appropriating or misappropriating particular readings or selections of scripture for polemical purposes, as ostensibly infallible support for challenges to papal authority or the politics of Catholic rule or controversial aspects of Catholic tradition. The intermittent excesses and overstatements of this approach, expecting and requiring scripture to have the last word to say on everything, contributed in the long term to rational scepticism about the scriptures, which in its turn prompted reconsiderations and reimaginings of biblical materials, a challenge taken up by George Eliot and subsequent novelists such as Rider Haggard. The process illustrates one of the harsh ironies of religious history: the crude version of the Protestant narrative of the triumph of scriptural authority over Church tradition contained within it the seeds of its own destruction, the emerging counter-narrative of partly misconceived scriptural authority approaching crisis and radical challenge. But early reformers such as Philipp Melanchthon had been prepared to be more conciliatory towards Church tradition. Melanchthon was largely responsible for the shaping of the Lutheran Augsburg Confession of 1530, presented to Emperor Charles V. This does not directly mention the authority of scripture as an article of faith, although scripture is frequently invoked, along with other authorities. The key

---

[1] Discussed by David Daniell, *The Bible in English* (New Haven and London: Yale University Press, 2003), pp. 85–90.

The Crisis of Biblical Authority   61

Lutheran doctrine of justification by faith, rather than trusting to good works alone, is set out in Article 20, which condemns 'childish and needless works' such as set fasts, pilgrimages, worshipping the saints, and the use of rosaries. Support for the doctrine is adduced not just from John's Gospel (John 14:6) and Ephesians (2:8, 9) but from the tradition of the universal (or 'Catholic') Church, specifically the church fathers Augustine and Ambrose.[2] Article 22, the final article of the dogmatic section of the *Confession*, sums up the reformed position as consisting of nothing discrepant with the scriptures, or the Church universal (*Ecclesia Catholica*), or even the historic teaching of the Roman Church (*Ecclesia Romana*) as represented by the writings of the church fathers.[3]

A more polemical second part defends the Lutheran reformers by outlining how they have addressed abuses that have crept into the Roman Church. But even here there is little direct confrontation between the authority of scripture and the authority of the Church since obnoxious practices and traditions, including administering communion in one kind only, clerical celibacy, and monastic vows, are attributed to unwarranted innovations, in breach of the ancient practices, pronouncements, and canons of the Church, as well as contrary to scripture. The fifth article in this section attacks the inauthentic 'human traditions' (*traditiones humanae*) and special observations and practices thought to merit grace and provide satisfaction for sin. These are condemned not just because they obscure the doctrine of grace and the commandments of God but because they belittle the ordinary duties and decencies of life: 'that the father brought up his children, that the mother nurtured them, that the prince governed the commonwealth' were all dismissed as merely worldly and imperfect acts.[4] It is interesting that well-conducted secular life is seen not as an inferior replacement for but as a vital expression of the Christian life, a view that Christian socialists such as Charles Kingsley and F. D. Maurice, and religiously liberal Victorian novelists such as George Eliot and Mary Ward coming after them, championed vigorously in the face of what they saw as callous

---

[2] *Augsburg Confession* part 1, art. 20 'Of Good Works'. Latin text and English translation in Philip Schaff, ed., *The Creeds of Christendom*, 6th ed. (1931), 3 vols, (repr. Grand Rapids, MI: Baker Books, 2007), III, pp. 20–2.

[3] *Augsburg Confession* part 1, art. 22, Schaff III, pp. 26–7.

[4] *Augsburg Confession* part 2, art. 5, Schaff III, pp. 43–4.

62 *The Crisis of Biblical Authority*

indifference or worse within the institutional Church. This, rather than the indiscriminate all-sufficiency of the scriptures, is perhaps the central moral legacy of the Reformation.

Luther himself, more confrontational and uncompromising than Melanchthon, was more disposed to distance himself from the Catholic past, his own as well as his countrymen's, particularly in the matter of the Bible. In his *Tischreden* ('Tabletalk'), he is recorded as airily dismissing the far-fetched spiritual meanings and elaborately allegorical methods of exegesis he had mastered when he was a monk. It is clear, however, that his reading of scripture, like Wycliffe's, still allows for figurative as well as literal reading of scripture, an approach closer to and more consistent with the imaginative appropriations and extrapolations of Victorian novelists than is usually recognized. Convinced that all scripture refers ultimately to Christ, he tended to read the Old Testament metaphorically, for what it seemed to say about Christ prophetically and figuratively, rather than for what it said in its own terms.[5]

Later Reformation Confessions were more aggressive in asserting the primacy of scripture on its own and in playing down the role of tradition, including traditions of specialized or allegorical readings of scripture. The first Helvetic Confession (1536) began with a solemn affirmation of the authority of scripture, proclaimed as the 'Word of God', which in the second Helvetic Confession (1566) was strengthened to the 'true word of God', independent of any merely human authority. The Lutheran Formula of Concord of 1576 began in the same way.[6] Attitudes to scripture were hardening, particularly after the Council of Trent (1545–63), which at its fourth session in April 1546 reaffirmed as Roman Catholic teaching the equal authority of the unwritten traditions of the Church and of scripture as sources of truth, and asserted the sole right of the Church to interpret the Bible. Calvin himself prepared the French Confession of Faith of 1559, with his pupil Antoine de la Roche Chandieu, which began not with scripture but with God, but then proceeded immediately to

---

[5] Martin Luther, *Tabletalk* (editorially dated Summer or Fall 1532), quoted in Darrell R. Reinke, 'From Allegory to Metaphor: More Notes on Luther's Hermeneutical Shift', *Harvard Theological Review* 66 (July 1973), 386–95 (388).

[6] *Confessio Helvetica Prior*, art. 1 'De Scriptura Sacra', Schaff III, 210; *Confessio Helvetica Posterior*, cap. 1 'De Scriptura Sancta, Vero Dei Verbo', Schaff III, p. 237; *Formula Concordiae* 1, Schaff III, p. 93.

The Crisis of Biblical Authority   63

explain how God revealed himself through the creation and through the scriptures.

But how do we know scripture to be scripture? Do we not depend on the traditions and authority of the Church to tell us? This question, the basis of Netter's objection to Wycliffe, was often asked. It was answered in the French Confession: the definition of scripture, that is, the identification of the canonical books, is ascribed not to the Church but directly to the 'testimony and inward illumination of the Holy Spirit', a recurring theme in Calvin, and this makes it easier to dismiss what can be represented as the merely human authority of the institutional Church or of other bodies.[7] The Belgic Confession of 1561, devised under specifically Calvinist auspices, defends the authority of the scriptures, independent of the Church and of custom, in similar terms, 'because the Holy Ghost witnesseth in our hearts that they are from God, whereof they carry the evidence in themselves.'[8]

Calvin, systematic in everything, can be represented as systematically opposed to allegorical interpretation of scripture and the supreme upholder of the Reformation principle of *sola scriptura*, the authority of scripture alone, independent of Church tradition. There are indeed plenty of places in the *Institutes* and elsewhere where he attacks allegorical reading of scripture, and in his commentary on 2 Corinthians he freely denounces Origen as the founder of perniciously allegorizing interpretation, 'the most disastrous error that Scripture is not only useless but actually harmful unless it is allegorized'. But on closer inspection it becomes clear that Calvin is not making a case for the naive biblical literalism adopted by too many of his followers: his main objection is not to allegory as such but to allegorical reading as a basis for doctrine. As he puts it, 'Allegories ought not to go beyond the limits set by the rule of Scripture, let alone suffice as the foundation for any doctrines.' Tendentious allegorized readings are too easily imported into the text and cannot be regarded as inherently scriptural or authoritative. He observes that transubstantiation and confession, as a sacrament, are defended by dubious allegorical readings of particular passages, which is no defence at all. Long after Calvin's time, his scepticism about basing doctrine on allegory was

---

[7] *Confessio Fidei Gallicana*, art. 3, Schaff III p. 361. See also John Calvin, *Institutes of the Christian Religion*, ed. J. T. McNeill, trans. F. L. Battle Library of Christian Classics (Philadelphia: Westminster Press, 1960), 1.9.3.

[8] *Belgic Confession*, art. 5, 'De auctoritate Sacrae Scripturae', Schaff III, pp. 386–7.

64 *The Crisis of Biblical Authority*

reflected in Protestant (and even to some extent Catholic) hostility to the papal definition in 1854 of the dogma of the Immaculate Conception of the Virgin Mary. Scriptural support for this was claimed from the Old Testament, from the 'garden inclosed, and fountain sealed' (Song of Songs 4:12) and the closed gate in the east of the temple (Ezekiel 44:1–3), which were traditionally applied to the closed womb of the Virgin. It was not just Calvinists who were unconvinced.[9] But Calvin, like Luther, was no naive biblical literalist: allegorical or non-literal reading, when consistent with scripture as a whole, was not necessarily a problem for him.

Lutheran and Calvinist views of scripture helped to mould the identity of the emerging Church of England in the sixteenth and seventeenth centuries. Archbishop Cranmer's original idea seems to have been to draw on the German and Swiss Reformers to formulate an evangelical Catholic creed that could provide a bond of union of all Protestant churches. This did not happen, but Cranmer went on to produce a set of Forty-Two Articles of Religion, published in 1553, in the reign of Edward VI, which drew on the Lutheran Augsburg Confession. These were revised and modified in the reign of Elizabeth I into the Thirty-Nine Articles, published in Latin in 1563 with an English version in 1571. The Lutheran influence was reinforced by drawing substantially on the Würtemburg Confession of 1551, an updated restatement of the Augsburg Confession, which in 1552 had been presented unavailingly to the Council of Trent. Article 30 of the Würtemburg Confession, 'De Sacra Scriptura', closely resembled Article 6 of the Thirty-Nine Articles, 'Of the Sufficiency of the Holy Scriptures for Salvation'. The Würtemburg Confession, Article 32 'De Ecclesia', stipulated that the Church had the right to interpret scripture, which may have been intended as a conciliatory gesture towards the Roman Catholic position, but the corresponding English Article 20, 'Of the Authority of the Church', said only that the Church was a 'witness and keeper of Holy Writ' and cautioned it against requiring or teaching anything contrary to scripture.[10]

---

[9] John Calvin, *The Second Epistle of Paul the Apostle to the Corinthians* [1548], trans. T. A. Smail (Edinburgh: Oliver and Boyd, 1964), p. 43, commenting on 2 Cor. 3:6; *Institutes* 2.5.19; see also 3.4.5; 4.17.22. For nineteenth-century controversies concerning the Immaculate Conception, see Schaff I, pp. 108–28.

[10] Schaff (I, pp. 614–29) prints the Latin text of the Thirty-Nine Articles in parallel columns with the Latin of the corresponding articles in the Augsburg and Würtemburg Confessions.

The Crisis of Biblical Authority 65

The Church as it operated in the England of Elizabeth I was not quite the same as the Church envisaged in Augsburg or Würtemburg or indeed in Geneva or Rome. The nature of true religion and of the Church, the bride of Christ, and the precise nature of the authority that should shape and direct it, were urgent questions in an era of bitter religious division and religious wars, as they had been in earlier ages. John Henry Newman's attempt to re-establish an essentially Catholic tradition in the Church of England was historically problematic, since Cranmer and the Elizabethans had not necessarily regarded the Church of England as he did. 'Show me, dear Christ, thy spouse, so bright and clear' John Donne had asked in 1620, at the beginning of the Thirty Years War.[11] Whether or not John Jewel, Bishop of Salisbury, was a direct source for Donne, he had effectively addressed the same issue in his celebrated *Apology for the Church of England* (1562). Donne had asked:

> Doth she, and did she, and shall she evermore,
> On one or on seven or on no hill appear?

Jewel, belittled by Newman's friend Robert Hurrell Froude as 'an irreverent Dissenter' and increasingly disparaged, along with Cranmer, by Newman himself, had turned not to Catholic tradition but directly to the Bible for answers:

> . . . it is not so hard a matter to find out God's church, if a man will seek it earnestly and diligently. For the church of God is set upon a high and glistering place, in the top of an hill, [Isa. 2:2] and built upon the foundations of the apostles and prophets. [Ephesians 2:20][12]

But, closer to earnest Victorian seekers after truth than they might have realized, he conceded that it was not always easy to find and recognize the truth:

> It hath been an old complaint, even from the first time of the patriarchs and prophets, and confirmed here by the writings and testimonies of every age, that the truth wandereth here and there as a stranger in the

---

[11] John Donne, 'Holy Sonnets' 18, *Selected Poetry*, ed. John Carey, Oxford World's Classics (Oxford: Oxford University Press, 1996), p. 207.

[12] John Jewel, *An Apology for the Church of England* (1562), trans. Ann Bacon (1564), ed. J. E. Booty (Ithaca, NY: Cornell University Press, 1963), p. 76. For Froude and Newman's attitude, see Peter Nockles, *The Oxford Movement in Context: Anglican High Churchmanship, 1760–1857* (Cambridge: Cambridge University Press, 1994), p. 124.

66   *The Crisis of Biblical Authority*

world and doth readily find enemies and slanderers amongst those that know her not.[13]

The reference to 'a stranger in the world' paraphrases the New Testament account of Christians as 'strangers and pilgrims on the earth' (Hebrews 11:13), which was to become an important theme for Protestant Bible readers and for (more or less) 'secular' fictions and quest narratives, but the whole passage also closely resembles Tertullian's account of [Christian] truth as but a sojourner on the earth, finding foes among strangers, something that becomes clearer when one compares Tertullian's Latin and the original, Latin, text of Jewel.[14] Contemporary Roman Catholicism is robustly condemned for being unscriptural, the standard position of the Reformers, but the Church of England is defined not by opposing scripture to Catholic tradition going back to the church fathers but by suggesting that a true reading of the fathers shows no conflict with Bible-centred Protestantism: 'The old fathers Origen and Chrysostom exhort the people to read the Scriptures, to buy them books, to reason at home among themselves of divine matters.'[15]

The importance of scripture in the newly Protestant English Church, and the scriptural basis of its doctrine, could be brought out in preaching, but many parish priests lacked the education and the experience to preach effectively and at length. To help them, and to provide guidance for the new Church, two series of homilies were issued, in 1547 and 1571, many in the second series written by Jewel himself. They were formally commended as containing 'godly and wholesome doctrine' by Article 35 of the Thirty-Nine Articles. In the first series the value and authority of scripture was commended in the opening homily, 'A Fruitful Exhortation to the Reading and Knowledge of Holy Scripture', possibly written by Archbishop Cranmer. On one hand, the non-biblical or post-biblical traditions upheld by contemporary Roman Catholicism could not be countenanced:

---

[13] Jewel, *An Apology for the Church of England*, p. 7.

[14] Tertullian, *Apologeticum* 1: 'scit se peregrinam in terris agere: inter extranos facile inimicos invenire'; Jewel's Latin was 'Veritatem in terris peregrinam agere, & inter ignotos facile inimicos & calumniatores inuenire' (*Apologia Ecclesiae Anglicanae* (London, 1562), sig.Aiir.

[15] Jewel, *An Apology for the Church of England*, p. 87.

The Crisis of Biblical Authority 67

Let us diligently search for the well of life in the books of the New and Old Testament, and not run to the stinking puddles of men's traditions, devised by men's imaginations, for our justification and salvation.[16]

On the other hand, the homily also draws on patristic sources to make its points. The Council of Trent had affirmed the joint and equal authority of scripture and the traditions of the Church. The young Church of England, striving as always to steer a middle course or *via media* between Catholic and Puritan extremes, was reluctant either to appear to endorse the Council of Trent by privileging tradition, or to jettison tradition altogether and appear to espouse the more extreme manifestations of the principle of *sola scriptura* adopted by Anabaptists and others. The homilies showed considerable skill in reading the scriptures in a recognizably Protestant sense, which was also consistent with the traditions of the Church universal and the sermons of St John Chrysostom or St Augustine himself.

There was a more extended and systematic exposition of this, and other matters, in Richard Hooker's *Of the Laws of Ecclesiastical Politie* (1593), still being invoked in the nineteenth century by Coleridge in his *On the Constitution of Church and State* (1829) and by leaders of the Oxford Movement such as John Keble, who brought out a new edition in 1836.[17] So far from driving a wedge between the authority of scripture and Church tradition, Hooker denounced what Protestants identified as the non-scriptural traditions of the Roman Catholic Church, as being themselves unwarranted by the early, patristic, tradition of the Church: 'to urge any thing as part of that supernaturall and celestiallie revealed birth which God hath taught, and not to shewe it in scripture, this did the ancient Fathers evermore thinke unlawfull, impious, execrable.' On the other hand, he warned of the dangers of inappropriate uses of scripture: 'we must... take great heede, lest in attributing unto scripture more then it can have, the incredibilitie of that do cause even those thinges which indeed it hath most abundantly to be lesse reverendly esteemed'.[18] It was not his

---

[16] 'A Fruitful Exhortation to the Reading and Knowledge of Holy Scripture', *Certain Sermons Appointed by the Queen's Majesty*, ed. G. E. Corrie (Cambridge: Cambridge University Press, 1850), p. 1.

[17] *The Works of Richard Hooker*, arranged by J. Keble, 3 vols (Oxford and London: Rivingtons, 1836).

[18] Richard Hooker, *Of the Laws of Ecclesiastical Politie* [1593], book 2, chapter 5 and chapter 8 in *Works*, ed. W. Speed Hill et al., 6 vols (Cambridge, MA: Belknap Press, 1977–93), I, pp. 160, 191.

68 *The Crisis of Biblical Authority*

fault that too many Victorian churchmen disregarded his advice and in their narrow, literal-minded bibliolatry involuntarily contributed to the growing 'incredibilitie' of scripture. Hooker seems to have broadly anticipated the intuition of liberal churchmen and Victorian novelists: that aspects of the Bible could be revered and appropriated for their mythic and imaginative power without being vested with a scientific or historical authority they were never intended to bear.

The mainly Calvinist framers of the mid-seventeenth-century Westminster Confession and its associated catechisms, still current in dissenting circles in the nineteenth century and later, had much less interest in the church fathers and ancient tradition and were less conciliatory, insisting on amassing single-verse 'scripture proofs' for everything without regard to patristic precedent or even at times scriptural context. Interestingly, when Rowland Williams was prosecuted in the church courts for allegedly challenging the authority of the Bible in *Essays and Reviews* in 1860 his defence counsel, Fitzjames Stephen (himself the son and grandson of prominent evangelicals) argued that the difference between the Anglican and the Nonconformist tradition (the latter represented by the Westminster Confession) was precisely that the former was permissive and fairly non-specific where the latter was narrower and more prescriptive in relation to the scriptures.[19]

On the whole, a certain amiable vagueness served the Church of England well from the later seventeenth century into the first decades of the nineteenth century. The authority of the scriptures was formally enshrined not merely in the Thirty-Nine Articles but in the prayerbook services of the Church of England, which appointed Psalms and other scripture readings throughout the year, the latter in the King James or Authorized Version of the scriptures of 1611, 'appointed to be read in churches'. But biblical literalists and embattled traditionalists have always made too much of this. It was in a sense as much a matter of politics as of religion. Article 20 of the Thirty-Nine Articles, controversial with the Puritans and subsequently, had insisted that, 'The Church hath power to decree Rites or Ceremonies, and authority in Controversies of Faith'. The authority of a state Church as by law established, with the sovereign at its head, was perhaps greater in practice than the direct authority of the

---

[19] Fitzjames Stephen, *Defence of Rev. Rowland Williams, DD, in the Arches' Court of Canterbury* (London: Smith, Elder, 1862), pp. 73–9.

The Crisis of Biblical Authority 69

scriptures. From the sixteenth century onwards there had been religious dissenters who pushed the Reformation principle of *sola scriptura* further by challenging the biblical basis of bishops and prayer books, not to mention some of the formal teachings of the established Church but, within the Anglican fold, reading the Bible was often in effect a gently circumscribed activity, incorporated into the more general life and teaching of the Church rather than isolated and privileged in a way that might lead to controversy and dispute. Article 34, 'Of the traditions of the Church', recommended rebuking 'Whosoever through his private judgement, willingly and purposely doth openly break the traditions and ceremonies of the Church, which be not repugnant to the Word of God.' History suggested that searching the scriptures too aggressively or in a partisan spirit could cause trouble, leading the seventeenth-century historian and lawyer Thomas Selden to sigh: '*Scrutamini Scripturas* [search the scriptures]. These two Words have undone the World.'[20]

The political philosopher Thomas Hobbes had picked up on the specifically political aspect of the authority of scripture and the issue of private judgement. For him, as for Wycliffe, it was axiomatic that the authority of the Pope over the Church and over the use and interpretation of scripture was no longer acceptable. But rejecting the Pope did not involve rejecting the principle of regulation by authority. Without that, people would either take their own dreams and feelings as authority, exercising possibly wayward private judgement, or they would allow themselves to be led by some strange prince or fellow subject who might bewitch them into rebellion, leading to the 'first chaos of Violence and Civill warre'. Instead of attributing authority to the scriptures themselves, and trusting the indwelling spirit, in the manner of Calvin, to ensure that they would be read right, he suggested that to avoid interpretative and religious anarchy there needed to be regulation: the Civil Sovereign or at least the Sovereign Assemblies of Christian Commonwealths should have the power to judge what doctrines were fit for peace and to license those who might lawfully teach the people.[21]

---

[20] John Selden, *Table Talk* (London: E. Smith, 1689), p. 3, quoting John 5:39 in the Latin of the Vulgate. The remark is not precisely dated but was recorded sometime in the last twenty years of Selden's life, between 1634 and 1654.

[21] John Hobbes, *Leviathan* (1651), ed. Richard Tuck (Cambridge: Cambridge University Press, 1991), pp. 267–9, 299, 372.

70 *The Crisis of Biblical Authority*

Hobbes' religious views were vigorously attacked by the orthodox such as Bishop Bramhall,[22] but his concern about authority had touched a nerve. The peace of the Church and the state seemed to require some kind of control over the interpretation of scripture, and this became all the more apparent during the Commonwealth and Protectorate, when special readings of scripture and unconventional religion troubled the social order as well as other believers. The millenarian 'Fifth Monarchist' preacher John Simpson had publicly attacked Cromwell himself, the Lord Protector. The eccentric Quaker James Nayler, accused of purporting to be Christ himself as he rode into Bristol and his followers hailed him—as Christ had been hailed riding into Jerusalem on Palm Sunday—had been condemned and rather savagely punished by the Commons for 'horrid blasphemy' and being a seducer of the people. Could scripture on its own provide security against such excesses?

The issue of authority was picked up after the Restoration in *Origines Sacrae* (1662), a massive and influential treatise that had already run to a third edition by 1666. The author was the talented and ambitious preacher and apologist Edward Stillingfleet, later Bishop of Worcester, then Rector of Sutton in the recently restored Church of England. For Stillingfleet, the link between scripture and good order in the state could be traced back to Moses, the Jewish lawgiver and traditional author of the Pentateuch, the first five books of the Old Testament. He claimed that the manifest political utility of these writings itself argued for their authenticity:

> ... when they concern the rights, priviledges, and government of a Nation, there will be enough whose interest will lead them to prevent Impostures. It is no easy matter to forge a Magna Charta and to invent Laws ... Now the Laws of Moses are incorporated into the very Republick of the Jews, and their subsistence and Government depends on them.

The argument moves outwards from the Pentateuch to the Bible as a whole, from the Jewish nation to the kingdom of Heaven, using the

---

[22] John Bramhall, *The Catching of Leviathan, or The Great Whale. Demonstrating, out of Mr Hobs his own Works, That no man who is thoroughly an Hobbist, can be a good Christian, or a good Common-wealths man, or reconcile himself to himself* (London: John Crook, 1658).

The Crisis of Biblical Authority 71

same political language and presenting the scriptures as in effect a
constitutional document:

> The Scriptures contain in them the Magna Charta of Heaven, an Act of
> pardon with the Royal assent of Heaven, a Proclamation of good-will
> from God towards men; and can we then set too great a value on that
> which contains all the remarkable passages between God and the souls
> of men, in order to their felicity, from the beginning of the world?[23]

It was all very well for Stillingfleet to rest the Christian faith and the
ultimate felicity of the souls of men on the 'truth and divine authority
of the Scriptures' as proclaimed in the subtitle of *Origines Sacrae*, but
anxieties about unruly 'private judgement' and Hobbes' concern
about anarchic or subversive scriptural interpretation still had to be
addressed. Stillingfleet's response, with Hobbes in mind, was a mas-
sively erudite if ultimately wrong-headed and intellectually vulnerable
attempt to demonstrate that the scriptural record was supremely
authoritative, beyond the vagaries of idiosyncratic interpretation,
and vastly superior to what had passed for history in the ancient
world, because it was demonstrably consistent with reason, the knowledge available from the best classical and contemporary sources, and
what we would now call 'science'.[24]

He was soon embroiled in controversy, his natural environment for
the rest of his extremely successful career. The war he had started, or
renewed, had to be fought on two fronts, the first against the Roman
Catholic position that scripture on its own lacked authority, and even
coherence, and required the authoritative teaching and the traditions
of the Church to make sense of it; the second against modern sceptics
at home and abroad who had raised particular difficulties. Oddly,
these positions had much in common, converging on the question of
certainty that had also obsessed John Calvin.[25] How could men be
certain that the scriptures were true and that they conveyed the
original teaching of Christ? The question was urgent at the time,
but the answers varied: certainty was available only with the help

---

[23] Edward Stillingfleet, *Origines Sacrae: Or, a rational account of Christian faith, as
to the truth and divine authority of the Scriptures* (London: Henry Mortlock, 1662),
pp. 118, 618.

[24] See Robert Todd Carroll, *The Common-Sense Philosophy of Religion of Bishop
Edward Stillingfleet 1635–1699* (The Hague: Martinus Nijhoff, 1975).

[25] See H. Jackson Forstman, *Word and Spirit: Calvin's Doctrine of Biblical Authority* (Stanford: Stanford University Press, 1962), p. 124f, Calvin, *Institutes* 1.9.3.

72   The Crisis of Biblical Authority

and on the authority of the tradition of the Church, according to the Roman Church; or perhaps not at all, according to the sceptics. Between these extremes there was Calvin's position that the testimony of the Holy Spirit confirmed the scriptures in the minds of men, and Stillingfleet's position, which he shared with others such as the dissenter Robert Ferguson, author of *The Interest of Reason in Religion* (1675), that reason could prove the divinity of the scriptures. Stillingfleet found himself locking horns with John Sergeant, a Catholic convert who set out the Catholic position in *Five catholick letters concerning the means of knowing with absolute certainty what faith, now held, was taught by Christ* (1687–8).

Meanwhile, Spinoza in the *Tractatus Theologico-Politicus* (1670) had noted that while people might hope for a trustworthy tradition of teaching, going right back to the prophets, as claimed by the Pharisees, or look for an infallible interpretation of the scriptures from the Pope, this kind of certainty was simply not available: both kinds of authority had been vigorously challenged.[26] Spinoza also anticipated modern concerns in a way that Stillingfleet did not. Where Stillingfleet had rested his case on the historical and scientific reliability of scripture, a position that had become almost totally untenable by the nineteenth century, Spinoza more wisely observed that, 'God adapted revelations to the understanding and opinion of the prophets', who pronounced effectively on matters of charity and morality but were unreliable sources of knowledge 'either of natural or of spiritual phenomena.' The question of historical veracity was, in any case, rather beside the point since love of God sprang from knowledge of Him rather than of history. Scriptural narrative was not scientific and did not engage with secondary causes, how things actually came about, but presented material in a manner to appeal most effectively to the devotional imagination.[27] While the authorship of the Pentateuch was traditionally attributed to Moses, an apparent guarantee of its authority, this was inconsistent with internal evidence, a point Spinoza claimed had been hinted at by Aben Ezra as long ago as the twelfth century.[28]

---

[26] Spinoza, *Tractatus Theologico-Politicus* (1670), trans. R. H. M. Elwes, Bohn series (London: G. Bell, 1883), as *A Theologico-Political Treatise* (repr. New York: Dover, 1951), chapter 7, 'Of the Interpretation of Scripture', p. 107.

[27] Spinoza, *Tractatus*, chapter 2, 'Of Prophets', p. 40; chapter 4, 'Of the divine law', p. 61; chapter 6, 'Of Miracles', p. 91.

[28] Spinoza, *Tractatus*, chapter 8, 'Of the authorship of the Pentateuch'.

The Crisis of Biblical Authority   73

The French biblical scholar Richard Simon, regarded as the founder of Old Testament criticism, had been a member of the French Oratory and saw his work as a defence of Catholic orthodoxy and a response to Spinoza, anticipating Newman in claiming that scripture unaided by tradition could not decide questions of faith, and demonstrating the need for Catholic teaching to make sense of scripture. But his *Histoire critique du Vieux Testament* (1678), following Spinoza in denying that Moses or any one writer was the author of the Pentateuch, and demonstrating various kinds of internal incoherence, provoked both Catholic and Protestant hostility and led to his expulsion from his order.[29]

One of the other difficulties to be confronted in scripture and scriptural interpretation was new knowledge about peoples and places. Stillingfleet did his best, drawing on the updated biblical geography of Samuel Bochart's *Phaleg* (1646). But the biblical world as it had been considered by the early rabbis and the church fathers was manifestly smaller than the world as known to modern geography, which now included the Americas and all their indigenous peoples. Could all of them really be descended from Adam, or rather from the sons of Noah who survived the flood? In *Pre-Adamitae* (1655), translated as *Men before Adam* (1656), the French lawyer and diplomat Isaac La Peyrère, or Pererius, took the radical step of proposing additional branches of the human family going back before Adam, claiming that there was a case for seeing the Bible as the history of the Jews, not of all mankind . The intention was not so much to debunk or dethrone as to supplement the biblical account, to provide a revised theory of origins that would still accommodate rather than efface Adam and Eve, and maintain the basic credibility of the biblical narrative, but Pererius still offended the orthodox from the Pope downwards and *Pre-Adamitae* was almost instantly banned in the provinces of Holland, Zeeland, and Friesland.[30] Stillingfleet devoted a whole chapter to pre-Adamism, populations and humans

---

[29] Richard Simon, *Histoire critique du Vieux Testament* [1678], trans. N. S. (from a Latin version) as *Critical Enquiries into the Various Editions of the Bible* (London: Tho. Braddyll, 1684); C. M. Du Veil, *A Letter to the Honourable Richard Boyle, Esq., defending the Divine Authority of the Holy Scripture and that is alone is the Rule of Faith. In answer to Father Simon's Critical History of the Old Testament* (London: Thomas Malthus, 1683).

[30] See David N. Livingstone, *Adam's Ancestors: Race, Religion and the Politics of Human Origins* (Baltimore: Johns Hopkins University Press, 2008).

74 *The Crisis of Biblical Authority*

origins in *Origines Sacrae*, conceding that we knew little about the peopling of America but pointing out that indigenous American traditions were only about eight hundred years old. This could accommodate the possibility that the Americas were populated from the old world in post-Biblical times and so safeguard the traditional theory of a single Adamite ancestry for the whole human race. But he protested too much and too ingeniously, falling into the familiar trap of treating scripture as science and scientific history rather than theology.[31]

Continuing controversy about biblical authority arose not just from different ways of reading the Bible but from debate about exactly what it consisted of and how it had evolved. There were lists of the individual books of the Bible in the decrees of the Council of Trent (fourth session), in Article 6 of the Thirty-Nine Articles, and at the beginning of the Westminster Confession. But the lists were not identical. There was agreement about the books of the New Testament, but the Tridentine list of Old Testament books was longer than the others. The extra or apocryphal books, of later date, found in the Greek Bible but not in the Hebrew scriptures, were listed separately in the Thirty-Nine Articles as still useful for 'example of life and instruction of manners', and they are in fact used in this way in the Prayerbook, but they were not to be used to establish doctrine. The Westminster Confession, on the other hand, dismissed them completely: 'not being of divine inspiration, [they] are no part of the Canon of Scripture; and therefore are of no authority in the Church of God, nor to be any otherwise approved, or made use of, than other human writings.'[32] Reformation suspicions of merely human authority endured, and they could be extended to the actual content of the Bible itself. It was remembered that there had been some misgivings about Revelation in the early Church and that Luther himself had had doubts about the apostolic and canonical status of the Epistle of James, because it seemed to be unsound on the doctrine of justification by faith. In fact his doubts had extended to Hebrews, Jude, and Revelation as well, and for almost a century some Lutheran Bible publishers listed these four books separately at the end of the table of contents and labelled them 'apocryphal' or 'non-canonical.'[33]

---

[31] Stillingfleet, *Origines Sacrae*, pp. 534–76.
[32] Schaff III, pp. 491, 602.
[33] Bruce M. Metzger, *The Canon of the New Testament* (Oxford: Clarendon Press, 1987), pp. 242–5.

The Crisis of Biblical Authority   75

If what was included could be questioned, so could what had been excluded. The maverick Irish rationalist John Toland, author of the controversial *Christianity not Mysterious* (1696), took Protestant wariness of human traditions, priestcraft, and superstition several degrees further than most. He was aware of the critical work of Spinoza and Richard Simon on the scriptures and had drawn his own conclusions. In *Amyntor* (1699) he reviewed the excluded or apocryphal writings relating to the New Testament period in a way that threatened to destabilize the official canon. Some of the apocryphal books were undoubted forgeries, but if some of these were genuine products of the apostolic period—and were kept out of the canon on the authority of the church fathers—how reliable was that authority? Toland had come across a little-known Gospel of Barnabas, purporting to be a first-century eyewitness account of the life of Christ, though now generally accepted as a fifteenth-century Italian forgery, which offered a radically different account of Christian origins, rejecting the teachings of St Paul as innovations perverting the original gospel and claiming among other things that it was not Jesus but Judas who was crucified. Whether Toland was really taken in by this strange gospel or not, he argued it had come from the Ebionites, a very early sect of Jewish Christians based to the east of the Jordan. He used it in his book *Nazarenus* (1718) to illustrate the unstable variousness of early Christianity and to suggest that by following different, probably later, traditions institutional Christianity had lost its way. He left his readers with the uneasy impression that more or less pious fraud and ignorant credulity were characteristic of the period of the early Church, a theme slyly elaborated in Edward Gibbon's *Decline and Fall of the Roman Empire* (1776–88). Toland gave grounds for the supposition that there might have been a degree of arbitrariness or special pleading in what was included or excluded from the scriptures. From that perspective, could anyone ever be really certain that any of the canonical books of the New Testament were genuine?[34]

A different kind of destabilization of biblical authority arose from anxieties about the biblical text itself, endlessly copied, preserved in

---

[34] Jonathan Sheehan, *The Enlightenment Bible* (Princeton: Princeton University Press, 2005), pp. 39–43; David S. Katz, *God's Last Words: Reading the English Bible from the Reformation to Fundamentalism* (New Haven and London: Yale University Press, 2004), pp. 138–43.

76   *The Crisis of Biblical Authority*

numerous manuscripts that were understandably enough not all quite the same. John Mill, or Mills, Principal of St Edmund Hall in Oxford, laboriously compared or reviewed more than one hundred manuscripts over a thirty-year period and by 1707 he was able to report some 30,000 variants, mostly of a trivial nature. Mill himself was not dismayed by his findings, thinking that they would help to restore the purity of scripture, and this was also the view of the great classical scholar Richard Bentley, but others feared that the effect would be to encourage anti-Christian and Catholic sneers at Protestant reliance on an unreliable text. In his originally anonymous *Discourse of Free-Thinking* (1713) the deist Anthony Collins, already fascinated by the problems of canonicity, ironically praised churchmen for 'owning and labouring to prove the Text of the Scripture precarious', and found another convenient reason to discount the Bible altogether.[35] Another deist, Matthew Tindal, critical of priestcraft and organized religion, argued that Christianity was a version of an age-old religion of nature, reason, and morality. In his book *Christianity as Old as the Creation* (1730) he tried to separate religion as he understood it from the religious history conveyed in the biblical record, particularly in the Old Testament.

Most English believers, uninterested in or unaware of the more extreme claims of the deists, the microscopic detail of textual variants, and the complex issues of canonicity, continued to read or listen to the King James version more or less undisturbed. When Benjamin Hoadly, Bishop of Bangor, suggested in a sermon in 1717 that there was no specific warrant in the gospels for any visible Church authority, which would include that of the established Church of England, he delighted dissenters and outraged high churchmen such as the non-juror William Law. However, the so-called Bangorian controversy did not challenge or debate the authority of scripture as such. As for Toland, Collins, and Tindal, they were marginal men and troublemakers who could safely be disregarded. But the questions and unorthodox speculations of the English deists had more impact in Germany. Tindal was translated into German in 1741 and other translations of deistic works soon followed, deeply influencing the founding fathers of German biblical studies. H. S. Reimarus of Hamburg (1694–1768) prepared but did not publish an *Apology for*

---

[35] Sheehan, *The Enlightenment Bible*, p. 44; Collins is quoted in Katz, *God's Last Words*, p. 188.

The Crisis of Biblical Authority 77

Rational Worshippers of God, fragments of which were published (anonymously) in Wolfenbüttel after his death by his friend G. E. Lessing, and these 'Wolfenbüttel Fragments' included a plea for toleration of the deists and an argument that religion was older than the Bible, which echoed Tindal's *Christianity as Old as the Creation*.[36] Publication plunged Lessing into bitter controversy with the orthodox and irascible Pastor Goeze of Hamburg. Lessing's last word in the controversy, in effect, was his verse-play *Nathan der Weise* (1779). Set at the time of the crusades, it is a plea for religious tolerance among Christians, Jews, and Moslems in which an ingenious plot reveals that a Templar and the adopted daughter of a Jew are brother and sister, and that Saladin is actually their uncle. German scholars, and some British Unitarians who could read German, took up the challenges of what came to be identified as critical scholarship. The young George Eliot read Lessing with interest.

In the German universities what we might now call the Humanities had traditionally been taught in the Philosophy Faculty as a prelude to more advanced studies in theology, law, or medicine. But in the course of the eighteenth century the role of the Philosophy Faculty, and particularly of classical teaching within it, became much more important. The new University of Göttingen, founded in 1737, established a formidable tradition in classical philology under C. G. Heyne. Heyne realized there were fruitful points of contact between biblical and classical studies since both engaged with the earliest available expressions of human consciousness. He developed principles for the interpretation of Greek myths, adapted from the English scholar Robert Lowth's pioneering lectures on the sacred poetry of the Hebrews, *De Sacra Poesi Hebraeorum* (1753). The connections could also work the other way. Analytical methods for exploring composition, authorship, and authenticity applied to classical texts could be easily transferred to the equally ancient texts of the Bible. The orientalist J. G. Eichhorn, a student at Göttingen from 1770 and later a professor there, speculated boldly on the composition of the books of the Old Testament, apocryphal writings, and the New Testament in a manner that fascinated Samuel Taylor Coleridge,

---

[36] J. W. Rogerson, *Old Testament Criticism in the Nineteenth Century: England and Germany* (London: SPCK, 1984), p. 9; there is a useful account of the Fragments Lessing published in Henry Chadwick, *Lessing's Theological Writings* (London: A. and C. Black, 1956), pp. 14–19.

78 *The Crisis of Biblical Authority*

though Coleridge's marginal annotations indicate that he often vigorously disagreed. An early article, published in 1779, showed how Eichhorn had taken account of Heyne's views on myth to develop an essentially mythical understanding of the opening chapters of Genesis.[37] Eichhorn is usually credited with being the first to apply the phrase 'Higher Criticism' (*die höhere Kritik*) to biblical studies, which he does in the Preface of the second edition of his *Einleitung ins Alte Testament* (1787). He makes it clear that he is importing this term and his analytical method from humanistic—that is, classical—studies.[38] This approach allowed him to distinguish different strands of tradition from different periods brought together in the first five books of the Bible. Following the speculations of Jean Astruc,[39] he claimed two main sources for Genesis and carefully distributed the narrative between them. Since he was in the Göttingen Philosophy Faculty rather than the Theology Faculty he had all the more freedom to pursue his pioneering research.[40]

The cherished principle of academic freedom (*Lehrfreiheit*) was underwritten by the state in nineteenth-century Prussia. The new University of Berlin, established in 1810, envisaged that all professors, including theologians, would be 'liberated from all censorship',[41] and although such freedoms came under duress from time to time, they were formally confirmed in the Prussian constitution of 1850.[42] German academic theologians were free from the threat of prosecution in the church courts, unlike their counterparts in England, Scotland, and Ireland. This had obvious advantages, but a possible disadvantage was that it encouraged disregard of pastoral considerations and a rigorously scientific and rationalist approach to theology,

[37] For Heyne, Lowth, and Eichhorn, see J. W. Rogerson, *Myth in Old Testament Interpretation* (Berlin and New York: Walter de Gruyter, 1974), pp. 23. Coleridge's marginal comments on Eichhorn are published in S. T. Coleridge, *Marginalia* II, Camden to Hutton, ed. George Whalley (London and Princeton: Routledge and Princeton University Press, 1984), pp. 369–520.

[38] J. G. Eichhorn, *Einleitung ins Alte Testament*, 2nd ed., 3 vols (Leipzig: Weidmans Erben, 1787), I, p. vi.

[39] Jean Astruc, *Conjectures sur les mémoires originaux dont il paroit que Moyse s'est servi pour composer le Livre de la Genèse* (Brusells: Fricx, 1753).

[40] Thomas Albert Howard, *Protestant Theology and the Making of the Modern German University* (Oxford: Oxford University Press, 2006), p. 120.

[41] Howard, *Protestant Theology and the Making of the Modern German University*, p. 179.

[42] Howard, *Protestant Theology and the Making of the Modern German University*, pp. 256, 291.

The Crisis of Biblical Authority 79

which needed to demonstrate that it was as intellectually strenuous as any other discipline in the university, and that it shared the enlightenment commitment to free enquiry without presuppositions (*Voraussetzungslosigkeit*).[43] Academic employment and promotion in this as in other disciplines depended on demonstrably original research, and the absence of ecclesiastical or pastoral constraints stimulated radical theorizing about the Bible and other religious matters, at the cost of provoking pious anti-intellectualism in the churches and encouraging churchmen to distrust modern scholarship, a distrust that eventually spread to Victorian England. A potentially disastrous gulf opened up between academy and pulpit. The situation was described by the Prussian-educated scholar and theologian Philip Schaff as 'favourable to the freest development of theological science and speculation, but very dangerous to the healthful and vigorous development of church life',[44] This 'dangerous' but stimulating academic tradition of free enquiry played an important part in the developing religious thought of George Eliot and Mary Ward.

The rationalist theologian Wilhelm de Wette (1780–1849), a rising star recruited in 1810 for the new University of Berlin, had already benefited from this freedom. It had given him scope in his *Beiträge zur Einleitung in das Alte Testament* (1806–7) to develop and refine his theory of the Pentateuch as a work of poetry and theology, which in effect offered mythical rather than reliably historical narrative as a way of expressing the national and religious insights of the Israelites. When he turned his attention to the New Testament in a commentary (in Latin) on the theology of the crucifixion, published in 1813, he seemed to deny the traditional doctrine of the atonement on the basis of historical-critical evidence. His disconcertingly radical approach and his work on myth had a considerable influence on his students at Berlin, and on David Strauss's severely demythologizing *Leben Jesu* (1835–6), which also made use of Eichhhorn's researches. Strauss was further indebted to his old teacher Friedrich Schleiermacher, Dean of the Theology Faculty at Berlin, whose emphasis on feeling as the basis for religion encouraged Strauss to suggest that the gospel narrative should not be treated historically but spiritually, should be drawn

---

[43] Howard, *Protestant Theology and the Making of the Modern German University*, p. 29.

[44] Howard, *Protestant Theology and the Making of the Modern German University*, p. 266.

80   *The Crisis of Biblical Authority*

inwards as a source of personal meaning and inspiration. Though Strauss was violently denounced as an atheist, there is perhaps a sense in which his work stretches back through Schleiermacher to Reformation teaching and the anti-speculative view of the early Melanchthon that knowing Christ is a matter of knowing his benefits. Strauss's extensive bibliography and his detailed reference to the work of other scholars in the field brought together the fruits of several generations of German critical scholarship, all made available for more or less disconcerted English readers in 1846 in George Eliot's translation.[45]

George Eliot's social circle in Coventry in the 1840s had included Unitarians of the school of Joseph Priestley and she had in fact taken over the translation of Strauss from her friend Rufa Brabant, who had married the Unitarian biblical scholar Charles Hennell. In 1839 Strauss had written an enthusiastic preface for the German translation of Hennell's rationalist *Inquiry Concerning the Origin of Christianity*. Unitarians welcomed critical biblical scholarship and some of the alleged demystifications resulting from it; they felt it could strengthen their position that there was no satisfactory biblical basis for the doctrine of the Trinity. In the 1750s the young Joseph Priestley, already unconvinced of the 'inspiration of the authors of the books of Scripture as writers', had begun a detailed study of divergences between the Hebrew text of selected books of the Hebrew Bible and their counterparts in the Greek Old Testament.[46] His friend Thomas Belsham was largely responsible for the publication in 1808 of a controversial 'improved' translation of the New Testament, based not on the old and inadequate Textus Receptus, essentially Erasmus' text, derived from just a few late manuscripts, but on the new Greek text (1775–7) established by Johann Jakob Griesbach on critical principles and with reference to a much wider range of manuscripts. Griesbach was able to take full account of textual variants established by earlier scholars such as the Englishman John Mill. Interestingly, it was a later edition of Griesbach's text that was purchased both by the young Thomas Hardy and by his fictional protagonist Jude the

---

[45] For de Wette and his influence, see Rogerson, *Old Testament Criticism*, chapters 2 and 3, and Howard, *Protestant Theology and the Making of the Modern German University*, pp. 195, 209–10. For Schleiermacher and Melanchthon, see John R. Schneider, *Philip Melanchton's Rhetorical Construal of Biblical Authority: Oratio Sacra* (Lewiston, Queenston, and Lampeter: Edwin Mellen, 1990), p. 211.

[46] Joseph Priestley, *Autobiography*, introd. Jack Lindsay (Bath: Adams and Dart, 1970), p. 83.

The Crisis of Biblical Authority 81

Obscure. A later Unitarian figure, the Egyptologist Samuel Sharpe, produced his own translation in 1840, also based on Griesbach's text. German scholarship was well understood by the next generation of Unitarians. John Kenrick, perhaps the greatest nonconformist scholar of his day, Principal of the Unitarian Manchester College, had studied at Göttingen and attended lectures by Eichhorn and Schleiermacher. He may well have been the first Englishman to use the phrase 'the higher criticism' in imitation of Eichhorn's *die höhere Kritik*; he was certainly one of the first to take close account of German biblical criticism. In an 1827 article 'On the Mythical Interpretation of the Bible' in the *Monthly Repository* (modelled on Priestley's *Theological Repository*) he not only talks about 'the higher criticism' in Germany but he learnedly traces the current interest there in myth in the Old Testament to its origins in the Göttingen classicist C. G. Heyne's lectures on Apollodorus, where he had suggested that heathen mythology could represent truths clothed in symbolic and poetic language.[47]

In *Middlemarch*, set in the early 1830s, George Eliot's Mr Casaubon had been fruitlessly engaged in seeking a key to all mythologies. The problem was not mythology, which Eliot knew was a fruitful area of enquiry, but ignorance of German scholarship going back to Heyne and beyond, an ignorance he would have shared with the majority of Anglican clergymen in the 1830s.

Thanks partly to Eliot's translations of Strauss and Feuerbach, this ignorance did not last, even if German critics were often more feared than read. For some English Christians the Bible was regarded as a single, authoritative source; for others, influenced by the Oxford Movement, there was a different but still single or unified source in the tradition of the Church, described in static terms as what was believed everywhere, always and by all, the 'Vincentian' test of Catholicity (originally formulated by St Vincent of Lérins in the fifth century), which had been explicitly endorsed in 1836 in Tract 78 of *Tracts for the Times*. Particular tribute was paid by the compilers to the early church fathers for the care they took 'to preserve the truth

---

[47] [John Kenrick] 'On the Mythical Interpretation of the Bible', *Monthly Repository and Review*, 2nd ser. 1:9 (September 1827), 633–40; see Francis E. Mineka, *The Dissidence of Dissent: The Monthly Repository, 1806–1838* (Chapel Hill: University of North Carolina Press, 1944).

82 *The Crisis of Biblical Authority*

from corruption'.[48] In a sermon preached in Winchester Cathedral in the same year, John Keble paid similar tribute to primitive tradition, coming closer than his Protestant critics liked to the Tridentine attribution of equal authority to tradition and scripture: 'We are to look before all things to the integrity of the good deposit, the orthodox faith, the Creed of the Apostolical Church, guaranteed to us by Holy Scripture and by consent of pure antiquity.'[49]

But German Protestantism, and German scholarship, and well-informed novelists such as George Eliot and Mary Ward, favoured a more dynamic or process-focused model of religion, sometimes attributed to Hegel's influence though it can be traced back to Lessing. It may have been Lessing's theory of historical development set out in his *Die Eherziehung des Menschengeschlechts* ('The Education of the Human Race') (1780), which had laid the foundations of German Protestant liberalism, that lay behind the schoolmaster Frederick Temple's contribution to *Essays and Reviews*, 'The Education of the World'. This did not stop him from becoming Bishop of Exeter in 1869, despite fierce conservative opposition, and eventually he went on to become Archbishop of Canterbury. Rowland Williams, Professor of Hebrew at St David's College, Lampeter, was less fortunate. His contribution to the same volume, an essay on 'Bunsen's Biblical Researches', led to prosecution for heresy. Williams began by picking up on the recently articulated geological principle of uniformitarianism, or geophysical change as continuous process, as a way of stressing 'the Divine energy as continuous and omnipresent', linking it (as Lessing would have done) with 'the law of growth, traceable through the Bible, as in the world'. He praised the voluminous biblical researches and other writings of the Prussian scholar and diplomat Baron Bunsen, a Lutheran, commending his awareness of process and the sometimes erratic development of religious ideas, necessarily different at different times and in different contexts. Bunsen did not go quite as far as the English deist Matthew Tindal in arguing that Christianity was as old as Creation, but he suggested there must have been something like 'our faith' in men's minds before the Christian

---

[48] [Henry Manning and Charles Marriott] *Testimony of Writers in the Later English Church to the Duty of Maintaining quod semper, quod ubique, quod ab omnibus traditum est* [1836], new ed. (London: Rivingtons, 1839) p. 117.

[49] John Keble, *Primitive Tradition Recognised in Holy Scripture*, 2nd ed. (London: Rivingtons, 1837), p. 44.

The Crisis of Biblical Authority 83

era, renewed from generation to generation even if it was reflected or expressed only in imperfectly credible narratives and propositions that would hardly stand the test of time. Even the New Testament scriptures, discussed by Bunsen in the light of the researches of de Wette of Berlin, had been composed at different times and showed divergence and change over time in the treatment of religious ideas. And soon the 'first freedom of the Gospel' was overlaid with 'the confused thought and furious passions which disfigure most of the great councils'.[50] Bunsen had already crossed swords with the conservative High Churchman Christopher Wordsworth, nephew of the poet, suggesting on disputed evidence that the early Church in the time of Hippolytus (c.170–c.236) was still in transition and took its stand on scripture as it was then understood rather than on the authority of the Catholic creeds.[51] For Williams, as for Bunsen, the insistent appeal of Catholics and Tractarians to the authority of traditions allegedly stemming from Christian antiquity was misguided and unhelpful since it implied an illusory purity of doctrine accessible and maintained in an already-achieved steady state: 'While they imagine a system of Divine immutability, or one in which, at worst, holy fathers unfolded reverently Apostolic oracles, the true history of the Church exhibits the turbulent growth of youth; a democracy, with all its passions, transforming itself into sacerdotalism . . . Even the text of Scripture fluctuated in sympathy with the changes of the Church, especially in passages bearing on asceticism and the fuller development of the Trinity.'[52] This last charge, almost calculated to infuriate the biblical literalists, was supported by the textual variants and different manuscript traditions revealed by the minute scholarship of Griesbach and his successors, and it has been upheld in our own time in Bart Ehrman's detailed study *The Orthodox Corruption of Scripture. The Effect of Early Christological Controversies on the Text of the New Testament* (1993), but it was not popular at the time. Williams, fully aware of High Anglican hostility to Bunsen, probably expected fierce criticism from other quarters

---

[50] Rowland Williams, 'Bunsen's Biblical Researches', *Essays and Reviews* (1860) (London: Longman, 1861), pp. 50, 52, 82–5.

[51] C. C. J. Bunsen, *Hippolytus and his Age*, 4 vols (London: Longmans, 1852); Christopher Wordsworth, *Remarks on M. Bunsen's Work on St Hippolytus* (London: Rivingtons, 1855).

[52] Williams, 'Bunsen's Biblical Researches', *Essays and Reviews*, p. 86.

84   *The Crisis of Biblical Authority*

as well, and was not disappointed, but he defiantly praised his 'noble and Christian spirit'.[53]

The uncritically cherished Reformation principle of *sola scriptura* was given a hard time in *Essays and Reviews*. H. B. Wilson, discussing 'The National Church', pointed out that no scriptural author actually identified the books of the Old and New Testaments as the 'Word of God'. While this ultra-Protestant claim was made in other credal statements such as the Helvetic Confession (and, he might have added, the Westminster Confession) it was not to be found in the Thirty-Nine Articles. As far as he was concerned this represented a 'comparative freedom' of interpretation that was entirely beneficial, though he regretted the 'many evils' entailed by 'an extreme and too exclusive Scripturalism'.[54] Mark Pattison, soon to be Rector of Lincoln College Oxford, offered an historical and critical survey of rationalist divinity, 'Tendencies of Religious Thought in England 1688–1750', in which he maintained that this 'Protestant theory of belief', the supreme authority of 'self-evidencing Scripture', had worked well enough for a time. But he went on to suggest that in the course of the seventeenth century it had in effect been forced to give ground to substitutes, including Reason, which was applied not altogether conclusively or satisfactorily to attack the deists (with whom he seemed to have some sympathy) and to justify traditional church teaching.[55]

Benjamin Jowett, Oxford Professor of Greek and author of the theologically liberal *Commentaries on the Epistles of St Paul* (1855), like Pattison a friend of George Eliot, was even more severe in his controversial essay 'On the Interpretation of Scripture'. He claimed that while Roman Catholics hardly realize they have little or no direct scriptural support from the New Testament for most of their distinctive doctrines, Protestants abuse the scriptures by claiming biblical support for their teaching from particular verses at the cost of ignoring others: 'The favourite verses shine like stars, while the rest of the page is thrown into the shade.'[56] Like Lessing, and indeed Toland before him, Jowett felt the Bible should be read like any other book,

---

[53] Williams, 'Bunsen's Biblical Researches', *Essays and Reviews*, p. 93.

[54] H. B. Wilson, 'Séances Historiques de Genève. The National Church', *Essays and Reviews*, pp. 175–7.

[55] Mark Pattison, 'Tendencies of Religious Thought in England 1688–1750', *Essays and Reviews*, pp. 328–9.

[56] Benjamin Jowett, 'On the Interpretation of Scripture', *Essays and Reviews*, p. 366.

The Crisis of Biblical Authority 85

'by the same rules of evidence and the same canons of criticism'.[57] He noted that despite popular superstitions to the contrary the Bible, or rather the generally accepted original text and English translation of the Bible, was not immune from human errors and misinterpretations, sometimes perpetuated because they seemed to support preconceived opinions and traditional religious teaching. One of his examples of convenient error preserved for doctrinal reasons, which he could have taken from Gibbon's examples of pious fraud, was the persistence in the King James version of 1611 (though not in Luther's Bible) of a spurious verse, the so-called 'Johannine comma' (1 John 5:7), referring to the three witnesses in heaven: the Father, the Word, and the Holy Ghost. This was habitually used as a proof-text for the orthodox doctrine of the Trinity, not directly set out in scripture in which there is no word in the original Greek that corresponds to 'Trinity'.[58] The Latin Vulgate translation had included and given currency to this verse, but Erasmus, in constructing his pioneering new text of the Greek New Testament, first published in 1516, had found no evidence for it in the small number of Greek manuscripts available to him, so he omitted it. Greeted by a storm of protest from the orthodox, Erasmus undertook to restore the familiar reading if any manuscript evidence for it could be found. When a forged late manuscript including the disputed reading was produced, probably to order, he blandly accepted it as providing the necessary evidence and changed his Greek text accordingly for later editions, from 1522 onwards, keeping his suspicions to himself. This was the Greek text that lay behind the King James version and the Elzevir edition of the Greek text of 1633, which came to be identified as the Textus Receptus.[59]

J. W. Colenso, mathematician and Bishop of Natal, found himself trying to make some kind of modern sense of scripture in a culturally alien environment, like Rider Haggard in his African novels almost a generation later. It was a mixed blessing for Colenso that the first and most controversial instalment of his *The Pentateuch and the Book of Joshua Critically Examined* (1862–79) appeared in 1862, under the

---

[57] Jowett, 'On the Interpretation of Scripture', *Essays and Reviews*, p. 375.

[58] Edward Gibbon, *Decline and Fall of the Roman Empire* (1776–88), ed. David Womersley, 3 vols (London: Allen Lane, 1994), II, pp. 442–3 (chapter 37); Jowett, 'On the Interpretation of Scripture', *Essays and Reviews*, p. 352.

[59] See Katz, *God's Last Words*, pp. 11–12.

86   *The Crisis of Biblical Authority*

title 'The Pentateuch Examined as an Historical Narrative', in the middle of the furore attending *Essays and Reviews*, while Rowland Williams was being prosecuted in the church courts. Boldly taking as his motto 'We can do nothing against the Truth' (2 Corinthians 13:8), Colenso deliberately linked his work with *Essays and Reviews* and responses to it such as the orthodox *Aids to Faith* (1861). He had found his moment, and his sales were enormous, but so was the trouble he brought upon himself. In the course of working on a Zulu translation of the Bible for use in his missionary diocese he had been forced to confront anew the fundamental issue of what the Bible, and indeed Christianity, were really about and how essential religious meaning could be communicated across cultural divisions in the modern world. Rider Haggard's fictions of the numinous approached the same issue from a different angle. Colenso had become acutely aware of various statistical and practical anomalies in the text, which he found it impossible to explain away to his African assistant William Ngidi. Detailed engagement with particular passages brought home to him inconsistency and incoherence, which demonstrated the unhistorical or mythic nature of much Old Testament narrative.

Some of the problems had been identified long ago. In one of the Wolfenbüttel Fragments published by Lessing in 1777 Reimarus had called into question the detail and plausibility of the story of the departure from Egypt and the crossing of the Red Sea (Exodus 12–15), calculating that the crossing would have taken nine days.[60] De Wette of Berlin, whose *Einleitung* Colenso had studied, had taken the same passage as an example of popular tradition transformed by stages into poetic and miraculous narrative. Colenso in his turn reviewed the number of Israelites leaving Egypt: the Bible specifies some 600,000 men (Exodus 12:37), nine times the size of Wellington's army at Waterloo, as Colenso noted, but if women and children were added the total figure would be more like two million (Reimarus had suggested three million), which seemed an improbably large figure. He worked out that they would have formed an unwieldy procession at least twenty-two miles in length. He raised various practical difficulties. How could so many people have been mobilized so quickly? It is implied that the men were armed, but how could a slave population

---

[60] [H. S. Reimarus] 'Durchgang der Israeliten durch Roten Meer', in G. E. Lessing, *Werke*, ed. Julius Petersen and Waldemar von Olshausen, 25 vols (Berlin and Leipzig: Bong, 1925), XXII (*Theologische Schriften* II), pp. 111–21.

The Crisis of Biblical Authority 87

have acquired arms? How could the infertile region of Sinai have supported the extensive 'flocks, and herds, even very much cattle' (Exodus 12:38) that reportedly accompanied the Israelites? Here, and elsewhere in the Pentateuch, scripture quite literally did not add up. Colenso's researches, like those of his German predecessors, served to indicate that biblical narrative was often a mode of imaginative religious teaching rather than accurate historical record-keeping. It was in fact closer to the more serious and instructive fictions of the period than it was usually tactful to admit.

Colenso was already in trouble for suggesting that polygamous converts should not be forced to become monogamous, and for publishing *The Epistle of St Paul to the Romans Newly Translated, and Explained from a Missionary Point of View* (1861), which denied eternal punishment and other traditional doctrines. Now he was denounced for heresy and his Metropolitan, the Bishop of Cape Town, deposed and excommunicated him, only to run into various legal challenges that kept the controversy before the public for many years to come.[61]

The very public controversy about biblical authority associated with *Essays and Reviews* and Bishop Colenso was renewed when modern textual and philological scholarship was deployed to produce an authoritative revised version of the English Bible. Conservatives were predictably aghast. After two hundred and seventy years of the King James Bible there was considerable suspicion of the distinctly overdue Revised Version of the New Testament (1881), based not on the old inadequate Textus Receptus but on a scientifically reconstructed critical text prepared by two distinguished Professors of Divinity at Cambridge, B. F. Westcott and F. J. A. Hort. For biblical literalists it was symptomatic that the revisers had changed the familiar wording of 2 Timothy 3:16 ('All scripture is given by inspiration of God, and is profitable for doctrine, for reproof, for correction, for instruction in righteousness') to 'Every scripture inspired of God is also profitable for teaching, for reproof, for correction, for instruction which is in righteousness.' The new phrasing seemed dangerously weaker, as if the

---

[61] W. M. L. de Wette, 'Durchgang durch das rothe Meer', *Beiträge zur Einleitung in das Alte Testament*, 2 vols (Halle: Schimmelpfennig, 1806–7), II, pp. 209–15; J. W. Colenso, *The Pentateuch and Book of Joshua Critically Examined*, 7 vols (London: Longmans, 1862–79), I, pp. xiv, xx, 48–50, 63; Katz, *God's Last Words*, pp. 250–7.

88   *The Crisis of Biblical Authority*

translators were doubtful about the inspiration of scripture, even though it more accurately translated the Greek. The controversial gesture of inviting a distinguished Unitarian scholar, Dr Vance Smith, to join the revisers was not appreciated by extreme conservatives who seemed to blame him, quite unreasonably, for more or less everything they disliked about the 'Revised and Arianized Version'.[62] For James Carson, an ultra-orthodox medical doctor from Coleraine in Northern Ireland: 'It is so fixed now that the Unitarian, the Freethinker, and all who wish to get away from the inspired Word, can sail off without difficulty.' Carson unconsciously testified to wider anxieties at the time by continuing with the nautical metaphor: 'when they take away verbal inspiration from the Scriptures they leave us on the ocean without a rudder'.[63]

It was true that some late Trinitarian interpolations such as the notorious 'Johannine comma' of which Jowett had complained had finally been removed from the text, but most of the changes made little theological difference. To take just one example, modern textual criticism queried the familiar King James version phrase 'by prayer and fasting' (Mark 9:29), based on the Textus Receptus, since the Greek for 'and fasting' did not appear in two of the best Greek manuscripts, the fourth-century Codex Sinaiticus and Codex Vaticanus. The reference to fasting was also missing from early Latin and Georgian versions and a second-century quotation by Clement of Alexandria. The Revised Version scrupulously revised the English text to take account of the manuscript evidence that the phrase was a late addition. Such small points hardly mattered, but the critics had little sense of proportion. Crusty old Dean Burgon of Chichester had savagely attacked *Essays and Reviews* in his book *Inspiration and Interpretation* (1861), which had in its turn been cited by Bishop Colenso as an example of intellectually indefensible biblical literalism. Totally unabashed, Burgon now attacked the Revised Version, complaining colourfully, at length and in detail in a series of scholarly articles in the *Quarterly Review*, later collected and published as *The Reviser Revised* (1883). The revisers, devout and scholarly men, were

---

[62] William Morris, *The Revised and Arianized Version of the English New Testament: A Protest and Testimony* (London: Elliott Stock, 1881); Katz, *God's Last Words*, pp. 218–22, 250–3; Owen Chadwick, *The Victorian Church*. 2nd ed., 2 vols (London: A. and C. Black, 1970–2), II, pp. 90–7.

[63] James C. L. Carson, *The New Translation of the Scriptures*, privately printed for the author, 1881, pp. 8, 10.

The Crisis of Biblical Authority

attacked, quite outrageously, for having 'sown broadcast over four continents doubts as to the truth of Scripture, which it will never be in their power either to remove or to recall'. As if that were not enough, the new 'ill-advised practice' of recording alternative readings in the margins 'can only result in hopelessly unsettling the faith of millions'.[64] Burgon particularly detested Codex Sinaiticus and Codex Vaticanus, to which the revisers had attached so much importance, condemning them in the language of the police courts as 'two false witnesses' of 'ascertained evil character'.[65] Westcott and Hort's sophisticated and innovative attempt to recover the original Greek text was condemned as 'about as hopeful a proceeding as would be the attempt to erect an Eddystone lighthouse on the Goodwin Sands'.[66]

Burgon had been a poet in youth, author of the much-quoted description of Petra as the 'rose-red city half as old as time'. His colourful rhetoric was worthy of a better cause, though most of his causes were lost causes. It seems inherently unlikely that 'the faith of millions' was really unsettled by marginal notes, scholarly revisers or biblical critics, but it was good to be able to blame someone for the complex religious uncertainties of the day. Gladstone's highly rhetorical *Impregnable Rock of Holy Scripture* (1890), taking rather selective account of critical scholarship, was intended to reassure the faithful in times of doubt and perplexity, but it was too late: the damage had been done. There was a ready market for the scoffing but substantial *Plain Commentary on the First Gospel* by 'An Agnostic', which appeared the following year (1891). Biblical literalism, too often reading for the letter and missing the underlying spirit, was a habit that Origen and others had long ago tried to get beyond, with admittedly mixed results. The habit of reading for the letter was shared by unimaginative religious conservatives and unimaginative scoffers alike. But neither the old story of the timeless and all-sufficient authority of scripture nor the new story of successful scientific demolition of scripture, reducing it to the status of mere romance, could really be sustained without qualification. It was left to more

---

[64] [J. W. Burgon] 'New Testament Revision: The New English Version', *Quarterly Review* 153 (January 1882), 2.

[65] [J. W. Burgon] 'New Testament Revision: Westcott and Hort's Textual Theory', *Quarterly Review* 153 (April 1882), 355, 356.

[66] [J. W. Burgon] 'New Testament Revision: Westcott and Hort's Textual Theory' p. 368.

90   *The Crisis of Biblical Authority*

imaginative readers and imaginative writers, including novelists, to make modern narrative sense of God and the Bible.

It was against the background of mistreating and mistrusting Holy Scripture, often courting disappointment by reading it in the wrong way for the wrong things and then wondering where else authoritative certainty might now be found, that some Victorian novelists from George Eliot onwards began to write their own more secular scriptures. These narratives, often compelling and authoritative in their own way, were, like the Bible, about the meaning and direction of history and the continuing fortunes and interactions of the individual, society, nature, and indeed God. It is unfortunate that the early Lukács has misled us into thinking too exclusively of the novel as the epic of the world abandoned by God. Even before Lukács, Thomas Hardy himself helped to mislead us: the aggressive iconoclasm and anticlericalism of his later novels certainly discourage any kind of religious reading. It is also a matter for regret that some otherwise excellent critical studies of Victorian novels and novelists, while noting religious doubt and dissent, have tended to emphasize engagements with Darwin, Comtean positivism, secular humanism, and social and political history to such an extent that they have distracted our attention from underlying religious seriousness and the reimagining of biblical themes in apparently secular narratives.[67] The author studies that follow seek to redress the balance: they offer contextualized rereadings of selected 'secular' novelists, all of them brought up with the Bible and the Church of England, to suggest that so far from repudiating their inheritance they found imaginative ways of accommodating, modifying, and enriching it. As Timothy Larsen has recently reminded us through the case studies in *A People of One Book: The Bible and the Victorians* (2011), rejecting some traditional dogmas and repudiating some of what has been done with the Bible is not the same as rejecting the Bible. George Eliot comes first, not just because she has chronological priority or because she is one of the

---

[67] See for example Gillian Beer, *Darwin's Plots: Evolutionary Narrative in Darwin, George Eliot and Nineteenth-century Fiction* (London: Routledge, 1983); T. R. Wright, *The Religion of Humanity: The Impact of Comtean Positivism in Victorian Britain* (Cambridge: Cambridge University Press, 1986); Barry Qualls, *The Secular Pilgrims of Victorian Fiction* (Cambridge: Cambridge University Press, 1982); Elizabeth Ermarth, *The English Novel in History 1840–1895* (London: Routledge, 1997).

best-known and most studied Victorian novelists, but because in her commitment to the narrative imagination as a way of exploring ultimate human questions, and in her socially progressive reimagining of the narrative of salvation history as the growing good of the world, she provided a model for her own century and for ours.

4

George Eliot's Secular Scriptures

George Eliot, born Mary Anne Evans, rebelled against the religion of her upbringing, but not, it can be argued, against God or the Bible. As a child she was pious, intense, and austere. She had read her Bible in her schooldays with faith and hope. Her early letters are full of scripture quotations, for what higher authority could there be? She recalled in 1859 that she had been 'strongly under the influence of Evangelical belief, and earnestly endeavouring to shape this English-Christian life of ours into some consistency with the spirit and simple verbal tenor of the New Testament'.[1] Already a voracious reader with an appetite for the works of Sir Walter Scott and the historical yarns of G. P. R. James, as well as for Archbishop Leighton's much-reprinted *Practical Commentary upon the First Two Chapters of the First Epistle of Peter* (1693), she tried hard to convince herself that novels read merely for entertainment were harmful and that 'The weapons of the Christian warfare were never sharpened at the forge of romance.'[2] In a severely Calvinistic poem, published in 1840 in the *Christian Observer*, the leading evangelical periodical, she imagines her farewell to the present world and all its delights, including 'Books that have been to me as chests of gold'. But she will keep her Bible:

> Blest volume! Whose clear truth-writ page, once known,
> Fades not before heaven's sunshine or hell's moan,

---

[1] Eliot to Sara Hennell, 7 October 1859, *The George Eliot Letters*, ed. Gordon S. Haight, 9 vols (Oxford: Clarendon, 1954–78), III, 175. From about 1855 Mary Anne (or Marian) Evans wished to be known as 'Mrs Lewes' and she assumed the pen-name of 'George Eliot' with the publication of *Scenes of Clerical Life* in 1858: for convenience she will be referred to here just as (George) Eliot.

[2] Eliot to Maria Lewis, 16 March 1839, *The George Eliot Letters* I, 21–3.

George Eliot's Secular Scriptures

> To thee I say not, of earth's gifts alone,
> Farewell![3]

It was all too intense and too extreme to last. She had already felt small twinges of doubt. Bulwer Lytton's novel *Devereux* (1829) had introduced her to the 'amiable atheist' Bezoni, who brought with him the disturbing possibility that 'religion was not a requisite to moral excellence'. It was equally disconcerting to discover from visiting Methodist miners in the neighbourhood that religious feeling was no barrier to a low standard of morality. Her scepticism grew in conversations with the freethinking and severely intellectual Brays and Hennells, whom she met in Coventry in 1841. Charles Hennell had published a rationalist *Inquiry into the Origins of Christianity* (1838) and when the second edition appeared in 1841 she bought her own copy. By the time she was twenty-two she had lost her faith, or at least her faith in the literal sense of scripture, and the miraculous and supernatural elements of Christianity. In January 1842, scrupulous if uncharacteristically insensitive, she abruptly refused to accompany her beloved father to church because she could no longer share his beliefs. This precipitated four months of 'Holy War', as she called it, and she was almost turned out of the house, but eventually they agreed to differ.[4]

Already formidably well read, she was stimulated by the companionship of the Brays and, liberated from narrow religious views, she found her intellectual and literary apprenticeship was entering a new and strenuous phase. She had acquired some German (as well as French, Italian, Latin, and Greek), so now she was able to read and admire Lessing's play *Nathan der Weise*, an anti-dogmatic plea for religious tolerance that left Lessing open to the charge from religious conservatives that he had attacked the unique status and value of Christianity. She also read Goethe's allegedly immoral novel *Wilhelm Meister*, the archetypal Bildungsroman (or novel of personal development) and a model for her own fictions, which she later defended as manifesting a morality with 'a grander orbit than any which can be measured by the calculations of the pulpit and of ordinary literature'.[5]

---

[3] George Eliot, *Collected Poems*, ed. Lucien Jenkins (London: Skoob, 1989), p. 26.

[4] Gordon S. Haight, *George Eliot: A Biography* (Oxford: Clarendon Press, 1968), pp. 39–40.

[5] 'The Morality of *Wilhelm Meister*' [*Leader*, 21 July 1855] in George Eliot, *Selected Essays, Poems and Other Writings*, ed. A. S. Byatt (London: Penguin, 1990), p. 307.

94 *George Eliot's Secular Scriptures*

Perhaps encouraged by Goethe's admiration of Spinoza, she also began to translate some of Spinoza's work (from Latin) and before her father's death in 1849 she had embarked on a version of the *Tractatus Theologico-Politicus*.[6]

This was a bold and enterprizing project, even if it was never completed. She seems to have been attracted by Spinoza's attempt in a would-be theocratic age to challenge the largely unchallenged authority of scripture.[7] This took the form of a critical approach to the historical reliability of scripture, particularly in his sixth chapter on miracles, and his claim that scripture is unscientific in that it does not attempt to explain things by their secondary causes but presents them in a way that will appeal to the religious imagination. Spinoza had had considerable influence on the development of German religious thought, particularly through Friedrich Schleiermacher's celebrated *Reden über die Religion* (1799), eventually translated in 1893 as *Religion: Speeches to its Cultured Despisers*, and Coleridge was interested in him, but his work was not well known in eighteenth- or nineteenth-century England. 'Spinozism' was used mainly as a loose term of theological abuse, a synonym for pantheism or atheism. The *Tractatus* was not available in English translation until 1862, though by 1843 there was a pioneering essay on his work by the journalist G. H. Lewes, whom Eliot had yet to meet though they were to live together as man and wife from 1854 to his death in 1878. Another substantial essay appeared in 1855, written by J. A. Froude, one of the more notorious religious doubters of the period and the author of *The Nemesis of Faith* (1849), which Eliot had sympathetically reviewed for the Coventry *Herald*.[8]

Spinoza's views on scripture may have helped to prepare Eliot for her pioneering translation of David Strauss's massive, iconoclastically post-Christian *Life of Christ*, which she took over from her friend Rufa Hennell in January 1844 and published in 1846. This was

---

[6] Rosemary Ashton, *George Eliot: A Life* (London: Hamish Hamilton, 1996), pp. 47, 71.

[7] Discussed in J. Samuel Preus, *Spinoza and the Irrelevance of Biblical Authority* (Cambridge: Cambridge University Press, 2001).

[8] G. H. Lewes, 'Spinoza: His Life and Writings', *Westminster Review* 39 (May 1843), 372–407; J. A. Froude, 'Spinoza', *Westminster Review* 64 (July 1855), 1–37; Matthew Arnold, 'A Word More About Spinoza', *Macmillan's Magazine* 9 (December 1863), 136–42, a review of Robert Willis' pioneering English translation of the *Tractatus* (1862).

George Eliot's Secular Scriptures 95

followed by a translation, still the definitive version in English, of Ludwig Feuerbach's *Essence of Christianity* (1854), an extended argument to the effect that the essence and sources of religion are anthropological rather than theological, a projection of human concerns rather than divine or supernatural. She then proceeded to translate Spinoza's controversially pantheistic and rationalist *Ethics*, completed in 1856, although this translation remained unpublished in her lifetime because of a dispute with the publisher. It was eventually published in Salzburg in 1981.[9]

All this earnest and strenuous mental activity was interspersed with brilliant critical essays in the *Leader*, edited by Lewes, whom she met in 1851, and more extended pieces in the *Westminster Review*, which she was editing herself, such as her erudite and searching review of R. W. Mackay's *Progress of the Intellect* (1851). From 1856 her moral and religious explorations and her retreat from religious dogmatism were continued mainly by other means in her second career as George Eliot the novelist. She continued to explore connections between divinity (or 'the Unseen') and human goodness in an informal, residually numinous 'Religion of Humanity', which was influenced but not dominated by the progressive, secular positivism first developed by Auguste Comte in his *Cours de philosophie positive* (1830–42). Her poem of 1867 'O may I join the choir invisible', commending past and future moral courage, selfless generosity, and 'the growing life of man', was often used liturgically at services conducted by English positivists, and was set to music as an almost sacred cantata in 1883.[10] Her vision of moral and intellectual growth, which Comte had formalized as a three-stage model of historical development with theological, metaphysical, and positive phases, can also be linked with her German studies and translations: Strauss and Feuerbach, in writing about Christian origins and the evolution of religious thought, were deeply influenced by Hegelian ideas of inexorable historical process and continuous development.

This is reflected in Eliot's novels both in the treatment of individual lives and in their relation to the broader current of history,

---

[9] Haight, *George Eliot: A Biography*, pp. 199–200; Ashton, *George Eliot: A Life*, pp. 154, 402.

[10] T. R. Wright, *The Religion of Humanity: The Impact of Comtean Positivism in Victorian Britain* (Cambridge: Cambridge University Press, 1986), pp. 173–201, 84, 95; George Eliot, *Collected Poems*, p. 49.

96   *George Eliot's Secular Scriptures*

optimistically described at the end of *Middlemarch* as 'the growing good of the world'. Growth implied movement in a positive direction, which might not be precisely the dynamic of redemption and 'salvation history', or an approach to Augustine's City of God, but it was a bit like it. This, coupled with an ethic of sympathy and enduring compassion for suffering humanity, approximating to Christian charity, helps to explain the wide popularity of her fiction in her own time and ever since among churched and unchurched alike. Her novels were respected and enjoyed as secular scriptures. It helped that she never denied the possibility of the existence of God, and indeed she took exception to the 'studiously offensive' expression of atheism of Harriet Martineau's *Letters on Man's Nature and Development* (1851).[11] It did not help that because Lewes could not divorce his wife she lived with him without benefit of clergy. The Ulster Presbyterian Samuel Law Wilson, later Professor of Sacred Rhetoric and Catachetics at the Presbyterian College in Belfast, discussed 'The Theology of George Eliot' at some length and praised her for being a better and clearer teacher than Carlyle, but felt obliged to draw a moral: 'George Eliot became a freethinker, and, as very often happens, freethinking prepared the way for freeliving.'[12] The unconventional relationship with Lewes was bound to offend conservative opinion and strain old friendships, but even in her own time it did her reputation less harm than might have been expected. Post-Christian, perhaps, but never aggressively anti-Christian, she has constantly received the more or less respectful attentions of theologians as well as of literary critics and fellow agnostics such as Leslie Stephen, author of *An Agnostic's Apology* (1893), who published a short book on Eliot.[13]

Lewes passed on the story that Archbishop Trench of Dublin, on the platform at a church conference, was observed looking intently into the hat on his knee. On closer inspection it appeared that he was reading not the work of devotion some might have expected but *Middlemarch*.[14] We do not know exactly what the Archbishop thought he saw in his hat, but we have the verdict of a later churchman, the well

---

[11] Ashton, *George Eliot: A Life*, p. 82.
[12] S. Law Wilson, *The Theology of Modern Literature* (Edinburgh: T. & T. Clark, 1899), pp. 231, 251.
[13] Leslie Stephen, *George Eliot* (London: Macmillan, 1902).
[14] G. H. Lewes to John Blackwood [13 July 1872], *The George Eliot Letters* V, 291.

George Eliot's Secular Scriptures   97

read Methodist missionary Thomas G. Selby, that 'Nature meant her [Eliot] for a great theologian.' Selby goes on to suggest that her books 'illustrate many principles which are precise parallels and analogies to some of the fundamental principles of the faith whose historic credibility she had thought well to repudiate'.[15] More relaxed attitudes to questions of historicity and faith are now current, and in our own time the theologian Peter Hodgson has sympathetically analysed and discussed Eliot's work from a modern theological perspective.[16]

Thinking more of politics and society than of religion, Dr Johnson had urged his friend Boswell to clear the mind of cant: the least that can be said of religious critique in the work of Eliot is that it acts on this robust advice, restated after her time by Paul Ricoeur who presents atheism as it has developed in the work of Nietzsche and Freud as both a destructive and a religiously liberating force, engaging with what he sees as the 'rotten points' of religion and clearing the ground for 'a faith beyond accusation and consolation'.[17] Eliot, though no atheist, would have endorsed the implied critique of pitiless 'accusation' or narrowly sanctimonious morality too often associated with conventional religion, and indeed her polemical essay on 'Evangelical Teaching: Dr Cumming' notes the conspicuous absence from his teaching of 'sympathy with that yearning over the lost and erring which made Jesus weep over Jerusalem'.[18] She also felt uneasy about the selfishness of seeking glibly metaphysical 'consolation' as opposed to showing practical human sympathy. In an essay on 'Worldliness and Other-Worldliness: the Poet Young' she was particularly scathing about Young's 'egoism turned heavenward', noting that, indifferent to everyday human concerns he 'flies for his utmost consolation to the day of judgement'.[19]

In the course of the long and overcrowded history of Eliot criticism, she has been variously constructed as a Comtean positivist, a disciple of Herbert Spencer, and a Feuerbachian, but while the various

---

[15] T. G. Selby, *The Theology of Modern Fiction* (London: Charles H. Kelly, 1896), p. 8.

[16] Peter C. Hodgson, *Theology in the Fiction of George Eliot* (London: SCM, 2001).

[17] Alisdair MacIntyre and Paul Ricoeur, *The Religious Significance of Atheism* (New York and London: Columbia University Press, 1969), p. 60.

[18] George Eliot, 'Evangelical Teaching; Dr Cumming', *Westminster Review* 64 (October 1855), 439.

[19] George Eliot, 'Worldliness and Other-Worldliness: the Poet Young', *Westminster Review* 67 (January 1857), 1–42, esp. pp. 36, 41.

98   *George Eliot's Secular Scriptures*

post-Christian thinkers she had studied left their mark, she never wholeheartedly or enduringly subscribed to the teaching of any of them and it is unnecessarily reductive to try to read her novels as positivist parables or Feuerbachian fables. She made no claim to be a systematic religious (or anti-religious) thinker and addressed religious matters over a long period through dramatized situations rather than formal disquisition. The tentative pluralism of her phrase 'experiments in life' used to describe her writing can serve as a warning against trying to reduce her work to a fully worked-out secular gospel.[20]

The main format of Eliot's first published religious reflections, while she was still contemplating turning to fiction, was the periodical essay, usually a book review in which ideas developed not in a vacuum but in dialogue with the works under review. The family tensions and the rebellious anger and antagonism associated with her initial loss of faith gradually receded. Although she never returned to what she called 'dogmatic Christianity', by 1859 she could claim that 'I have no longer any antagonism towards any faith in which human sorrow and human longing for purity have expressed themselves; on the contrary, I have a sympathy with it that predominates over all argumentative tendencies.'[21] Sympathy and argumentative tendency are nicely balanced in some of her reviews of the 1850s in the progressive *Westminster Review*. The evangelical austerity that might once have condemned self-indulgent emotional vagueness and frivolous worldliness in manners and material culture, in order to emphasize more serious concerns, was only slightly displaced into argumentative endorsement of the painterly (and literary) doctrine of 'realism' in Ruskin's moral aesthetics; in a review of the third volume of *Modern Painters* Eliot writes:

> The truth of infinite value that he teaches is realism – the doctrine that all truth and beauty are to be attained by a humble and faithful study of nature, and not by substituting vague forms, bred by imagination on the mists of feeling, in place of definite, substantial reality. The thorough acceptance of this doctrine would remould our life . . .[22]

---

[20] Eliot to Dr J. F. Payne, 25 January 1876, *The George Eliot Letters* VI, 216–7.

[21] Eliot to François D'Albert Durade, 6 December 1859, *The George Eliot Letters* III, 230–1.

[22] George Eliot, 'Contemporary Literature: Art and Belles Lettres', *Westminster Review* 65 (April 1856), 626.

George Eliot's Secular Scriptures 99

Unfortunately, as she noted in another review, this doctrine had not reached many of the feebler lady novelists of the day who attempted to write on religious themes:

> as a general rule, the ability of a lady novelist to describe actual life and her fellow-men, is in inverse proportion to her confident eloquence about God and the other world, and the means by which she usually chooses to conduct you to true ideas of the invisible is a totally false picture of the visible.[23]

Only scrupulous realism could redeem and vindicate the novel form, about which Eliot had felt uneasy in her evangelical phase despite her guilty pleasure in it. There was more argument, and even less sympathy, in her stern review of 'Evangelical teaching: Dr Cumming'. Cumming's fashionable evangelical preaching, which seemed to her conspicuously lacking in genuine charity and moral sympathy, his rhetorical excesses, and his intellectually shoddy religious populism were all mercilessly dissected and deplored.[24]

Scenes of Clerical Life (1858), her first venture in fiction, can be seen as both a more extended response to Dr Cumming and a series of experiments sifting and testing what Eliot had come to see as the mixed quality of her partly discarded evangelical heritage. Moral and religious sympathy proves more durable than doctrine. Early reading of Cowper's *The Task* and of Wordsworth and Walter Scott had shown her that the commonest objects could be invested with beauty, and that the everyday lives of humble people, lovingly represented, could demonstrate moral dignity. In the first story, the Rev. Amos Barton's vanity, thoughtless insensitivity, and intellectual limitations as an evangelical preacher bring no particular credit to his faith but he is brought close to the heart of Eliot's residual religion of sympathy and suffering when his overworked wife dies and his alienated parishioners respond to his human distress as they never had to his preaching. In 'Mr Gilfil's Love-Story' Maynard Gilfil's spirituality comes out not in his yellowing sermons, short and shallow, but in the depth of his love for the bruised and suffering Tina. The title of 'Janet's Repentance' implies a conventionally evangelical conversion narrative of the kind that the new evangelical clergyman Mr Tryan

---

[23] George Eliot, 'Silly Novels by Lady Novelists', *Westminster Review* 66 (October 1856), 450.

[24] Eliot, 'Evangelical Teaching; Dr Cumming'.

100 George Eliot's Secular Scriptures

might have been expected to relish, but the topic is cleared of cant by a narrative tracing deliverance from the evil of self-absorbed despair in a degrading and brutal marriage and an awakening to a new life of devotion to others.

Self-sacrificing devotion, a recurring theme in Eliot's novels, can be seen as not only a practical expression of the imitation of Christ enjoined by her much-admired Thomas à Kempis but a transcendent value. She outlines her vision of the ethical sublime in 'O may I join the choir invisible', aspiring to:

> live
> In pulses stirred to generosity,
> In deeds of daring rectitude, in scorn
> For miserable aims that end with self,
> In thoughts sublime that pierce the night like stars,
> And with their mild persistence urge man's search
> To vaster issues.
> So to live is heaven . . .[25]

This was a view of heaven that contrasted sharply with the rhetoric of hellfire preachers and poets such as Young with his crude antitheses of heaven and hell, his 'bombastic absurdity', and 'vaulting sublimity that o'erleaps itself'.[26] Eliot's heaven was closer to the Wordsworthian sublime as it emerged in the *Lyrical Ballads* (1798), an imaginative intuition stimulated by the world of nature and the world as it is, linking the 'still, sad music of humanity' with:

> the joy
> Of elevated thoughts; a sense sublime
> Of something far more deeply interfused,
> Whose dwelling is the light of setting suns,
> And the round ocean, and the living air,
> And the blue sky . . .[27]

Adam Bede (1859), Eliot's first and most Wordsworthian novel, furnished with an epigraph from Wordsworth's *Excursion* (1814), which alludes to 'lapse or error' in 'nature's unambitious underwood',

---

[25] Eliot, *Collected Poems*, p. 49.

[26] Eliot, 'Worldliness and Other-Worldliness: the Poet Young', pp. 26, 21.

[27] William Wordsworth, 'Lines written a few miles above Tintern Abbey', lines 95–100, in William Wordsworth, *A Selection*, ed. Stephen Gill and Duncan Wu, Oxford Poetry Library (Oxford: Oxford University Press, 1994), p. 59.

George Eliot's Secular Scriptures 101

is set back in time. It begins in 1798, which coincides with the publication of the *Lyrical Ballads*, mentioned in chapter 5 of the novel. It reimagines aspects of New Testament narrative and teaching in the life of the English countryside, secular indeed, but also representing an approach to religious meaning. The Hebrew word *adam* can mean a man, as it does in Ecclesiastes 7:28, or mankind generally, as well as the first man, the biblical individual called Adam who in the New Testament is linked with spiritual renewal through Christ the redeemer, the second Adam (1 Corinthians 15:22, 45). *Adam Bede* takes advantage of this range of meaning to explore moral and religious issues and the possibilities of renewal in the life of man through suffering, leading to 'the fuller life which a sad experience has brought us',[28] while apparently concerning itself mainly with the (fictional) individual Adam Bede. The novel accepts that, by the time of writing, Methodism, discreetly doing duty for institutional religion more generally, may have lost some of its early fire: 'charisma' as Max Weber understood it dissipated into institutional or organizational channels. But it was not always like that. Eliot explores the early days of Methodism in the 1790s and uses that epoch as a metaphor for the fervent beginnings of Christianity itself in the Galilean countryside. Dinah Morris, partly modelled on Eliot's Wesleyan aunt, is no Christ figure, but she is for a time a kind of messiah in the original Old Testament sense of someone 'anointed' or set apart for some special function, in her case as a preacher. Her preaching function, like that of Eliot's aunt, was eventually curtailed by a decision of the Methodist Conference of 1803 forbidding women to preach, but not before she had had opportunities to commend and to give practical effect to what she thinks of as the love of the Saviour for humankind. Eliot makes no attempt to belittle her aunt's faith, even if she does not share it: what matters is love itself, not theological controversy about its origins. Early in the novel, the reader and the village community are lulled into special receptiveness by the Wordsworthian visionary splendour of a glorious summer evening, 'the level sunlight lying like transparent gold among the gently-curving stems of the feather grass and the tall red sorrel'. This provides the setting for Dinah's emotionally effective open-air sermon, which recalls not merely Wesley and his followers but the out-of-doors preaching and

---

[28] George Eliot, *Adam Bede*, ed. Valentine Cunningham, World's Classics (Oxford: Oxford University Press, 1996), chapter 54, p. 530.

102　　　*George Eliot's Secular Scriptures*

loving ministry of Jesus Himself, described by Dinah as 'doing good to poor people' and performing 'miracles to feed the hungry'.[29]

It is interesting that in the (probably) first-century *Didache* ('The Teaching of the Twelve Apostles'), which was rediscovered in 1873 after *Adam Bede* was published, a Eucharistic prayer picks up the same New Testament language of the feeding of the hungry multitude and applies it to the common life and unity of the Church: 'Even as this broken bread was scattered over the hills, and was gathered together and became one, so let Thy Church be gathered together from the ends of the earth into Thy kingdom'.[30] This suggests that Eliot, already embarked on a project of religious reimagining, had intuitively reinvented the sense of community as it had been articulated in the very early days of the Christian Church. Eliot's scriptural precedent or model for Dinah's preaching was the Sermon on the Mount and this is quoted in the *Didache*, if not directly from the gospels then from the tradition that lies behind the gospels.

There is a sense in which the *Didache* and *Adam Bede* are parallel works, both of them reworking, and providing pastoral context for, the material of the gospels. Early readers certainly found that Eliot's books 'don't rank as Novels but as second Bibles',[31] and this applied particularly to *Adam Bede*. Much later in the novel, when Bartle Massey offers the righteous but betrayed and embittered Adam some refreshment, considerately provided by the clergyman Mr Irwine, the bread and the wine recall the biblical Last Supper and function as a kind of informal sacrament, symbolizing renewal as Adam in his distress learns the lesson of mercy that brings him back into the community of love and sympathy and makes him part of it. After eating and drinking a little 'he stood upright again, and looked more like the Adam Bede of former days'.[32]

The sin and sorrow of the world, and the suffering at the heart of the novel, are linked by Dinah not just with the suffering of the crucified Christ but with God Himself, 'that Divine Love which is one with his sorrow'.[33] The pregnant Hetty's distress prompts the narrator to thoughts of the cross and the reflection that, 'No wonder

---

[29] Eliot, *Adam Bede*, chapter 2, pp. 18, 26.
[30] *Didache* 9:4, trans. I. H. Hall and J. T. Napier, Ante-Nicene Fathers VII (Grand Rapids, MI: Eerdmans, 1994) p. 380; compare Matt. 14: 20.
[31] John Blackwood to Eliot, 8 February 1877, *The George Eliot Letters* VI, 340.
[32] Eliot, *Adam Bede*, chapter 42, p. 429.
[33] Eliot, *Adam Bede*, chapter 30, p. 328.

George Eliot's Secular Scriptures   103

man's religion has much sorrow in it: no wonder he needs a Suffering God.'[34] This recalls the fifth chapter of Feuerbach's *The Essence of Christianity*, entitled (in Eliot's translation) 'The Mystery of the Suffering God', which addresses itself very specifically to links between human suffering and divine suffering not just in an incarnate Christ but in God Himself. But the notion of a suffering God is much older than Feuerbach. Eliot was not obliged to be an uncritical Feuerbachian, and Feuerbach's remorseless insistence that everything in Christianity is pure construction—a merely human projection of subjective feeling—is more extreme than anything in Eliot. Peter Hodgson suggests that suffering in *Adam Bede* has links with the ancient theory of 'patripassianism.'[35] This heterodox but emotionally compelling doctrine, one version of which claims that the Father was in a sense born of the Virgin and was a fellow sufferer with the Son, was associated with early heretics such as Praxeas (*c.a.* 200), denounced by the uncompromisingly orthodox Tertullian.[36] There are connections with Luther's emphasis on the cross and human suffering as that which can 'bring the Saviour more deeply into our hearts'.[37] There are also more modern analogues in A. N. Whitehead's process theology, developed in works such as *Religion in the Making* (1926) and *Process and Reality* (1929), and indeed in post-Holocaust and feminist theologies, which present God as no longer impassive and immutable but subject to process and change through direct involvement with suffering and historical development. There is a striking parallel, from an epoch between Eliot's time and our own, in the hymn 'God is love, let heaven adore Him', by Timothy Rees (1874–1939), who had encountered extremes of human desolation as a chaplain during the First World War and again as Bishop of Llandaff in south Wales in the Depression:

> And when human hearts are breaking
> Under sorrow's iron rod,

---

[34] Eliot, *Adam Bede*, chapter 35, p. 364.

[35] Hodgson, *Theology in the Fiction of George Eliot*, p. 57.

[36] Tertullian, *Against Praxeas* 2 (PL 1.156), *Writings*, trans. Alexander Roberts and James Donaldson (Grand Rapids, MI: William B. Eerdmans, 1997).

[37] Martin Luther, 'Sermon at Coburg on Cross and Suffering' [1530], *Works*, American Edition, vol. 51, trans. John W. Doberstein (Philadelphia: Michlenberg Press, 1959), p. 207.

104   *George Eliot's Secular Scriptures*

That same sorrow, that same aching
Wrings with pain the heart of God.[38]

The Mill on the Floss (1860) is another exploration of pain and suffering, in the life of Maggie Tulliver, giving her access to Eliot's version of the transcendent other, 'the Unseen Pity that would be with her to the end'.[39] But the narrative moves beyond suffering and painful renunciation to end with a sense of reconciliation in death, of recovery of a lost Eden of childhood affection and trust between Maggie and her brother Tom. Kant's formulation of the mathematical sublime in the *Critique of Judgement* described overwhelming effects of nature which by their extent and power defied measurement and comprehension, and romantic painters such as J. M. W. Turner and John Martin had provided many examples. These included pictures of tumultuous waterfalls, violent storms at sea, and catastrophic death by water as divine punishment, such as Martin's *The Destruction of Pharaoh's Host* (1830) and *The Eve of the Deluge* (1841). The catastrophic flood at the end of Eliot's novel, overwhelming and sublime, brings not destruction but paradise regained, a kind of renewal, suggesting the view of the Song of Songs (8:7) that 'Many waters cannot quench love.' As in the biblical lament of David for Saul and Jonathan (2 Samuel 1:23), which provides the last words of the narrative and an epigraph for the novel as a whole, death need not bring division: 'in their death they were not divided'.

The biblical frame of reference is reinforced by allusion to spiritual classics, which contributed to the formation of both Maggie Tulliver and the young George Eliot. The landscape of the novel is linked for Maggie with the journey of Christiana in Bunyan's *The Pilgrim's Progress*.[40] Bunyan's pilgrimage narrative, including the passage through 'The Valley of Humiliation', which Eliot uses as her title for Book Four of the novel, provides a metaphor for Maggie's constantly frustrated secular progress. Thomas à Kempis's *Imitation of Christ*, which George Eliot had encountered in Richard Challoner's much-reprinted translation (1737), describes the need to accept the crucifixion of self-sacrifice, confirming Maggie's act of renunciation

---

[38] Timothy Rees, *Sermons and Hymns* (London and Oxford: Mowbray, 1946), p. 110.

[39] George Eliot, *The Mill on the Floss*, ed. Gordon S. Haight, World's Classics (Oxford: Oxford University Press, 1996), book 7, chapter 5, p. 515.

[40] Eliot, *The Mill on the Floss*, book 1, chapter 5, p. 41.

George Eliot's Secular Scriptures   105

in the last movement of the novel: 'I have received the Cross, I have received it from Thy hand; I will bear it, and bear it till death, as Thou hast laid it upon me.'[41] The novel's conclusion gestures towards peace and renewal but stops short of the glibly accepting piety and blandly proffered consolation that would have neutralized Maggie Tulliver's rebellious passion and suffering: 'Nature repairs her ravages—but not all . . . To the eyes that have dwelt on the past, there is no thorough repair.'[42]

More efficient repair of human damage is offered in *Silas Marner* (1861). The narrative has the simplicity of a fairy tale. The solitary and embittered Silas Marner, robbed of his hoarded wealth, finds the abandoned Eppie by his hearth and by caring for her discovers a new purpose in life. In a sense the miser's gold is replaced by the golden-haired child. The narrative functions as a kind of extended parable of salvation, which provides humanitarian fulfilment of the messianic prophecy of Isaiah that 'a little child shall lead them' (Isa. 11:6). The Bible also describes angels leading the faithful to safety from Sodom, a model for the City of Destruction from which Bunyan's Pilgrim set out for the Celestial City. Eliot suggests that men still need to be taken by the hand and led from threatening destruction—a moral, religious, and a humanitarian imperative—and Eppie shows how 'the hand may be a little child's'.[43]

The messianic, or sub-messianic, theme of deliverance from injustice and wrong in specific contexts, illuminated by implicit or explicit moral vision, becomes stronger in Eliot's later novels. These engage with individual moral agents in relation to a wider social and public, sometimes political, life and the processes by which that shared life may evolve. If the ultimate model is the life and teaching of Christ himself, there are other models in the Old Testament prophets and in Thomas Carlyle's *On Heroes, Hero-Worship and the Heroic in History* (1841), which includes a discussion of 'The Hero as Prophet'. Carlyle had also written a biography of a fervid failed prophet and sometime radical, his friend John Sterling, which Eliot had reviewed very sympathetically, seeing Sterling's story as one that she would go on

---

[41] Eliot, *The Mill on the Floss*, book 7, chapter 4, p. 515 alluding to Thomas à Kempis, *Imitation of Christ* 56.4.

[42] Eliot, *The Mill on the Floss*, 'Conclusion', pp. 521–2.

[43] George Eliot, *Silas Marner*, ed. Terence Cave, World's Classics (Oxford: Oxford University Press, 1996), chapter 14, p. 130.

106   *George Eliot's Secular Scriptures*

to tell in many of her novels, 'the struggle of a restless aspiring soul, yearning to leave a distant impress of itself on the spiritual development of humanity...'[44]

Prophetic aspiration and prophetic witness in times of crisis had been more effective in earlier ages. Eliot's next novel, *Romola* (1863), is set during a crisis in fifteenth-century Florence. The great Lorenzo de' Medici had died, French influence threatened Florentine autonomy, and the prophetic voice of the charismatic radical preacher Savonarola was a major influence on public life. The public situation brings religion and politics, prophecy and history, and individual lives into sometimes abrasive contact, and while Savonarola is quite sympathetically presented there is a sense both of puritanical excess in his 'bonfire of the vanities' and of the dangers of power, which threaten the integrity of the prophetic office. The ambivalence of Savonarola's radical vision is evident from the fact that it inspires both the saintly Romola, whose selflessly compassionate care for others, including children, makes her a Madonna figure in the novel, and the passionately vengeful Baldassare. Romola realizes that the 'wicked folly' of the mad Camilla is excited if not expressly sanctioned by Savonarola, and that he is powerless to restrain her religious mania.[45]

For the historical narrative to have some moral currency with nineteenth-century readers there had to be some sense of connections and parallels. Savonarola's rhetorical fervour may have links with the nineteenth-century tradition of evangelical preaching, represented not just by the obnoxious Dr Cumming but by the celebrated Thomas Dale whom Eliot had gone to hear when she visited London in 1838 and, more recently, by the Baptist C. H. Spurgeon.[46] By way of contrast, the Renaissance exuberance of Politian's celebration of classical deities in the novel has its unspoken romantic counterpart in Schiller's poem 'The gods of Greece', nostalgic for the old gods who have fled to poet-land. This is perhaps why Tito's Mediterranean paganism, which makes him a kind of sun-god, an antitype to Savonarola, is so seductively attractive.

---

[44] George Eliot, 'Contemporary Literature of England', *Westminster Review* 57 (January 1852), 247.

[45] George Eliot, *Romola*, ed. Andrew Brown, World's Classics (Oxford: Oxford University Press, 1994), chapter 52, p. 419.

[46] Haight, *George Eliot: A Biography*, p. 22.

George Eliot's Secular Scriptures　　　107

Tito's self-serving evil, which emerges only gradually, has no 'active malignity'. It is not the 'motiveless malignity' that Coleridge associated with Iago in Shakespeare's *Othello* so much as a self-centred absence of moral courage under duress. As the narrator observes, 'The repentance which cuts off all moorings to evil, demands something more than selfish fear', even though 'he would still have been glad not to give pain to any mortal.'[47] However, he is brilliantly duplicitous in public life and equally perfidious as a husband. His wronged wife Romola, like Adam Bede before her, develops through suffering and the cross, through renunciation and 'yearning passivity',[48] and her individual emotional pilgrimage under Savonarola's spiritual direction is a kind of microcosm or anticipation of larger historical processes that Savonarola tries but fails to direct. The characteristically agonising progress towards a better world, 'the great world-struggle of developing thought', for her as for Eliot 'is continually foreshadowed in the struggle of the affections, seeking a justification for love and hope'.[49]

Felix Holt, the Radical (1866), set at the time of the first great Reform Bill of 1832, is in effect a response to the movement towards further parliamentary reform in the 1860s. Once again the political situation is tense and difficult, but this time there is no charismatic messianic figure bidding to redeem and deliver the nation or even the local community from turbulent times. All is not lost, however. Eliot, like Scott in *Woodstock* and *Old Mortality* and like Carlyle, editor of Cromwell's *Letters and Speeches*, was fascinated by the moral fervour of seventeenth-century Puritanism, and she had been reading Daniel Neal's *History of the Puritans* (1732–8). The moral witness and anti-establishment religious radicalism of that 'rusty old puritan' Rufus Lyon, a dissenting minister, are linked with the intricate inheritance plot of the novel and the radical campaign for parliamentary reform. Law, which regulates inheritance and provides a measure of stability even in difficult times, is the novel's central mechanism and one of its central metaphors. A reformed society must have moral legitimacy.[50] Lyon looks forward to 'that crowning time of the millennial reign,

---

[47] Eliot, *Romola*, chapter 23, p. 212–13.
[48] Eliot, *Romola*, chapter 41, p. 346.
[49] Eliot, *Romola*, chapter 52, p. 420.
[50] Discussed in Norman Vance, 'Law, Religion and the Unity of *Felix Holt*', in Anne Smith, ed., *George Eliot: Centenary Essays and an Unpublished Fragment* (London: Vision Press, 1980), pp. 103–23.

108 *George Eliot's Secular Scriptures*

when our daily prayer will be fulfilled, and one law shall be written on all our hearts, and be the very structure of all thought, and be the principle of all action'.[51] This prophetic vision of fundamental law is more radical than the politicians: it underpins the novel's critique of unreformed England, which it represents as still governed by dysfunctional and sometimes morally dubious landed interests and a largely ineffective established church. As always in Eliot, personal integrity and moral courage are crucial, the essential basis of any enduring social order. The future of the nation seems to lie not so much with selfishly ambitious politicians and public figures as with thoroughly decent private individuals such as Esther Lyon, who renounces wealth and social position and marries the radical Felix Holt, a man always likely to be poor.

The same period and the same sense of rapid, unnerving social and political change are explored again on the broader canvas of *Middlemarch* (1871–2), Eliot's most ambitious and successful novel. As in *Felix Holt*, existing community leaders are lacking in prophetic fire and moral vision and are unable or unwilling to provide the enlightened leadership necessary to carry the town and the country forward into a challenging future. Bulstrode the banker is a powerful and influential figure but he is morally compromised in the course of the novel and the would-be radical politician Mr Brooke is a lightweight figure of fun. The saints of old had shown the way to better things, discharging a sub-messianic function in their own day, and the novel is in a sense a soberly realist modernised version of exemplary saints' lives. As Eliot worked on *Middlemarch* she had been reading, and reading about, the long-winded fifteenth-century poet John Lydgate.[52] The crusading Middlemarch doctor, Tertius Lydgate, finds his idealism has to adjust to unpropitious circumstances and he becomes a merely fashionable doctor instead of a great medical reformer. His comparative defeat may glance ironically at John Lydgate's *Fall of Princes* (1431–8), while his frustrated personal pilgrimage may have connections not just with Bunyan but with Lydgate's *The Pilgrimage of Man* (1426–30), a translation of the Cistercian monk Guillaume de Deguileville's *Pèlerinage de la vie humaine*.

---

[51] George Eliot, *Felix Holt, the Radical*, ed. Fred C. Thomson, World's Classics (Oxford: Oxford University Press, 1988), chapter 13, p. 127.

[52] See George Eliot's *'Middlemarch' Notebooks: A Transcription*, ed. J. C. Pratt and V. A. Neufeldt (Berkeley: University of California Press, 1979), pp. 6, 97, 98.

George Eliot's Secular Scriptures   109

Dorothea Brooke is named after one saint and her progress in life is explicitly compared with that of another, Teresa of Avila. Like Lydgate, she has brought a lofty idealism to her adult life, which is bruised but in her case channelled rather than defeated by contact with practical realities and constrained circumstances. Unlike St Teresa she does not found a new religious order, but she does at least contribute in small ways to 'the growing good of the world', the phrase Eliot uses in the last paragraph of the novel to generalize from her significance and achievement.

The impulse to various kinds of reform that pervades the novel is accompanied by aspirations to uncover underlying principle, whether Casaubon's doomed search for a key to all mythologies or Lydgate's search for basic human tissue. Neither quest is successful but the various narrative strands of the novel are drawn together to disclose another underlying principle, a secular gospel of human interconnectedness and social benevolence. In Dorothea's case, the path to chastened self-realization and mature understanding of her society has involved personal crisis and the death of private joy, a passage through Bunyan's slough of despond, which is invoked in an epigraph.[53] But her new awareness is presented as a kind of religious conversion to a new life as a new day dawns. Eliot had always admired the poet Cowper's large-hearted capacity to respond to ordinary humanity—the carter and the cottager's wife[54]—and she gives the now chastened Dorothea a similar enlarged vision:

> On the road there was a man with a bundle on his back and a woman carrying her baby; in the field she could see figures moving – perhaps the shepherd with his dog. Far off in the bending sky was the pearly light; and she felt the largeness of the world and the manifold wakings of men to labour and endurance. She was part of that involuntary, palpitating life, and could neither look out on it from her luxurious shelter as a mere spectator, nor hide her eyes in selfish complaining.[55]

The seventeenth century had had fewer difficulties than the nineteenth in reconciling faith and knowledge and there is a pattern of

---

[53] George Eliot, *Middlemarch*, ed. David Carroll, World's Classics (Oxford: Oxford University Press, 1997), chapter 79 (epigraph) p. 769, which quotes Bunyan's description of the slough of despond. See Vincent Newey, 'Dorothea's Awakening: the Recall of Bunyan in *Middlemarch*', *Notes and Queries* 31 (1984), 497–9.

[54] Eliot, 'Worldliness and Unworldliness: the Poet Young', p. 40.

[55] Eliot, *Middlemarch*, chapter 80, p. 776.

110   *George Eliot's Secular Scriptures*

usually ironic reference to seventeenth-century figures throughout the novel. Naively eager for heroic self-sacrifice, 'enamoured of intensity and greatness', Dorothea had read Pascal and Jeremy Taylor, had imagined herself married to the blind Milton and had transformed the mediocre and rather plain-looking Mr Casaubon into an image of John Locke. Casaubon himself carried the name of the much greater scholar Isaac Casaubon (1559–1614) and was authorially associated with the unflattering catalogue of ailments that Burton's *Anatomy of Melancholy* (1621) attributed to 'hard students'.[56] But there is no irony about the arduous Bunyanesque pilgrimage Dorothea has undergone, while the 'manifold wakings of men to labour and endurance' and the sense of being an integral part of that wider life unironically recall a seventeenth-century hymn, the well-known 'Morning Hymn' of Thomas Ken, lustily sung by Adam at the beginning of *Adam Bede*:

> Awake my soul, and with the sun
> Thy daily stage of duty run.
> . . . By influence of the Light divine
> Let thy own light to others shine.[57]

Eliot's most extended negotiation of prophetic and messianic ideas can be found in *Daniel Deronda* (1876). The Jewish and Zionist theme, famously deplored by F. R. Leavis who wished it excised from the novel,[58] provides a natural point of connection between politics and religion, even if it also risks a loss of balance and entanglement in the thicket of narrow but rigorous moral imperatives in public and private life, which Matthew Arnold had recently labelled 'Hebraism'.[59] Eliot negotiates the risk with considerable grace and skill by pursuing several different if ultimately related narrative threads, as she had done in *Middlemarch*, and ensuring that moral concern and moral action are embedded in rather than obtrusively separated from a well-specified cultural and social world.

---

[56] Eliot, *Middlemarch* chapter 1, pp. 8, 20; chapter 2, p. 16; chapter 5 (epigraph), p. 41.

[57] First published in Thomas Ken, *A Manual of Prayers for the Use of the Scholars of Winchester College* (1695).

[58] F. R. Leavis, *The Great Tradition* (London: Chatto, 1948), pp. 80–5.

[59] 'Hebraism and Hellenism' was the title Matthew Arnold gave to the fourth chapter of *Culture and Anarchy*, published in book form in 1869. The chapter first appeared as an article, 'Anarchy and authority, part 3', *Cornhill* 17 (June 1868), 745–60.

George Eliot's Secular Scriptures   111

Both Gwendolen and Deronda need to find their way in life. The rich variety of possibilities, the European scale of the action, and the mystery surrounding Deronda's origins, complicate the plot, which owes much more than most of Eliot's novels to the much-disparaged tradition of romance. Her early admiration and emulation of Ruskin's moral as well as aesthetic doctrine of realism is not abandoned, but she has acquired the confidence and the experience to vary the narrative mode. A teasing epigraph from Molière's *Les Précieuses Ridicules* at the head of chapter 4 alludes to Madeleine de Scudéry's interminable romances and suggests that in them and in the play it is the deferring of marriage that keeps the plot going. That is in effect what happens in *Deronda*. The question of how and who Gwendolen will marry, recalling Jane Austen's comedies of manners, turns into something much darker with her disastrous marriage to Grandcourt, but in a sense the marriage plot starts over again even before his death and the reader wonders just how the entwined lives of Gwendolen and Deronda and her increasing dependence on him will end. Eliot makes use of the stylized concentrations and complications of the action in the stage-play, with sudden explanations and recognition scenes. Tongue-in-cheek, in an epigraph to chapter 41, she quotes Aristotle's *Poetics* on necessary improbability in tragic plots. The improbabilities of Shakespeare's *Winter's Tale* (which is largely based on Robert Greene's prose-romance *Pandosto*) are brought into the novel at an early stage when Gwendolen plays the part of Hermione, presented as a statue coming to life at the end of the play. She awakes not just to life but to Gothic horror as a panel flies open to reveal a picture of a dead face, as if to hint at sinister troubles ahead.[60] Deronda's story, like the story of Eppie in *Silas Marner*, is in a sense a foundling legend that comes from the romance tradition. Versions of this can be found in the twelfth-century French romance *Guillaume de Palerne* and in the folk tales of many cultures: the abandoned baby, brought up unaware of its parentage, often turns out to be a prince (or princess, like Perdita in Shakespeare's *The Winter's Tale*), and there is usually a kingdom to inherit or a prince to marry by the end of the story.[61] Giuseppe Mazzini's ambitions for divided Italy, or Deronda's

---

[60] George Eliot, *Daniel Deronda*, ed. Graham Handley, World's Classics (Oxford: Oxford University Press, 1988), chapter 6, p. 49.

[61] *Guillaume de Palerne* was the basis for the fourteenth-century English romance *William of Palerne*. For Russian and Romanian tales of royal foundlings, see Leonard

112 George Eliot's Secular Scriptures

ambition to make his people a nation again, represent an updated version of the romance possibility of coming into one's kingdom.

The sympathetic account of the Jewish sense of tradition, and of the vision of a homeland for the Jews, which gradually emerge in the novel, are important in their own right, but also do duty for a range of recent or contemporary instances of the problem of establishing and governing a righteous nation, one of the themes of Old Testament history—a problem postponed and complicated in the modern age by social inequality, racial injustice, and oppression. The American Civil War, the controversy over Governor Eyre's ruthless suppression of a rebellion in Jamaica in 1865,[62] and the Italian struggle to achieve a free and united Italy were vivid and recent memories for the original readers of the novel. Abraham Lincoln and Mazzini, whom Eliot had got to write for the *Westminster Review*,[63] were contemporary examples of the sub-messianic heroes on whom the delivery of righteousness and freedom had always depended throughout history, and Mazzini, admired by Deronda,[64] is a kind of model for his final messianic quest to save his people and bring them again to their promised land. As Mary Wilson Carpenter has pointed out, Christian as well as Jewish visions of history are at work in the narrative.[65] On the evidence of scattered biblical texts, Christ had been traditionally described as prophet, priest, and king, a formulation particularly associated with Calvin and emphasized in doctrinal formulations such as the *Heidelberg Catechism* of 1563 and the *Shorter Catechism* of the Westminster Assembly (1648).[66] In *Daniel Deronda* these offices are in a sense distributed between the novel's two moral exemplars, Mordecai with his visionary Old Testament rhetoric that recalls Scott's covenanters in *Old Mortality* and Rufus Lyon in *Felix*

A. Magnus, trans.,'The Foundling Prince', in *Russian Folktales* (London: Kegan Paul, 1915), and Petre Ispirescu, *The Foundling Prince and Other Tales*, trans. Julia Collier-Harris and Rea Ipcar (Boston: Houghton-Mifflin, 1917).

[62] See Bernard Semmel, *The Governor Eyre Controversy* (London: McGibbon & Kee, 1962).

[63] Haight, *George Eliot: A Biography*, p. 99

[64] Eliot, *Daniel Deronda*, chapter 42, p. 457.

[65] See Mary Wilson Carpenter, *George Eliot and the Landscape of Time: Narrative Form and Protestant Apocalyptic History* (Chapel Hill: North Carolina Press, 1986).

[66] John Calvin, *Institutes of the Christian Religion*, ed. J. T. McNeill, trans. F. L. Battle, Library of Christian Classics (Philadelphia: Westminster Press, 1960), 2.15. The triple formulation of the office of Christ has been traced back to Eusebius, *Ecclesiastical History* 1.3.6–9.

George Eliot's Secular Scriptures   113

Holt, and Deronda, Mordecai's (and Eliot's) messiah figure. Deronda is equipped by education, wealth, and social standing for leadership in the public world of national and international affairs. He also functions as an almost oppressively righteous secular priest and confessor, particularly to Gwendolen. Grandcourt's barbed sneer 'I suppose you take Deronda for a saint?'[67] provokes Gwendolen to unflattering comparison. Grandcourt could never be a Deronda. Deronda is not just a secular saint with 'charisma' or attractive gifts of character, personality, and intellect, which correspond to the spiritual gifts commended in the New Testament: it gradually emerges that he is a messianic figure in the Old Testament sense, metaphorically anointed or set apart for the special function of leading his people, like a king in the Davidic tradition. He has all the moral and personal qualifications for public life and benign statesmanship that Grandcourt conspicuously lacks. Cynical and ruthless, Grandcourt supports racist oppression; he is self-centred and unjust in this as in his private life, in which he is oppressive and tyrannical as a husband. As Gwendolen comes to realize, this is in sharp contrast with Deronda's righteousness, compassion, and generosity in public and private.

Deronda's quasi-messianic sense of mission was not exactly traditional Christianity but it represented a powerful reimagining of its vision and moral imperatives as applied to an emerging issue in contemporary public life. George Eliot's residually Christian morality soon attracted the scorn of the more radically post-Christian Friedrich Nietzsche, who snorted condescendingly at 'little moralistic females à la Eliot' and attributed to her a characteristically English inconsistency in not rejecting the morality as well as the metaphysics of traditional Christianity.[68] But for her Christianity could still be seen and reconfigured as a religion of humanity. Its partly outmoded scriptures with their grand narrative of salvation history could now be reread or revised as narratives of the mystery of goodness, self-sacrifice, and love in society and history, or they could be replaced by her own narratives on the same theme. Other novelists would reread, revise, and replace in different ways. Chief among them after Eliot was Thomas Hardy.

---

[67] Eliot, *Daniel Deronda,* chapter 48, p. 503.
[68] Friedrich Nietzsche, *Twilight of the Idols* (1889), IX.5 in *The Portable Nietzsche,* ed. and trans. Walter Kaufmann (London: Chatto & Windus, 1971), p. 515.

5

Thomas Hardy: The Church or Christianity

Thomas Hardy, much more overtly negative about traditional Christianity than George Eliot in his novels, has been less congenial to theologians, even though recent essays by Pamela Dalziel and Mary Rimmer suggest a sustained religious seriousness played down by Hardy himself.[1] In his last novels he courted the hostility of conventional churchmen, particularly in *Tess of the d'Urbervilles* (1891) and *Jude the Obscure* (1895), and he was not disappointed. In 1896 the Methodist T. G. Selby condemned Hardy's 'terrible and inflammatory impeachments' of moral and religious principle and the 'hopeless note' in much of his writing.[2] Selby's more conservative contemporary, Samuel Law Wilson, complained of 'dabbling in beastliness and putrefaction' in the later novels and the 'wail of moral helplessness' of his sinning heroes and heroines.[3] G. K. Chesterton's verdict of 1913, patronizing and slapdash though it is, that 'Hardy became a sort of village atheist brooding and blaspheming over the village idiot' is hard to dislodge. It is not inconsistent with Hardy's diary entry of

---

[1] Pamela Dalziel, 'The Gospel According to Hardy' and Mary Rimmer, '"My Scripture Manner": Reading Hardy's Biblical and Liturgical Allusions', in Keith Wilson, ed., *Thomas Hardy Reappraised: Essays in Honour of Michael Millgate* (Toronto: University of Toronto Press., 2006). For a valuable, more extended, study of Hardy and the Bible, see Shuji Awano, *Paradox and Post-Christianity: Hardy's Engagements with Religious Tradition and the Bible* (Yokohama: Shumpûsha, 1999).
[2] T. G. Selby, *The Theology of Modern Fiction* (London: Charles H. Kelly, 1896), pp. 92, 129.
[3] S. Law Wilson, *The Theology of Modern Literature* (Edinburgh: T. & T. Clark, 1899), pp. 382, 396.

Thomas Hardy: The Church or Christianity 115

29 January 1890: 'I have been looking for God 50 years, and I think that if he had existed I should have discovered him.'[4]

And yet, as his recent biographer Claire Tomalin puts it, 'atheist or agnostic as he was—he was not sure which - he could never quite get away from the Christian God'.[5] This was partly a matter of childhood custom and social convention. In the world of the novels, particularly the early ones, institutional religion and Bible reading are still accepted as part of the social scene. Hardy's inherited affection for hymns and church choirs provides background for the comedy of *Under the Greenwood Tree* (1872). The mangled prayer book allusions and biblical quotations of Joseph Poorgrass in *Far from the Madding Crowd* (1874) are amusing rather than subversive, and the humorously named Parson Thirdly does no harm even if he does little real good either. Church architecture, religious dissent, and debate about infant baptism, all of which had once exercised the young Hardy, contribute to the rather melodramatic plot of *A Laodicean* (1881), and the title alludes to the church of the Laodiceans described in the New Testament as 'neither cold nor hot' (Revelation 3:16). But this is not really a religious (or anti-religious) novel: the Laodicean heroine is undecided and capricious in love rather than spiritually lukewarm.

Hardy's engagements with God and the Bible are, however, imaginative and moral rather than just a matter of social and cultural background and casual allusion. An early notebook of 'Studies, Specimens & c.', evidence of his literary apprenticeship, shows a fascination—one that never left him—with the language of the Book of Common Prayer, the prayer book psalms, and other parts of the Old Testament. The copy of the Bible that he used in his twenties has many marked passages, particularly in the Book of Job.[6] He had read his New Testament not just in the King James version but in the original Greek, and owned a modern (1859) edition of the Griesbach Greek text, first published in 1775-7, which he bestows on his hero

---

[4] G. K. Chesterton, *The Victorian Age in Literature* [1913] (London: Oxford University Press, 1966), p. 62; Florence Emily Hardy, *The Early Life of Thomas Hardy, 1840-1891* (London: Macmillan, 1928), p. 293.

[5] Claire Tomalin, *Thomas Hardy: The Time-Torn Man* (London: Viking, 2006), p. 223.

[6] Pamela Dalziell and Michael Millgate, eds, Thomas Hardy, *Thomas Hardy's 'Studies, Specimens & c.'* (Oxford: Oxford University Press, 1994), pp. 23, 34, 40-4, 68-9, 113, etc.

116   *Thomas Hardy: The Church or Christianity*

Jude the Obscure.[7] 'The letter killeth' (2 Corinthians 3:6), the text that had licensed allegorizing Origen's departure from narrowly literal readings of scripture, provided the epigraph for *Jude*, his bitterest novel.

Like Origen, Hardy did not reject the Bible but sought to read it for what he took to be the spirit rather than the letter. Like George Eliot, he had fallen out of love with organized religion and the narrow views and censoriousness too often associated with it. But it would be too much to claim that he repudiated Christianity altogether. He was post-Christian rather than anti-Christian, imaginatively responsive to some of the radical challenges of the Bible, retaining some relabelled Christian-humanist baggage. This included a selective attraction to Comte and the progressive Comtean 'Religion of Humanity'.[8]

Whatever Hardy's views of institutional Christianity, he had much in common with Eliot as a religiously significant writer. He owned and read at least some of Eliot's translation of Strauss's *Life of Jesus*.[9] The first number of the originally anonymous serial version of Hardy's *Far from the Madding Crowd* prompted R. H. Hutton to observe in *The Spectator* on 3 January 1874, 'If [it] is not written by George Eliot, then there is a new light among novelists', and on 24 December 1874 the young Henry James observed rather loftily in *The Nation* that 'the author has evidently read to good purpose the low-life chapters in George Eliot's novels'.[10]

The common sympathetic concern in Hardy and Eliot with 'low life'—the moral and spiritual dignity and difficulties of humble, ordinary people in rural settings—was a shared legacy from the Wordsworth of 'Michael' or 'The Old Cumberland Beggar', and perhaps also from the poetry of Crabbe and Burns. But the detailed work of Jan Jędrzewski and Pamela Dalziel on Hardy, and Elisabeth Jay on Eliot, has helped to demonstrate that they also shared aspects

---

[7] Michael Millgate, *Thomas Hardy: A Biography Revisited* (Oxford; Oxford University Press, 2004), p. 64.

[8] Hardy and Comte are discussed in T. R. Wright, *The Religion of Humanity: The Impact of Comtean Positivism in Victorian Britain* (Cambridge: Cambridge University Press, 1986), pp. 202–17.

[9] Thomas Hardy, *The Literary Notebooks*, ed. L. A. Björk, 2 vols (London: Macmillan, 1985), I, p. 381. Apparently the pages were uncut after p. 192.

[10] R. H. Hutton in *The Spectator*, 3 January 1874, quoted in Laurence Lerner and John Holmstrom, eds, *Thomas Hardy and his Readers* (London: Bodley Head, 1968), p. 23; Henry James in *The Nation* (New York), 24 December 1874, also in Lerner and Holmstrom, p. 30.

Thomas Hardy: The Church or Christianity   117

of a more specifically religious heritage.[11] Hardy as well as Eliot had grown up with the evangelical habit of Bible reading and serious reflection, which never left him and which led to complex but by no means wholly negative critical engagements with theological issues. Even the very hostile Samuel Law Wilson, considering Hardy's earlier fiction and the poetry, was forced to admit that 'though exiled from the great Father's house, he has not ceased to cast some longing, lingering looks behind'.[12]

Despite Hardy's anti-religious grumblings, the label of atheist does not sit entirely comfortably on him. Unwilling to appear as a propagandist rather than an artist, he refused to join the Rationalist Press Association, and late in life he refused to be included in the secularist Joseph McCabe's *Dictionary of Modern Rationalists* (1920).[13] In his poem 'Lausanne: In Gibbon's Old Garden' (1897) in *Poems of the Past and Present* (1901) he saluted the iconoclastic historian of the Roman Empire with fellow feeling as a maligned truth-teller, but made no attempt to renew Gibbon's sly ironies and insinuations against the early Church. 'A Cathedral Façade at Midnight' in *Human Shows* (1925) accepts as fact that reason had eclipsed 'The coded creeds of old-time godliness', but not without regret.[14] Whatever reason might suggest, scriptural narrative and its cultural consequences retained their hold on Hardy's imagination. In 'In the British Museum' in *Satires of Circumstance* (1919) he uses the persona of a working man to convey a sense of simple wonder that a 'time-touched stone' from the Areopagus in Athens 'once echoed/The voice of Paul'.[15] The poem alludes to the occasion (Acts 17:23) when St Paul, visiting Athens, had opportunistically used an altar inscribed 'to the unknown God' to preach the Christian God. With comparable opportunism the sceptical scientist T. H. Huxley had in 1869 coined and appropriated the term 'agnostic' from the original New Testament Greek of this

---

[11] Jan Jędrzewski, *Thomas Hardy and the Church* (Basingstoke: Macmillan, 1996); Elisabeth Jay, *The Religion of the Heart: Anglican Evangelicalism and the Nineteenth-Century Novel* (Oxford: Clarendon Press, 1979).

[12] Wilson, *The Theology of Modern Literature*, p. 407.

[13] Wright, *The Religion of Humanity*, p. 202; Florence Hardy to Joseph McCabe, 18 February 1920, *The Collected Letters of Thomas Hardy*, ed. R. L. Purdy and M. Millgate, 7 vols (Oxford: Clarendon Press, 1978–88), VII, p. 162.

[14] 'A Cathedral Façade at Midnight', *Thomas Hardy: Complete Poems*, ed. James Gibson (London: Macmillan, 1976), p. 703.

[15] 'In the British Museum', *Thomas Hardy: Complete Poems*, pp. 381–2.

118   *Thomas Hardy: The Church or Christianity*

phrase (*agnosto theo*), itself the title of another poem by Hardy. But Hardy's outlook was imaginative rather than scientific. Unlike his friend Edward Clodd, who dedicated his *Primer of Evolution* to Huxley in 1895, and unlike Huxley himself, he could not altogether convince himself that God and religious thought were of purely antiquarian interest with no bearing on the moral life of man. The nature of God might still be unknown and mysterious but it could not be altogether discounted.

If Hardy was not a conventional believer he was not a conventional unbeliever either, and he could be at least as wary of scientific rationalism and the positivist 'Religion of Humanity' as he was of institutional Christianity.[16] By temperament more a depressive than a thoroughgoing sceptic, he was a sombre ironist, fond of sardonic titles for his late volumes of verse such as *Time's Laughingstocks* (1909) or *Satires of Circumstance* (1914), and if his God existed he had a similarly bitter sense of humour and an apparent indifference to suffering humanity. A natural heretic, Hardy was intrigued by the idea of a non-active and passionless God, an early heresy that had been vigorously attacked by the ultra-orthodox Tertullian.[17] A similar view of deity—majestic, remote, and serenely impassive—had been developed by the Roman poet Lucretius, pioneer of scientific materialism and much admired by agnostics and freethinkers and by Hardy himself. The comparison with Lucretius was hinted at by at least one of Hardy's contemporaries, the *fin-de-siècle* poet and critic Lionel Johnson.[18]

Yet it has to be stressed that Hardy was not a systematic theologian or philosopher but a poet and novelist with a keen sense of the dramatic and the ironic, and an instinct for the imaginative possibilities of mood and situation. We need to take account of the variable and provisional nature of Hardy's religious vision as it is disclosed in his creative work over the years. As he observed in the 1892 Preface to *Tess of the D'Urbervilles*, Tess was 'charged with impressions' rather

---

[16] Timothy Hands, *Thomas Hardy: Distracted Preacher?* (Basingstoke: Macmillan, 1989), p. 118.

[17] Tertullian, *De Testimonio Animae* ('The Soul's Testimony') 2, noted in Hardy's *Literary Notebooks*, II, p. 91.

[18] Lucretius, *De Rerum Natura* II, 1090–104; Lionel Johnson, *The Art of Thomas Hardy* (London: John Lane, 1895), p. 254. For Lucretius in nineteenth-century literature, see Norman Vance, *The Victorians and Ancient Rome* (Oxford: Blackwell, 1997), pp. 83–111.

Thomas Hardy: The Church or Christianity   119

than formal convictions, and 'A novel is an impression, not an argument'. *Jude* was similarly defended in the Preface to the first edition (1895) as 'a series of seemings, or personal impressions'. Later still, in the 'Apology' prefixed to his *Late Lyrics and Earlier* (1922), he lays claim only to 'a series of fugitive impressions which I have never tried to co-ordinate'.[19]

Some of these impressions, bleak and powerful, are presented in strongly visual form. They may at times approximate to what Longinus and others had described as the sublime. Visualizations (*phantasiai*) or 'image productions' (*eidolopoiiai*) had been identified by Longinus as a common and effective way of conveying the weight and grandeur of the sublime in tragic and epic poetry, particularly Homer.[20] Even if Hardy had not encountered Longinus at first hand, he had read his Homer and his Greek tragedy, not to mention Virgil, Shakespeare, Milton, and the Psalms, favourite sources of illustration in later writers on the sublime such as Addison, Burke, and Kant. He was also sensitively aware of the tradition of European landscape painting and the visual sublime, culminating in the work of Turner. In the opening chapter of *The Return of the Native* (1878) the narrator claims, rather glumly, that, 'The time seems near, if it has not actually arrived, when the mournful sublimity of a moor, a sea, or a mountain, will be all of nature that is absolutely in keeping with the moods of the more thinking among mankind.'[21] This reflection, perhaps calculated to offset the pre-Darwinian moments of delight occasioned by Wordsworthian nature, arises from the description of the sombre vastness of 'Egdon Heath' at dusk—wild, ancient, and unchanged, sublime rather than conventionally beautiful. The chapter title, 'A Face on which Time Makes Little Impression' simultaneously humanizes the heath as a character in the novel and makes it alien, changeless, indifferent to the affairs and passions of man, a metaphor for the withdrawn and inactive God favoured by

---

[19] Thomas Hardy, *Tess of the d'Urbervilles*, ed. Juliet Grindle and Simon Gatrell, World's Classics (Oxford: Oxford University Press, 1988), pp. 4–5; *Jude the Obscure*, ed. Patricia Ingham, World's Classics (Oxford: Oxford University Press, 1985), pp. xxxv-vi; *Complete Poems* p. 557.

[20] Longinus, *On the Sublime*, ed. D. A. Russell (Oxford, 1964) 15.

[21] Thomas Hardy, *The Return of the Native*, ed. Simon Gattrell, World's Classics (Oxford: Oxford University Press, 1990), p. 10. For Hardy and visual culture, see J. B. Bullen, *The Expressive Eye: Fiction and Perception in the Work of Thomas Hardy* (Oxford: Clarendon Press, 1986).

120   *Thomas Hardy: The Church or Christianity*

Tertullian's heretics. This grimly ironic approach to the sublime resists and frustrates conventional expectation. If it represents a mode of imaginative access to a transcendent Other, that Other is not easily assimilated to conventional religion or the God of Genesis or the Psalms, let alone the New Testament, who providentially sustains as well as creates the universe and the lives of men and women.

The stars in their courses in *Two on a Tower* (1882), Hardy's novel about star-gazing star-crossed lovers, represent a differently ironic version of the sublime. Addison's sustained engagements in the *Spectator* with the Homeric, Miltonic, and biblical sublime had led to his celebrated paraphrase of Psalm 19, 'The spacious firmament on high', seeing in the order of the 'spangled heavens' the divine hand of the Creator. More than seventy years later Immanuel Kant had concluded the *Critique of Practical Reason* (1788) by linking the starry heavens and the moral law within as sources of perpetual admiration and reverence. But Hardy's astronomer Swithin is ultimately intimidated rather than exalted by the sublime prospect of the starry heavens, inspired with a sense not of reverence but of human insignificance. In the *Critique of Judgement* (1790) Kant had distinguished between the sublime as unmanageable immensity, the mathematical sublime, and the dynamic sublime that had the power to move the mind to fear and terror. Swithin and his companion Lady Constantine pass swiftly from one form of the sublime to the other:

> At night, when human discords and harmonies are hushed, in a general sense, for the greater part of twelve hours, there is nothing to moderate the blow with which the infinitely great, the stellar universe, strikes down upon the infinitely little, the mind of the beholder; and this was the case now. Having got closer to immensity than their fellow-creature they saw at once its beauty and its frightfulness. They more and more felt the contrast between their own tiny magnitudes and those among which they had recklessly plunged, till they were oppressed with the presence of a vastness they could not cope with even as an idea, and which hung about them like a nightmare.[22]

Kant's formulation of the 'mathematical sublime' marks the extent to which sublime effects may be a matter of scale in relation to the human subject, a concern not just of poets and painters but of

---

[22] Thomas Hardy, *Two on a Tower*, ed. Suleiman M. Ahmad, World's Classics (Oxford: Oxford University Press, 1993) chapter 8, p. 64.

Thomas Hardy: The Church or Christianity 121

professional architects such as Hardy. In *Tess* the vastness of the plain around Stonehenge, like many of Hardy's landscapes, dwarfs the people on it. It is associated not so much with a Christian or theistic sense of the transcendent as with the mystery and the pitiless harshness of an older world of sun-worship and blood-sacrifice, and provides Hardy with the backdrop for Tess's last night of freedom and her arrest.[23] The reader is left to draw the obvious conclusion that Tess herself may be a kind of sacrificial victim of a harsh, self-righteous, and unpitying society.

Hardy, like Lucretius and Milton before him, like Milton's illustrator John Martin and other exponents of the apocalyptic sublime, had a vivid and emotionally charged spatial imagination with an instinct for cosmic vastness and terrestrial panorama as well as for human encounter. This came into its own in *The Dynasts* (1903–8), his epic verse-drama of the Napoleonic Wars. In the 'Fore Scene' of Part First, the sky opens and the whole of Europe is disclosed, but the audience is presented not with a vision of civilization or some magnificent Blakean embodiment of heroic energy but with 'a prone and emaciated figure'. The point of view then sinks downwards through space to reveal wretched and distressed peoples in the grip of European war.[24] As John Wain has noticed, the ever-shifting perspectives of the epic drama, variously Olympian and intimate, anticipate the technique of cinema.[25] They encompass the vast disease-ridden military encampment at Walcheren, a bird's-eye view of the expanse of sea on which the battle of Trafalgar would be fought, the whole terrain of Waterloo, and close-ups of individual exchanges, the conversations of stage-coach passengers, admirals, generals, beacon-keepers, and deserters.

Longinus had had access to the Greek Old Testament and famously used the reported divine command in Genesis, 'Let there be light', as an example of the sublime, the expression of an appropriate perception of divine power on a cosmic scale.[26] The Genesis creation account had already been imaginatively invoked in Milton's *Paradise Lost*, and the sublime creation of light had an enormous influence on

---

[23] Hardy, *Tess of the d'Urbervilles*, chapter 57, p. 381.

[24] Thomas Hardy, *The Dynasts* (London: Macmillan, 1910), p. 6.

[25] John Wain, 'Introduction' to *The Dynasts* (London: Macmillan, 1965), p. x, quoted in T. R. Wright, ed., *Thomas Hardy on Screen* (Cambridge: Cambridge University Press, 2005), pp. 9, 20, 52.

[26] Longinus, *On the Sublime* 9, alluding to Gen. 1:3.

122   *Thomas Hardy: The Church or Christianity*

poetry and culture in the eighteenth century, including Haydn's oratorio *The Creation* (1798), with a libretto that owed a lot to *Paradise Lost*. Haydn's bold musical evocation of primal chaos is dramatically succeeded by much more conventionally ordered tonalities to register the sublime simplicity of the moment when new-created light dawned on the world and the chorus swells from *piano* to *fortissimo* as it sings 'and there was light'. Hardy's sensitivity to manifestations of possibly divine light and power is not inconsistent with his habitual irony. As the theologian John Milbank has observed, the concept of the sublime had come to rearticulate the idea of transcendence, 'the most ultimate and primal reality imaginable'.[27] But it is perfectly possible to be imaginatively aware of both ends of the scale, the ultimate and the immediate or practical, and to find irony in the apparently impossible and impassable distance between them. Given the limiting conditions under which we live, can visionary gleams ever lead to anything more than that?

Jude the Obscure is a study of light that failed. Early in the novel the young Jude has an intimation of the sublime. He is fascinated by the distant prospect of Christminster (Oxford), first seen as points of light gleaming like a topaz in the setting sun. This is represented as a quasi-apocalyptic vision of the 'heavenly Jerusalem', recalling the biblical holy city 'having the glory of God: and her light . . . like unto a stone most precious', an enchanting centre of learning and religion.[28] It also recalls the celestial city in Bunyan's *The Pilgrim's Progress*. But Jude's journey is a kind of inverted or frustrated *Pilgrim's Progress* ending not with the celestial city but with despair. The coherence of pilgrimage narrative and of the realist tradition is allowed to break down into fragmentary allusion and disconnected reverie in Christminster, to all intents and purposes Oxford, as Jude hears a medley of voices from Oxford's intellectually and religiously varied past and comes to realize his own voice can never join them.

Hardy had been fascinated with Bunyan's narrative since as a boy of ten he had been terrified by an illustration of Apollyon fighting Christian.[29] In a notebook dated 1867 he transcribed a favourite

---

[27] John Milbank, 'Sublimity: The Modern Transcendent' in Regina Schwartz, ed., *The Sublime: Philosophy, Literature, and Theology Approach the Beyond* (New York and London: Routledge, 2004), p. 211.

[28] Hardy, *Jude The Obscure*, pp. 16–17; Rev. 21:11.

[29] Hardy to J. W. Mackail, 24 December 1924, *Collected Letters* VI, p. 299.

Thomas Hardy: The Church or Christianity   123

passage: 'There, said they, is the Mount Zion, the heavenly Jerusalem, the innumerable company of angels, and the spirits of just men, made perfect...'[30] The pilgrim's vision of Mount Zion gradually faded for the mature Hardy, but the journey motif exploited by Bunyan survived not only as a recurring narrative device, a way into the carefully specified environments of his novels, but as a model of inspiring individual and social possibility, however frustrated in practice.

This way of using Bunyan had a radical pedigree. Even before Marx and Marxist commentators, as Jonathan Rose has shown, nineteenth-century political radicals could read Bunyan as one of them, as a rebel. As early as 1839 we have a secular, socialist *Political Pilgrim's Progress* serialized in the Chartist journal *The Northern Liberator*, tracing a journey from the City of Plunder to the City of Reform.[31] Where Charles Kingsley, the Christian socialist, believed that individuals and nations that had lost their way could find it again and find God, and socialist secularizers brought up on Bunyan could hold on to some kind of politico-economic version of the heavenly Jerusalem or the celestial city, Hardy looked for a better future but did not find it, or at least not here and not yet.

In Bunyan's delightful land of Beulah, beyond the valley of the shadow of death, the contract between Bride and Bridegroom is symbolically renewed,[32] and there are more mundane traces of this in Victorian pilgrimage novels such as *Jane Eyre* in which journey's end for the protagonist may include the fulfilment of marriage. But in Hardy marriage contracts tend to end badly, if they are ever achieved in the first place. The late poem 'Faintheart in a Railway Train' (1920), in *Late Lyrics and Earlier* (1922), resurrects another character from *The Pilgrim's Progress* and transmutes the pilgrim quest into a lover's quest that never actually happens, because Hardy's Faintheart is too timid to get out of the train to speak to the enchanting lady he has observed. This has the effect of returning Bunyan's Faintheart to the more secular and customary business of never winning fair lady.

The ironic reworking of *The Pilgrim's Progress* is sharper and more sardonic in *Jude*. The vision of Christminster as the heavenly

---

[30] Hardy, *Literary Notebooks* II, pp. 463–4.

[31] Jonathan Rose, *The Intellectual Life of the British Working Classes* (New Haven: Yale University Press, 2001), p. 105.

[32] John Bunyan, *The Pilgrim's Progress*, ed. W. R. Owens (Oxford: Oxford University Press, 2003), p. 146.

124   *Thomas Hardy: The Church or Christianity*

Jerusalem of Bunyan and of the Book of Revelation inspires Jude's life's pilgrimage. But Christminster turns out to be not the bright vision of his dreams but a place of darkness, misery, and disappointed hopes, at least for him. When Bunyan's Mr Valiant-for-Truth left the world it was described as a triumph: 'So he passed over, and the Trumpets sounded for him on the other side',[33] inspiring some of Vaughan Williams' most triumphant religious music. But when Jude dies at the end of the novel it is in solitude and despair and the trumpets that sound from the brass band by the river are not sounding for him: they are part of the privileged entertainments of the university from which he has always been excluded. His last words are the bitter recriminations in the third chapter of the book of Job. Job's fortunes recovered after all his trials, but Jude knew that happiness and prosperity would never be his.

There are different strands in Hardy's appropriation of the pilgrimage idea, representing the unresolved tension between the pessimistic and progressive aspects of his outlook. Jude's journey to despair, like Tess's uncomfortable intuition that we live on a blighted star,[34] suggest that the world is hostile or at least indifferent to individual happiness and fulfilment, since it confers no special favours and humans are but strangers and pilgrims in it, without entitlement or the right of permanent settlement in such a place. Michael Henchard, first encountered as a travelling man who has been on a long journey, a labourer looking for work, seems to have arrived—in social and material terms—when he becomes mayor of Casterbridge, only to find it all slips away from him. But the pilgrimage idea can also signal progressive or purposive journeying to some more or less secular version of Bunyan's celestial city, to a better place. This parallels the ambivalence of the quasi-Darwinian phrase 'evolutionary meliorism', which the later Hardy used to sum up his outlook.[35] 'Evolutionary' implies savage competition in the struggle for life, the harsh economy of suffering and waste enforced by the blind forces of nature, grimly divorced from questions of merit or moral worth. The indications of blighted life among the trees in *The Woodlanders*, evidence of nature's unfulfilled intention, are the most vivid indication of this in the novels, metaphors for the blighted lives of Giles Winterbourne and Marty

---

[33] Bunyan, *The Pilgrim's Progress*, p. 288.
[34] Hardy, *Tess of the d'Urbervilles*, pp. 35, 37.
[35] 'Apology' prefacing *Late Lyrics*, in *Complete Poems*, p. 557.

Thomas Hardy: The Church or Christianity   125

South. But 'meliorism', perhaps influenced by Hardy's reading of Comte, suggests progress towards a better mode of existence. It implies that the evolutionary process, however bleak, might have ultimately positive consequences: that eventually circumstances and institutions will get better in a manner consistent with the progressive socialist reading of Bunyan. This rather muted version of ultimate progress towards some kind of secular approximation to Augustine's City of God links Hardy, and Hardy's narratives, with other residually Christian teleologies such as George Eliot's 'growing good of the world', even if the promise of better things is not delivered or fulfilled in time to benefit his tragic protagonists, born ahead of their time, or to supply many unequivocally happy endings.

The rigid social hierarchy challenged in Hardy's early unpublished novel *The Poor Man and the Lady* is still in place in *Jude*. So is the radical instinct to confront it and to look towards a better future. In *Tess* and *Jude* this radicalism extends to the outspoken condemnation of the contemporary practice of institutional Christianity, and overt and controversial sympathy for unconventional sexual morality, which has not yet gained social acceptance. This spirit of rebellion was reflected in one of Hardy's earlier titles for *Jude*: *Hearts Insurgent*. Hardy presents a world that needs to move beyond the inadequacy and the injustice of narrow views. While it might now be possible to see this boldly progressive moral vision as a secularized version of salvation history it was not appreciated in those terms at the time. It seemed closer to the revolutionary spirit of Nietzsche than to the gospels. It even seemed to invite comparison with the extreme view attributed to Dostoevsky's Ivan Karamazov by his enemy: that if God was dead, if belief in God and human immortality had ceased, then everything, even cannibalism, was permitted.[36]

But Hardy actually stops well short of this. His poem 'God's Funeral' (1908–10) is not a celebration of release from bondage but an exercise in sombre nostalgia: as the funeral passes, the speaker is left 'dazed and puzzled'. Hardy wrote in 1902 that Nietzsche's ruthless moral teaching could bring 'disaster to humanity'.[37] His enduring

---

[36] Fyodor Dostoevsky, *The Brothers Karamazov* (1880), trans. David Magarshack (Harmondsworth: Penguin, 1958), part 1, book 1, chapter 6.

[37] Thomas Hardy, 'M. Maeterlinck's Apology for Nature', *Academy and Literature*, 17 May 1902, p. 451; see Eugene Williamson, 'Thomas Hardy and Friedrich Nietzsche: The Reasons', *Comparative Literature Studies* 15 (December 1978), 403–13.

126   *Thomas Hardy: The Church or Christianity*

commitment to human compassion in times of war and peace, which Nietzsche would have dismissed as mere weakness, a feature of 'slave morality', was ultimately formalized as the 'Spirit of the Pities' in *The Dynasts*. Throughout his writing career Hardy registered a sustained protest against tolerated cruelty and failures of charity. Insofar as charity is at the heart of Christian morality, Hardy's attacks on the Church and churchmen are not so much an indictment of Christianity as of failures of Christian love, failures, in a sense, to be Christian enough. There are haughty and useless churchmen in Hardy such as Angel Clare's insufferable brothers in *Tess* and the two clergymen whom Jude and Sue overhear irrelevantly arguing about the merits of the eastward position for the priest at communion just after the devastating death of the children. If such priests are identified with the useless scribes and Pharisees of the New Testament the novels begin to look more Christian in essentials than one might have expected. On the other hand, the humane indictment of cruelty immediately runs into the problem of how to justify what seems to be divinely tolerated evil. How can a benign all-powerful God be so cruel as to permit the suffering, natural and man-made, which disfigures the world He created?

This problem, the problem of theodicy, was not new. As Hardy was well aware, for Voltaire and others the appalling Lisbon earthquake of 1755 had been more than enough to unsettle any simple confidence in divine providence. Hardy's notebooks, which include many extracts from his friend John Morley's *Voltaire* (1872, reprinted 1886), also record, from the 1855 edition of G. H. Lewes' *Life of Goethe*, that 'Goethe's religion was all taken out of him by the Lisbon earthquake.'[38] Natural disaster and the mindless and reckless profusion of nature, producing species and human lives that it could not sustain, called into question Wordsworth's blithe formulation 'Nature's holy plan' in his 'Lines written in early spring', which is bitterly repudiated by the narrator of *Tess of the d'Urbervilles*.[39]

The sense that neither God nor the amoral natural order as it had been redescribed for Hardy's generation by Darwin, and Darwin's popularizer T. H. Huxley, can be relied on to ensure human happiness and fulfilment is the dark thread that runs through most of Hardy's novels, with varying degrees of intensity. There are some

---

[38] Hardy, *Literary Notebooks* I, p. 14.
[39] Hardy, *Tess of the d'Urbervilles*, p. 28.

Thomas Hardy: The Church or Christianity 127

compromises with popular taste, particularly in the earlier novels. Disaster, desertion, obsession, and murder darken the pastoral landscape of *Far from the Madding Crowd* (1874), serialized in the *Cornhill*, but it ends with Gabriel Oak finally marrying Bathsheba. Diggory Venn is allowed to marry the widowed Thomasin at the end of *The Return of the Native* (1878), though in a footnote Hardy insists austerely that he would have preferred to leave her a widow. Where possible, in place of formulaic happy endings and implicitly providential plots—derived from conventional religious assurance and the artificial conventions of stage comedy—Hardy tends to favour tragic plots with elements of melodrama and farce, which grimly mock in their excesses the very idea of a divine economy or a benevolently plotted universe.[40]

The most grimly farcical of all his novels is perhaps *Two on a Tower* (1882) in which the rather severe Bishop of Melchester makes a conventionally good match by becoming the husband of Viviette, Lady Constantine. Her child born after the marriage is not his: he does not know that she has agreed to this union in a moment of despair after she finds she has become pregnant by the young astronomer Swithin, the man she thought she had legally married when, unknown to them both, her brutal absentee first husband was still alive. The bishop conveniently dies and Swithin comes back to Viviette. In the last chapter of the novel she dies melodramatically of an overstrained heart, touched by sudden joy after despair, in a manner that recalls Gloucester at the end of Shakespeare's *King Lear*. Swithin, her true lover, gives her full credit for generosity and unselfishness, the biblical charity that 'seeketh not her own'.[41] The suggestion is that there may be more essential Christianity in Viviette than in the bishop.

In Hardy's moral and imaginative universe Christian charity is, however, more easily commended than the traditional doctrine of Christ. There is evidence of nostalgia for old religious traditions and popular belief, such as the Christmas poem 'The Oxen' (1915). But for all practical purposes, he seems to have ruled out miracle and the supernatural, the virgin birth, and the resurrection. The redemption of a dark and fallen world by a messiah or by sub-messianic figures

---

[40] See Gillian Beer, *Darwin's Plots: Evolutionary Narratives in Darwin, George Eliot and Nineteenth-century Fiction* (London: Routledge, 1983), esp. pp. 236–58.

[41] Hardy, *Two on a Tower*, p. 280; 1 Cor. 13:5.

128   *Thomas Hardy: The Church or Christianity*

seems hardly possible. Opportunities and 'charisma' or spiritual gifts, to be bestowed on individuals who might make a difference or hasten a better future, tend to be in short supply or are misdirected. Jude is intellectually gifted but frustrated by self and circumstance: his dreams of being a scholar and then a bishop or a dean are old-fashioned and perhaps more individualistic than spiritual, perhaps more involved with social climbing than with social improvement, even though he becomes a powerful witness to a world gone wrong, with what he describes as 'all creation groaning'. His grim biblical reference, picked up by the narrator later in the novel, pointedly ignores the rest of the passage, which looks forward from groaning and travailing in pain to redemption and salvation, and assures the faithful that 'all things work together for good to them that love God'.[42]

Charisma in Hardy mainly takes the form of morally ambivalent personal magnetism or sexual attractiveness, more likely to do harm than good. Fitzpiers in *The Woodlanders* or Angel Clare in *Tess* are educated, scientific, modern-minded outsiders, men who make a strong impression in the local community, potential reformers. But Fitzpiers is a dilettante, a philanderer, and an amoral scoundrel, and if Angel Clare has shaken off some outmoded attitudes he is not liberal or modern-minded enough in sexual matters to abandon the hypo-critical double standard, to accept Tess as the essentially pure woman that the subtitle insists she is, or to deserve the 'idolatry' or quasi-religious devotion she bestows on him as her substitute for God.[43]

In *The Return of the Native* Clym Yeobright returns from the intellectual ferment of Paris to his native place with a quasi-messianic sense of a teaching mission, a new undogmatic gospel of human possibility to be preached and lived. His quixotic determination to 'throw up his business to benefit his fellow creature' sets him apart from safe and comfortable mediocrity, and although the outcome is actually less dramatic, this leaves him open to be persecuted or 'to be applauded as a prophet, revered as a priest, or exalted as a king'.[44] The same formula had been imaginatively appropriated in Eliot's *Daniel Deronda*. 'Prophet', 'priest', and 'king' are biblical attributes of Christ, commended in the line, 'My Prophet, Priest and King' in the Calvinist

---

[42] Hardy, *Jude the Obscure*, pp. 356, 409; Rom. 8:22–8.
[43] Hardy, *Tess of the D'Urbervilles*, p. 212.
[44] Hardy, *The Return of the Native*, pp. 170–1.

Thomas Hardy: The Church or Christianity 129

evangelical John Newton's popular hymn, 'How sweet the name of Jesus sounds'.[45] Eustacia sees Clym as 'like a man coming from heaven' though her interest is personal and sexual rather than religious.[46] There is a deliberate allusion to Christ's Sermon on the Mount at the end of the novel, as Clym preaches or gives moral lectures on Sunday afternoons on Blackbarrow to assembled villagers.[47] But Hardy presents him as a forerunner, ahead of his time for this country place, 'a John the Baptist who took ennoblement rather than repentance for his text'.[48] A good man but half-blind, his limited vision is a metaphor as well as a handicap: he will never set the world on fire. In the first edition of the novel he is described as still 'less than thirty' but Hardy revised that in the 1895 edition to 'less than thirty-three', the age at which it is supposed that Christ was crucified, to reinforce the ironic parallel.[49] What real difference will be made by either Clym's life or his death?

For all Clym's noble intentions and ambitions, more immediate and practical good is probably achieved in the novel by the reddleman Diggory Venn, a kind of Wordsworthian solitary. His first appearance in the novel is when he helps Thomasin Yeobright in her great trouble when there is a humiliating problem with the marriage licence on her wedding day. The surname Venn is not uncommon in the south-west of England, but it is also the name of the famous evangelical divine Henry Venn, author of *The Complete Duty of Man* (1763) and his son John Venn, rector of Clapham and one of the founders of the Church Missionary Society. It may have been Hardy's intention to make Diggory Venn the embodiment of an entirely secular gospel. In his decency and resourcefulness he resembles the good shepherd Gabriel Oak in *Far from the Madding Crowd*. Gabriel is not himself a Christ-figure but he takes his name from the messenger-angel who brought Mary the news that Christ would be born to her.

In *The Mayor of Casterbridge* personal limitations and changing conditions in the corn trade lead to the eclipse of Henchard and the rise of Farfrae. The close but difficult relationship between King Saul

---

[45] Newton's hymn, first published in his collection of *Olney Hymns* (1779), was included in the first edition of *Hymns Ancient and Modern* (1861) of which Hardy had a copy.

[46] Hardy, *The Return of the Native*, p. 108.

[47] Hardy, *The Return of the Native*, p. 389.

[48] Hardy, *The Return of the Native*, p. 170.

[49] Hardy, *The Return of the Native*, p. 389.

130   *Thomas Hardy: The Church or Christianity*

and the young David in the Old Testament provides a model for the relationship between old Henchard and young Farfrae—tradition and modernity, instinct and calculation—and this helps to confer archetypal dignity on Hardy's narrative.[50] But the Old Testament analogy is not pushed too far. In religious art David can be a type of Christ, born of 'the house and lineage of David' (Luke 2:4), and this connection is made by Victorian painters such as Dante Gabriel Rossetti, as George Landow has noted,[51] but Hardy stops well short of pressing this aspect of the parallel. Farfrae is an innovator or modernizer, but he is a shrewd operator of some personal attractiveness, not a social reformer or a messianic redeemer capable of delivering Casterbridge, Henchard, or anyone else from the burden of sin or any other kind of oppression.

If Hardy's heroes fail to sustain the burden of even the weakest kind of 'weak messianism' is there any possibility of salvation or redemption, any grounds for hope? His poem 'The Darkling Thrush', dated 31 December 1900 in *Poems of the Past and the Present* (1901), proposed as a kind of epitaph for the nineteenth century, allows the desolate hopelessness of the bleak dead landscape of winter to be transformed by the unexpected song of a thrush, perhaps signalling 'some blessed Hope whereof he knew/And I was unaware'. The word 'blessed' and the capitalized Hope suggest a totally unexpected gleam of what might be Christian hope, one of the three theological virtues, biblically grouped with faith and charity.[52]

Yet all too often in Hardy hopes are dashed and deliverance and happiness fail to materialize, either in religious or secular terms. The psalmist had proclaimed that, 'The righteous shall be glad in the Lord' (Ps. 64:10) and Aristotle in the *Nicomachean Ethics* had identified living and acting well with being happy. The two sentiments, and the ethical traditions behind them, are in a sense combined in the phrase *bene agere et laetari*, 'to act well and be happy', invoked by Hardy's struggling Jude as a way of focusing his aspirations. The quasi-proverbial tag comes from Spinoza's *Ethics*, respected and admired

---

[50] See Julian Moynahan, '*The Mayor of Casterbridge* and the Old Testament First Book of Samuel', *PMLA* 71 (1956), 118–30.

[51] George P. Landow, *Victorian Types, Victorian Shadows: Biblical Typology in Victorian Literature, Art and Thought* (Boston: Routledge, 1980), p. 139.

[52] Hardy, *Thoms Hardy: Complete Poems* p. 150; for faith, hope, and charity, see 1 Cor. 13:13; see also Norman Vance, 'Hardy's "The Darkling Thrush" and G. F. Watts's *Hope*', *Victorian Poetry* 33 (Summer 1995), 295–8.

Thomas Hardy: The Church or Christianity   131

by George Eliot and by other Victorian agnostics. It describes the conduct and condition of the self-fulfilled wise and free man who has phlegmatically accepted that all things follow from the necessity of the divine nature. But this ideal and the Olympian calm associated with it are unrealized and unrealizable in this angry novel, for Jude is given no scope to be self-fulfilled or free. This is partly attributable to his own failings, but he is also a victim of circumstances and a still-evolving, still very imperfect social order.[53]

There is a similar pattern of frustration in one of Hardy's bleaker short stories, 'The Grave by the Handpost' in *A Changed Man* (1913). A father, an old soldier bitterly disappointed in his soldier son, has committed suicide and is buried at a crossroads rather than in consecrated ground. The guilt-smitten son arranges for the biblical words 'I am not worthy to be called thy son'—the confession of the penitent Prodigal Son (Luke 15:18–19)—to be inscribed on his father's tombstone. But the tombstone is never erected, and years later the hope of reunion and reconciliation, implied in the forgiveness of the Prodigal in the biblical story, is not realized, even in death, because the son's express wishes are accidentally overlooked and he is not buried beside his father. In the same story, the death of both father and son is associated with the singing (to a 'dull air') of a carol by Philip Doddridge that includes the lines, 'He comes the prisoners to release/In Satan's bondage held'.[54] Hardy would have known, and probably expected his readers to know, that the first line of the carol sung in such doleful circumstances was the spectacularly inappropriate 'Hark, the glad sound! the saviour comes', and the events of the story suggest that, nineteen centuries later, the biblical promise of liberation and joy still awaits fulfilment.

But Hardy's glum ironies often depend not only on knowledge of scripture (and the hymn book) but on continuing respect for the underlying sense of scripture. Human heedlessness and lack of charity as well as sheer accident contribute to frustrate any kind of reconciliation of the latter-day prodigal son, but none of that invalidates the possibility or the importance of divine as well as human forgiveness and generosity, which the original parable teaches. The

---

[53] Aristotle, *Nicomachean Ethics* 1.4; Spinoza, *Ethics* 4, proposition 50, scholium; proposition 73, scholium; Hardy, *Jude the Obscure*, p. 74.

[54] Thomas Hardy, 'The Grave by the Handpost', in *The Distracted Preacher and Other Tales* (Harmondsworth: Penguin, 1979), p. 336.

132   *Thomas Hardy: The Church or Christianity*

ultimate irony is the discrepancy between the teaching and example of Christ and the work of the Church on earth. The harsh ecclesiastical custom of not burying a suicide in consecrated ground, which leads to the humiliating burial at the crossroads, could be seen as the human act which in this instance helps to frustrate, but not to discredit, the essentially Christian process of penitence, spiritual healing, and reconciliation with God and man.

The absence of convincing messianic saviour-figures in Hardy's imagined world does not completely preclude intuitions of possible redemption, or at least some kind of ultimately consoling religious understanding of life and history. But consolation is not cheaply available in Hardy. Prehistoric, Roman, Saxon, and medieval settlement, and the more recent excitements of the Napoleonic wars, had all left traces on the countryside in which he grew up and that encouraged sombre historical reflection. Annals of bloodshed, oppression, and past cruelties left little to celebrate, contributing to the background sense of tragedy in novels such as *The Mayor of Casterbridge*, but there was much to ponder. One outcome of prolonged reflection on such matters was his poem portentously entitled 'In Time of "The Breaking of Nations"' in *Moments of Vision* (1915). This refers to the Old Testament severity of God's judgement against Babylon, breaking in pieces the nations and destroying kingdoms, as described in Jeremiah 51:20. The original idea came to Hardy during the Franco-Prussian war of 1870. But the theme of undramatic continuity ironically counterpointing violent public rupture and discord was quietly matured over more than forty years and eventually published during the First World War. God is not mentioned in the poem and the reflection that 'this will go onward the same/Though Dynasties pass' is strongly humanistic, an affirmation of the resilience of human life without God.[55] Yet the poem is also tacitly religious, embodying a kind of secular realization of divinely sustained continuity, the promise in the same chapter (Jeremiah 51:5) that 'Israel hath not been forsaken'.

The poem also reminds us that, whether in ancient Babylon or in modern Europe, dynasties—and what Hardy called 'Dynasts'—could come and go. His great epic drama of the Napoleonic Wars, presided over by the Immanent Will, was called *The Dynasts*, for ultimately

---

[55] Hardy, *Thomas Hardy: Complete Poems*, p. 543.

Thomas Hardy: The Church or Christianity   133

religious rather than political or literary reasons. It is in a sense his boldest attempt at an alternative or secular scripture, an extended reimagining of the relations of God, man, nature, and history. Hardy had occasionally invoked the Greek tragedians Aeschylus and Sophocles in his novels, as if to suggest that pre-Christian tragic necessity rather than Christian providence governed the life and death of Tess of the d'Urbervilles or the luckless characters of *Jude the Obscure*. But when a scholarly reader asked if the 'Dynasts' of his title came from Aeschylus, from the Greek term *dynastas* used to describe the apparent power of the wheeling stars bringing in the seasons at the beginning of the *Agamemnon*, Hardy replied that it came not from Aeschylus but from the Greek of the Magnificat, the song of Mary that has been the hope and the consolation of radical Christians throughout the ages.[56] The revolutionary biblical idea of putting down the mighty, the dynasts (Greek *dynastas*), from their seats, or thrones (Greek *ek thronon*) (Luke 1:52) is transferred unironically into the drama, paraphrased by the Chorus of the Pities in the concluding scene:

> To Thee whose eye all Nature owns,
> Who hurlest Dynasties from their thrones,
> And liftest those of low estate
> We sing . . .[57]

The intercalated lyric musings of the Spirit of the Pities in *The Dynasts*, presented alongside the speeches of the inexorable Spirit of the Years, dramatize a perpetual tension between Pity and the pitiless sequence of events as they unfold year by year. In theological terms this confrontation could be redescribed as the work of Mercy and Grace in tension with the iron logic of Judgement. In literary terms it represents a vast expansion of the dialectic of opposed strophe and antistrophe in the structure of the choruses commenting on the unfolding action in Greek tragedy. But where in Greek choruses a concluding epode could resolve formal difference, Hardy seems determined to avoid the spurious consolation of glib and easy resolutions. Yet the trajectory of *The Dynasts* suggests that the ultimate resolution in human history may come when, by evolutionary processes of amelioration, the blind unconscious Immanent Will

---

[56] Hardy to R. Bosworth Smith, 20 February 1906, *Collected Letters* III, p. 197.
[57] Hardy, *The Dynasts*, p. 522.

134   *Thomas Hardy: The Church or Christianity*

eventually acquires full consciousness, and the harshness and cruelty of nature and recorded history gradually pass over into a more benign and sympathetic dispensation.

While this is hardly orthodox theology it still has what might be described as a theological shape, a progressive teleology providing some grounds for hope. It anticipates and invites comparison with the linkage of physical and psychic nature and historical movement towards a unifying 'Omega' point of assembled consciousness in the controversial religious teaching of the Jesuit scientist Teilhard de Chardin, particularly in *The Phenomenon of Man* (1955). Imaginative fusion of Darwinian and Spencerian evolution with the traditional biblical scheme of 'salvation history' lies behind both writers. In some ways Teilhard's work develops from Henri Bergson's *Creative Evolution*, published in 1907 with an English translation in 1911. This is itself a response to Darwin and Spencer, and at least one early commentator on *The Dynasts* noticed parallels with Bergson, though Hardy had not actually read Bergson at the time.[58] As Hardy noted himself in 1907, his fantasy of an evolving consciousness in the Immanent Will resembled the evolutionary 'New Theology' proposed by the liberal dissenter R. J. Campbell, minister of the City Temple in his controversial book *The New Theology* published in 1907. Like Hardy, Campbell was trying to develop what he called 'the religious articulation of the scientific method' and, again like Hardy, he was looking for a solution to the problem of theodicy, a way of not being 'appalled by the long story of cosmic suffering'.[59]

For Hardy, as for many others, the First World War made it much harder to defend any kind of optimism about human affairs. The ultimately progressive dynamic of *The Dynasts* seemed unwarranted. But Hardy's response was not that of a betrayed and disappointed secular humanist so much as that of the puzzled and God-haunted man of Christian nurture that he had always been, still trying to make some sense of what he read in his Bible. On Christmas Day 1914 he wrote that 'the present times are an absolute negation of Christianity'.[60]

---

[58] Hardy to Caleb Williams Saleeby, 21 December 1914, *Collected Letters* V, pp. 69–70.

[59] Hardy, *Literary Notebooks* II, pp. 353–7. The press-cutting about Campbell's 'New Theology' is inscribed in Hardy's hand 'very like the "Immanent Will" of the Dynasts'.

[60] Hardy to Rev. E. C. Leslie, 25 December 1914, *Collected Letters* V, p. 72.

6

Mary Ward and the Problems of History

Mary Arnold, better known as Mary Ward or Mrs Humphry Ward, made the most of her connection with her famous uncle, Matthew Arnold, and the family tradition of social, religious, historical, and literary earnestness. But in literature, as in everything else, family connections and family loyalties can be a mixed blessing. It was unfair of Oscar Wilde to describe *Robert Elsmere* (1888), Mary Ward's most important novel, as 'simply Arnold's *Literature and Dogma* with the literature left out', but he was sorely tempted.[1] Impaling two Arnolds on a single barb was too good an opportunity to miss. Like Lytton Strachey a generation later, Wilde could never resist the opportunity to tilt his lance at the old-fashioned but still-lingering tradition of Victorian moral earnestness, and attempts to renegotiate traditional thinking about religion and the Bible were a familiar aspect of that earnestness.

Ward was variously behind and ahead of her times in ways that have intrigued and annoyed modern critics such as Judith Wilt.[2] She was radical and unconventional in her religious outlook, creatively engaged with reimaginings of the biblical sublime and the messianic and with the future of the Church in the modern world. But the conservatism of some of her social views, particularly her opposition to votes for women and her hereditary Victorian high seriousness, continued into the reign of Victoria's grandson George V, were a source of exasperation to young iconoclasts such as Strachey. This exasperation helped to explain his savagely unfair

---

[1] Oscar Wilde, 'The Decay of Lying: A Dialogue', *The Nineteenth Century* 25 (January 1889), 40.

[2] See Judith Wilt, *Behind her Times: Transition England in the Novels of Mary Arnold Ward* (Charlottesville, Virginia: University of Virginia Press, 2005).

136   *Mary Ward and the Problems of History*

attack on her grandfather Dr Thomas Arnold in *Eminent Victorians* (1918). 'The Doctor' had indeed been formidably eminent and though he died before Mary was born he had left a daunting legacy to later Arnolds: Oxford Professor of Modern History, classical scholar, liberal Broad Churchman, public moralist, legendary headmaster of Rugby School, and, for his pupils at least, iconic embodiment of terrible righteousness.[3]

The most prominent Arnold in the next generation was Mary's agnostic uncle, Matthew Arnold, another public moralist whose literary and ethical rereadings of the Bible had considerable influence on her. As well as writing *Literature and Dogma* (1873) and *God and the Bible* (1875), not to mention *Culture and Anarchy* (1869), Uncle Matt had also been Oxford Professor of Poetry, a leading poet and a pioneering Inspector of Schools. Another uncle, William Delafield Arnold, had been Director of Education in the Punjab and author of *Oakfield, or, Fellowship in the East* (1854), a severely moral novel about life in India. Mary's father, Thomas Arnold the younger, had been an Inspector of Schools in Tasmania and, later, Professor of English Literature in what became University College Dublin, producing a much-reprinted *Manual of English Literature, Historical and Critical* (1862), substantial editions of John Wycliffe (1869–71) and *Beowulf* (1876), and other scholarly works in the intervals of vacillation between Catholicism and Protestantism. His sister Jane, Mary's godmother, married the politician William Forster, who introduced the great Education Act of 1870 and served a bruising term as Chief Secretary for Ireland.[4]

Mary Arnold, who wrote as Mrs Humphry Ward, her married name, inherited the burden of Arnoldian earnestness to such an extent that in 1904 (when she was already a well-established middle-aged writer and a public figure in her own right) the cartoonist Max Beerbohm represented her as a solemn young girl reproaching her Uncle Matthew for frivolity: 'Why, Uncle Matthew, oh why,

---

[3] For Strachey, Mary Ward, and Thomas Arnold, see Michael Holroyd, *Lytton Strachey: A Critical Biography*, 2 vols (London: Heinemann, 1967–8), I, p. 443; for Arnold's effect on his pupils, see A. P. Stanley, *Life and Correspondence of Thomas Arnold, D.D.*, 2 vols (London: Fellowes, 1845), I, p. 165.

[4] There is a collective biography of the Arnolds by Meriol Trevor, *The Arnolds: Thomas Arnold and His Family* (London: Bodley Head, 1973); see also Bernard Bergonzi, *A Victorian Wanderer: the Life of Thomas Arnold the Younger* (Oxford: Oxford University Press, 2003).

Mary Ward and the Problems of History 137

will not you be always wholly serious?'[5] Even if the wistful poet had turned mocking social commentator in prose works such as *Culture and Anarchy* this exaggerates the differences between them. The sombrely reflective Arnold of 'Stanzas from the Grande Chartreuse' or 'Dover Beach' who had elegized the ever-receding sea of faith was much admired by his niece, and much quoted in the novels. But it is true that there was nothing remotely frivolous about Mary Ward. The dedicated social work of her hero Robert Elsmere among the poor of London was matched by her own energetic involvement with the Passmore Edwards Settlement as organizer, fund-raiser, and publicist. According to the *Daily News* of 11 February 1898 this was 'Robert Elsmere's Scheme at Work'. Her particular successes were play-centres for children, summer schools, and special schools for the physically handicapped, which proved a model for the rest of the country.[6] As if that was not enough, she was also a pioneer of higher education for women, secretary of an 'Association for the Education of Women' founded in 1877, and a moving force behind Somerville Hall in Oxford, opened in 1879.[7]

Her own higher education was completely informal but extremely rigorous. Irregularly taught at the various schools she attended, as a young woman she set herself to properly learn Latin, French, and German when she realized she would need them for scholarly work.[8] She also learnt Spanish; classical Greek came a little later. It was fortunate for her that the family had moved to Oxford in 1865 and that she continued to live in Oxford for a time after her marriage to Humphry Ward, Fellow of Brasenose, in 1872. After she left school in 1867 she was taken in hand by a family friend, Mark Pattison, the immensely learned Rector of Lincoln College, one of the contributors to *Essays and Reviews*. From him she learned that texts, ideas, and scholarship are all shaped by history and need to be studied critically and in context. He himself had written authoritatively about eighteenth-century religious thought and was embarked on a massive history of European learning since the Renaissance. He encouraged her to develop an academic specialism, to 'get to the bottom of

---

[5] Included in Max Beerbohm, *The Poet's Corner* (London: Heinemann, 1904), plate 4.

[6] John Sutherland, *Mrs Humphry Ward: Eminent Victorian, Pre-eminent Edwardian* (Oxford: Oxford University Press, 1990), pp. 214–29.

[7] Sutherland, *Mrs Humphry Ward*, pp. 63–5.

[8] Sutherland, *Mrs Humphry Ward*, p. 29.

138   *Mary Ward and the Problems of History*

something', and she began work in the Bodleian Library on early Spanish literature and history.[9] Her early article on the Spanish *Poema del Cid*, published in *Macmillan's Magazine* in 1871, demonstrates that by the age of twenty she had developed a strong historical sense, an awareness that expressive possibilities are historically conditioned, limited by their moment. Twelfth-century Spain had needed heroes to protect true believers against the Moors, and the heroic *Poema del Cid* was 'the only possible expression of the mind of Spain at the time'.[10] That this principle of historical limitation and conditioning could apply to the religious as well as the secular past, to the history of religious thought as well as to intellectual history, had already been suggested by Pattison and other contributors to *Essays and Reviews*, and it was a lesson the young Mary Arnold carried into the writing of *Robert Elsmere* and its rather belated sequel, *The Case of Richard Meynell* (1911).

Early Spanish history was particularly dangerous territory for those of conventionally religious nurture. The superstitious credulity of the churchmen of the period had stimulated the lethal ironies of Edward Gibbon in *Decline and Fall*, and the more general issue of the evidential weakness and the unreliable nature of testimony in religious matters had been discussed by Hume.[11] The traditional Protestant solution to the problem of extravagant miracle-stories in the early and medieval Church was to distinguish between the apostolic period covered by the New Testament and everything that came after, blaming the Catholic Church rather than the Christianity of the Bible for strange legends and pious frauds. But Gibbon was unwilling to draw such a sharp distinction. Like Hume before him, he looked for evidence that could be tested, and he could find no external confirmation of even biblical miracles. Enlightenment scepticism, particularly as applied to the New Testament account of Christian origins, migrated to Germany and then came back to England through George

---

[9] Mary Ward, *A Writer's Recollections* (London: Collins, 1918), pp. 105–6.

[10] Mary Arnold, 'The Poem of the Cid', *Macmillan's Magazine* 24 (October 1871), 486. This is almost her only work published under the name of Mary Arnold: she married Humphry Ward in 1872 and her subsequent work was signed Mary Ward or Mrs Humphry Ward.

[11] Edward Gibbon, *Decline and Fall of the Roman Empire* (1776–88), ed. David Womersley, 3 vols (London, 1994), chapter 37; David Hume, *An Enquiry concerning Human Understanding* [1748], ed. Peter Millican, World's Classics (Oxford: Oxford University Press, 2007), Section X 'Of Miracles'.

Mary Ward and the Problems of History 139

Eliot's translation of David Strauss's demythologizing life of Jesus. Strauss was an influence on the rationalizing *Vie de Jésus* (1863), the first volume of *Origines du Christianisme* (1863–83) by Ernest Renan, whom Mary Ward first met in 1874.[12] These disturbing works were soon followed by the home-grown *Ecce Homo* (1866) by the historian J. R. Seeley, which Mary Ward read in 1874. This was also the year in which an anonymous writer, eventually identified as W. R. Cassels, published *Supernatural Religion: An Inquiry into the Divine Revelation*, attacking the authenticity of the New Testament and sparking off lively and prolonged controversy.[13] For Strauss and Renan, and for other advanced thinkers, the main obstacle to taking biblical narrative at face value was miracle and the supernatural. This was the view adopted by Matthew Arnold in *Literature and Dogma* (1873). For him, miracles did not happen and the supernatural had to be discounted: the natural truth of Christianity as a life-enhancing moral system was its best defence. The Bible was still important, but it needed to be approached with critical discrimination rather than taken literally or treated as some kind of magical book.

Mary Ward trod a similar path away from Christian orthodoxy, retaining a strong emotional attachment to the humanity and ethical example of Christ while distancing herself from miracles and Trinitarian dogma. What she had in common with George Eliot and Thomas Hardy was a strong moral and imaginative commitment to the spirit if not the letter of the New Testament. But this did not show immediately. Her Spanish studies brought her to the attention of other Oxford scholars. Spanish expertise was hard to find and in 1878 she was invited to contribute articles on early Spanish churchmen to the magisterial *Dictionary of Christian Biography* edited by William Smith and Henry Wace (1877–87). These included an account of Montanus, Bishop of Toledo, and a long, learned, and rather dry discussion of the historical works of Isidore of Seville. This was solid, exacting, scholarly work. Her fellow contributors, including her father, were among the leading scholars of the day. The 209 articles she eventually completed would not have disgraced any

---

[12] Sutherland, *Mrs Humphry Ward*, p. 66; Ward, *A Writer's Recollections*, pp. 155–7.

[13] Ward, *A Writer's Recollections*, p. 165. Among the more effective responses to *Supernatural Religion* was a series of articles in the *Contemporary Review* by the leading New Testament scholar J. B. Lightfoot.

140   *Mary Ward and the Problems of History*

university-bred scholar embarked on an academic career. There could be little formal recognition of her achievement in a university that was only beginning to acknowledge the possibility of women students and tutors, but she was delighted when in 1883 Oxford invited her to examine in modern languages, the first woman examiner of men in either Oxford or Cambridge.[14]

This early historical work stimulated reflection on moral and religious history as recounted in the Bible and illustrated changing ways of reading it. It deeply affected her practice as a novelist, encouraging narratives that went beyond the novelist's usual preoccupation with personal development to address larger issues of social and historical process, as George Eliot had done, prompting her to respect and assess cultural and intellectual evidences. The interest in evidence was unsurprising. She was knowledgeable and intellectually curious to start with, and had made the most of living in Oxford as the daughter and then the wife of university teachers. The historians J. R. Green, E. A. Freeman, and Mandell Creighton were all personal friends. The redoubtable William Stubbs, Regius Professor of Modern History, had personally checked and approved her work for the *Dictionary of Christian Biography*. Uncle Matthew had given her introductions to various European scholars, and the great Sanskrit scholar Friedrich Max Müller, an Oxford neighbour, had supplied an introduction to Renan. One sometimes feels she could have supplied a bibliography for almost anything, instantly. She had breathed the atmosphere of critical scholarship and progressive social thought from an early age. In addition to her friendship with Mark Pattison she had met that other notorious *Essays and Reviews* contributor Benjamin Jowett, Master of Balliol, and the influential political philosopher and preacher of lay sermons T. H. Green, a fellow of Balliol, who appears as Grey in *Robert Elsmere*. She also encountered and helped to entertain famous visitors such as George Eliot and the French historian Hippolyte Taine.[15] The vexed question of the nature of evidence for miracles in the tradition of the Church, in and after the days of the first apostles, is important to the plot of abandoned orthodoxy in both *Robert Elsmere* and *Richard Meynell*, but evidence itself is central to her work as a novelist, as it was for George Eliot. Her

---

[14] Sutherland, *Mrs Humphry Ward*, p. 73.
[15] Sutherland, *Mrs Humphry Ward*, pp. 35, 60, 66; Ward, *A Writer's Recollections*, pp. 85–6.

Mary Ward and the Problems of History   141

novels were as solidly evidence-based as the best historical writing of the time, drawing on extensive reading as well as personal observation and experience, and what she did not already know she made it her business to find out.

Early evidence gathering can be documented from her notebook entries for *Robert Elsmere*.[16] The next novel, *The History of David Grieve* (1892), further illustrates the process of writing fiction as cultural and moral history. Early in the narrative the protagonist encounters local recollections of the Brontës at Haworth, much as Mrs Gaskell would have done for her *Life of Charlotte Brontë*, presumably a source for this part of the novel, and that leads him on to read *Shirley* and discover reformist intellectual and political ambitions, which launch him on his career as a radical secularist.[17] The author, herself interested in if not fully committed to secularist agendas, makes sure that the right names are dropped into the text in the right places to chart David's progress: in the first chapter of the novel, still a child, still a believer, he is reading an old translation of Josephus, the main source for first-century Jewish history. But he runs away to Manchester and encounters the sceptics of an earlier generation: Diderot, Voltaire, Tom Paine, Richard Carlile, the much-prosecuted radical publisher, and then, later, the posthumously published Wolfenbüttel fragments that had raised such difficulties in Germany about the historical truth of scripture.[18]

The author had done at least some of the reading she attributes to her hero, and more besides. The radical Samuel Bamford is mentioned in passing in the novel, which suggests she has taken a look at Samuel Bamford's *Passages in the Life of a Radical* (1844).[19] Alexander Somerville's *The Autobiography of a Working Man* (1848) provided her with details of the career of another radical autodidact, this time a Scot, which are taken into her own narrative and are reliable

---

[16] For the *Robert Elsmere* Notebook, see William S. Peterson, *Victorian Heretic: Mrs Humphrey Ward's Robert Elsmere* (Leicester: Leicester University Press, 1976), Appendix A, pp. 213–220.

[17] Mary Ward, *The History of David Grieve* (London: Smith and Elder, 1892), book 1, chapter 7, pp. 77–8. There is no scholarly edition of this or of many of Ward's novels and the 1911 Westmoreland edition of her works is incomplete and issued without her direct supervision, so if there is no scholarly edition references are to first editions.

[18] Ward, *David Grieve*, book 1, chapter 1, p. 6; book 2, chapter 2, pp. 135–6, and chapter 4, p. 159; book 4 chapter 10, p. 555.

[19] Ward, *David Grieve*, book 2, chapter 4, p. 159.

142   *Mary Ward and the Problems of History*

evidence of that kind of life. She also talked to working men such as the printer Frederick Rogers and was able to assemble evidence for the Manchester section of the novel through conversations with her brother William, a journalist on the *Manchester Guardian*.[20] Later in the novel, a course of reading in recent French literature prepares her protagonist for new experiences in bohemian Paris, and again the right names are dropped to establish the rather raffish cultural ambience for which it appears that the author herself has little sympathy. David's growing sense of cultural and moral difference from the stricter world of his youth is reinforced by encountering fictional heroes and heroines for whom 'marriage does not apparently exist'. He has read enough French novels to know something in advance about the life and work of French artists, the Salon, and the jury system. Voltaire, Diderot, and d'Holbach have yielded pride of place in his mind to George Sand. There are references to Henry Murger's *Scènes de la vie de Bohème*, Octave Feuillet (mentioned again, disapprovingly, in her later novel *The Case of Richard Meynell*), and Flaubert's *Madame Bovary*.[21] The fictitious artist Regnault's new painting of Salome and Herodias—strange, brilliant, pitiless—haunts David's imagination for days. This evidence of the *avant-garde* is (for once) fabricated, but it is carefully done to make it anticipate contemporary culture: the Francophile Oscar Wilde's disturbing French play *Salome* was first produced in 1892, the year before the novel was published.

In other novels, well-documented reference to earlier patterns of historical or moral development could provide a useful way into anatomies of modern times. One model was supplied by the painter William Hogarth in his popular, richly detailed, visual narratives of *A Harlot's Progress* (1730), *A Rake's Progress* (1732–3), and *Industry and Idleness* (1747). Even without the captions, successive paintings in the same series told their own story: the last two pictures of *Industry and Idleness* show the idle apprentice hanged at Tyburn and the industrious apprentice acclaimed as Lord Mayor of London. The implied inevitability of the sequences for particular character

---

[20] Frederick Rogers, *Labour, Life and Literature: Some Memories of Sixty Years* [1913], ed. David Rubinstein (Brighton: Harvester, 1973), pp. 287–8; Sutherland, *Mrs Humphry Ward*, p. 134.

[21] Ward, *David Grieve*, book 2, chapter 10, pp. 242–5; book 3, chapter 2, p. 270, and chapter 5, pp. 299.

Mary Ward and the Problems of History   143

types—the roads to success or, more often, disaster—allow the morbidly self-aware Langham in *Robert Elsmere* to insert himself into a 'dismal Hogarthian series, image leading to image, calamity to calamity', to imagine the worst if he goes ahead with marriage to the rebellious and beautiful musician Rose.[22] But moral narrative in Mary Ward can be more complex than it is in Hogarth, and surrendering to a faint-hearted sense of historical inevitability may itself be the road to disaster. Rose's sister Catherine, married to Robert Elsmere when he was still an Anglican clergyman, is profoundly hostile to the heterodox ethical theism her husband gradually espouses, and that places the marriage under great strain, but the marriage is saved not just by mutual love but by Catherine's emotional intelligence, a shared if differently theorized commitment to suffering humanity, and a refusal to accept that moral or marital disaster is inevitable.

More generally, the narrative of *Robert Elsmere* suggests that the death of God may not after all be historically inevitable, even if science, scholarship, and problems about the evidence for miracles suggest orthodox Christianity has run its course: perhaps the cause of religion can be saved through the kind of heroic reorientation and reimagining of essential Christianity and the moral teaching of the Bible attributed to Elsmere himself. This was a characteristic Arnoldian theme: Mary's grandfather Thomas Arnold had given it as his opinion that: 'The Church, as it now stands, no human power can save.'[23] But that had not been acquiescence in a simple narrative of inevitable decline and fall so much as a deeply religious statement and a plea for rethinking the nature and function of the Church.

Another Hogarthian series, *Marriage à la Mode* (1743–5), rebuked cynical marriage for social advantage or financial gain by illustrating the stages of the disastrous outcome. This provided a basis for *Daphne, or Marriage à la Mode* (1909), one of Mary Ward's less successful novels. This is a rather stern moralizing narrative of contemporary life, which dissects a modern marriage undertaken for the wrong reasons between an impoverished English aristocrat and a fabulously wealthy self-willed American. The epigraph from Herrick emphasizes the age-old yet constantly renewed theme of marrying for money:

---

[22] Ward, *Robert Elsmere*, ed. Rosemary Ashton, World's Classics (Oxford: Oxford University Press, 1987), chapter 36, p. 434.

[23] Stanley, *Life and Correspondence of Thomas Arnold, D.D.*, I, p. 287.

144   *Mary Ward and the Problems of History*

> When all birds else do of their music fail
> Money's the still-sweet-singing nightingale.

But once again Ward complicates the simple Hogarthian narrative of inevitable consequences: in this case the unhappy outcome could have been avoided. The husband comes to love the wife he married for money, and the marriage might have worked but for a fatal combination of groundless jealousy, the unscrupulous use of wealth, overpermissive American divorce laws, and what the author rather mean-spiritedly presents as a godless and heartless sense of female entitlement. This aspect of the novel is really a covert attack on what Ward sees as the thinking behind contemporary agitation for votes for women, an issue on which she had taken a very public conservative stance in the Women's National Anti-Suffrage League established in 1908, with disastrous consequences for her reputation in progressive circles.[24]

It is tempting to think that Mary Ward had recourse to pre-existent narrative patterns and adapted old stories because she had difficulty in constructing plots of her own. But even if there is some truth in this it is not the only reason. Niall Ferguson and other 'counterfactual' historians have demonstrated the benefits of rerunning historical sequences on a 'what if' basis as a way of testing alleged inevitabilities and the role of contingency, a technique whimsically anticipated in James Thurber's short story in the *New Yorker* 'If Grant had been drinking at Appomatox' (1930).[25] In effect Ward does something similar as a way of illuminating the nature of social and historical processes: if Chateaubriand, journalist, dreamer, diplomat, and author of *Le Génie du Christianisme* (1802), or Byron and the notorious Lady Caroline Lamb (1785–1828), or the humbly born portrait painter George Romney (1734–1802) who neglected and practically disowned his wife for thirty years while he moved in fashionable society, or the glittering Holland House circle (active 1797–1845),

---

[24] Sutherland, *Mrs Humphry Ward*, pp. 299–304.

[25] James Thurber, 'If Grant had been drinking at Appomattox', *New Yorker*, 6 December 1930, collected in Thurber, *The Middle-aged Man on the Flying Trapeze* (New York: Harper, 1935); Niall Ferguson, ed., *Virtual History: Alternatives and Counterfactuals* (London: Picador, 1997); see also David Sylvan and Stephen Majeski, 'A Methodology for the Study of Historical Counterfactuals', *International Studies Quarterly* 42 (1998), 79–108.

Mary Ward and the Problems of History 145

had lived at the beginning of the twentieth century how would things have developed? What could be attributed to historical contingency, the particular circumstances of their day, and what would have happened anyway, in any age? These are the questions that lie behind Ward's novels *Eleanor* (1900), *The Marriage of William Ashe* (1905), *Fenwick's Career* (1906), and *Eltham House* (1915) respectively.

Biography and history reconstructed as contemporary experiments in living in this way have at least the potential to illuminate both past and present and to say something about the way the world has been changing, or has not significantly changed, or not for the better. These novels suggest that education and opportunity might now be better, particularly for women, but not invariably, and not always to their advantage. The progressive and secular but not necessarily anti-religious project of the growing good of the world, which Ward inherited from George Eliot, has demonstrably still some way to go. Self-sacrificing women are still likely to be victims of unscrupulous and ambitious men. Eleanor Burgoyne, the heroine of *Eleanor*, is a good example. She is the inspiring friend and literary assistant of the brilliant, unreliable, egotistical writer and politician Edward Manisty. As Peter Collister has pointed out, Manisty corresponds to Chateaubriand, also brilliant, unreliable, and egotistical, and Eleanor corresponds to his once-beloved Pauline de Beaumont, who helped him with the writing of his celebrated *Le Génie du Christianisme*.[26] Manisty rather ungratefully falls in love with a younger woman, Lucy Fox, just as Chateaubriand had transferred his affections to Madame de Custine.

But more interesting than Chateaubriand's contribution to the plot is the attempt to provide Manisty with a literary project representing an updated Italian version of *Le Génie du Christianisme*. Edmund Burke's *Reflections on the Revolution in France* (1790) had deplored the revolutionary onslaught on religion, and there are Burkean moments in the post-revolutionary Chateaubriand when he urges a reawakening of the religious sense and reveals a fugitive romantic nostalgia for the old order and the old stability in Church and state. His book certainly did him no harm politically when the French monarchy was restored after the fall of Napoleon. Chateaubriand's emphasis on the socio-political significance of religion in the nation,

---

[26] Peter Collister, 'Mrs Humphry Ward's *Eleanor*: a late-Victorian portrait of Chateaubriand and Pauline de Beaumont', *Neophilologus* 65 (October 1981), 622–39.

146 *Mary Ward and the Problems of History*

and on religious experience rather than religious dogma or biblical literalism, commended itself to the Arnoldian in Mary Ward, but could it work a century later, in the contemporary Italian context—or had the world moved on? The Italian *risorgimento*, the fight for modern Italy against the temporal power of the papacy and the conservative Catholic tradition associated with it, had appealed to George Eliot and it fascinated English liberals such as the young Cambridge historian G. M. Trevelyan, the biographer of Garibaldi, who would soon marry Mary Ward's daughter, Janet. But despite earlier triumphs, modern Italy was currently in the doldrums and suffering reverses in Abyssinia. What could be done to preserve the young Italian nation? Manisty's book proposes turning the clock back and abandoning the project of secular modernity altogether. It embodies a counter-revolutionary Burkean vision for modern Italy that is profoundly if cynically traditionalist and neo-Catholic. Even he comes to realize that what worked in early nineteenth-century France in the aftermath of the revolution will not work in modern Italy where neither the dogma nor the politics associated with traditional Catholicism command the respect they did in the *ancien régime*. The historian in Mary Ward counterfactually transplants Chateaubriand to modern Italy to help her readers to see that, despite Catholic claims to the contrary, religious ideas and institutions either change or lose their hold over time.

More rigid and conservative in morals than in religion or politics, Mary Ward could nevertheless register moral changes. Morality might be less lax, at least in public, than it was a hundred years earlier, but it was not always more compassionate or more even-handed. Her Byron figure Geoffrey Cliffe, the amoral, dangerously attractive traveller and writer in *The Wooing of William Ashe*, still has the capacity to wreck other lives with comparative impunity (though by way of compensation the author consigns him to a remote foreign war in Bosnia and makes sure there is nothing heroic or Byronic about his death). The wayward and unstable Kitty Ashe, fatally in love with him—corresponding to the eccentric, outrageous, and damaged Lady Caroline Lamb—is less indulged by society, more helpless, and more manipulated by men, and ultimately more of a victim than her Regency counterpart. Where Lady Caroline Lamb survived into her forties, the turbulent life of the fictional Kitty Ashe is cut short in her twenties. William Ashe himself, the wronged husband and statesman corresponding to the historical William Lamb, who

Mary Ward and the Problems of History 147

eventually became prime minister as Lord Melbourne, is a more vulnerable, less Olympian, less worldly, figure, more in need of the domestic support he does not have.

Fenwick's Career gives greater agency to an ill-treated woman, the wife of an ambitious and abrasive artist who leaves her behind when he moves to London to seek his fortune. Humphry Ward, no longer an Oxford tutor, was now a journalist and art critic and he collaborated on a study of Romney, published in 1904, which gave Mary Ward the outline for her novel.[27] But where Romney's long-deserted wife seems to have been able to do little about her situation Fenwick's more modern wife, misinformed by gossip, misreading her husband's prolonged absence as infidelity and deliberate desertion, has the spirit and the opportunity to take herself off to a new life in Canada with her daughter. If she has suffered, Fenwick suffers too, feeling she has deprived him of his daughter. This introduces a kind of symmetry missing from the original narrative: when reconciliation eventually takes place, after various misfortunes and misunderstandings, each partner is represented as having something to forgive: each needs the other. This conservative vindication of the institution of marriage, given some plausibility by shortening the interval of separation from thirty years to twelve, is reinforced by the character and example of Ward's Louise de Pastourelles. Where Romney was long enslaved by an unscrupulous married woman, Emma Hamilton, now remembered chiefly as Nelson's mistress, Fenwick's generous friend Louise is rather different, even if his wife is led to believe that she is another Lady Hamilton. She is in fact another deserted wife, married to a scoundrel who has left her for an actress, but she still feels committed to her husband and will not consider divorcing him unless he requests it.

Modern divorce and female empowerment inside and outside marriage are considered again in *Eltham House*. Women are represented as now politically powerful and influential behind the scenes, for good or ill, irrespective of the right to vote. Virginia Woolf, who violently disliked Mary Ward, a friend of her father's, savagely condemned the novel in a letter as a 'vile book' by a 'mangy old hack',[28] but it deserves more respect than it has usually been given. It is a kind

---

[27] Humphry Ward and William Roberts, *Romney: a Biographical and Critical Essay*, 2 vols (London: Agnew, 1904).

[28] *Letters of Virginia Woolf*, ed. Quentin Bell and Angelica Garnett, 3 vols (London: Hogarth Press, 1975–77), II, p. 68.

148 *Mary Ward and the Problems of History*

of throwback to the aristocratic glamour of the 'silver fork' school of fiction developed by Bulwer Lytton and Disraeli in an earlier age, and has indeed rather too much beauty and wealth in it, as an unnamed friend of the author's cited in the Foreword had observed. But it is a humane and well-crafted novel, much more generous and compassionate towards divorce than *Daphne* a few years earlier. It explores the gendered and spiteful nature of social exclusion as it affects the divorced heroine Caroline, a brilliant and energetic political hostess, and her wealthy, politically ambitious second husband Alex Wing who eventually succeeds to a peerage.

The glittering couple are modelled on the Hollands. Elizabeth Vassall Fox, Lady Holland (1770–1845) abandoned her first husband in 1796 to run away with the third Baron Holland (1773–1840). The deserted husband was eventually persuaded (or bribed) to divorce her. Such matters had much less impact on political life in the eighteenth century. While society women did not call on Lady Holland any more than they did on Caroline Wing, Lord Holland's career in public life was apparently unaffected by the scandal: he was included in various Whig ministries and received at Court. In a later age, Alex Wing is snubbed by his party and seen as an electoral liability, at least for the time being, though there are hints that women still pay more heavily than men in such matters and that in time he might still be allowed to make his mark. Both Holland House and Eltham House were set up to be great political centres, but the Wings at Eltham House could not succeed as the Hollands at Holland House had done because of censoriousness, particularly among politically influential women, towards public revelations of adultery of the kind that had ruined the political careers of Charles Stewart Parnell and Charles Dilke a few years before. While the reader is left in no doubt that Caroline has sinned, Ward shows how she is maligned and misrepresented, and made to pay a disproportionately heavy price for her sin. There is little sympathy for the unscrupulous intrigue and inhumanity of respectable society women, or the censorious 'Nonconformist conscience', or Caroline's intolerable and harshly self-righteous first husband who makes her a stranger to her own child. Where the Holland House story ended well, the Eltham House story ends badly: the marriage more or less falls apart when Alec's impatient and unrealistic political ambitions are frustrated, despite his vast fortune and his wife's heroic support. Caroline dies while still in her twenties, her life and social disgrace a sacrifice to an insensitive

Mary Ward and the Problems of History 149

husband and lover unworthy of her, whereas Lady Holland outlived her husband and died in her seventies.

Deeply conscious of history and of historical process as well as of contemporary social problems, committed to promoting and imaginatively projecting an ultimately religious vision of the growing good of the world, Mary Ward aspired in fiction and in life to deliver the present from what could now be perceived as the oppressive burdens and inadequate intellectual horizons inherited from the past, and to present to an expanding democratic readership the challenges and benefits of rational reform in the state and in social and religious thought. Acutely aware of how her father's vacillations between rival more or less doctrinaire constructions of Christianity had not just damaged his career but effectively destroyed his marriage, and impoverished and broken up his family, she had her own doubts about orthodox Christianity. Yet she had no doubt about the urgent work that needed to be done in the world, particularly in areas of massive social deprivation such as the East End of London. Oscar Wilde was thinking partly of her when he spoke disparagingly of the 'great and daily increasing school of novelists for whom the sun always rises in the East End'.[29] The religiously inspired sense of social mission that had animated Christian socialists such as Charles Kingsley and F. D. Maurice in the 'hungry' forties might need a different theoretical and metaphysical basis if one could no longer be quite so sure of the historical basis of the gospels and the perhaps dated affirmations of the Thirty-Nine Articles, but the sense of social mission had not gone away. In cases of acute social need it should still be possible to mobilize the ethical and humanist residue of traditional Christian teaching, what Seeley's *Ecce Homo* had untheologically described as the 'Enthusiasm of Humanity, the essential spirit of Christianity'.[30]

This mobilization is the project underlying Ward's most celebrated novel, *Robert Elsmere*, widely discussed for years afterwards not just as a novel but as a challenging contribution to religious discussion. Gladstone's long review in the *Nineteenth Century* was one of many. The book merited a chapter all to itself in T. G. Selby's *Theology of Modern Fiction* (1896) and another a little later in Samuel Law Wilson's *Theology of Modern Literature* (1899). Long before that

---

[29] Wilde, 'The Decay of Lying', p. 38.

[30] J. R. Seeley, *Ecce Homo* (London: Macmillan, 1865), p. 249.

150   *Mary Ward and the Problems of History*

the furore had spread from Britain to North America and Australia.[31] None of her later works attracted the same degree of attention. None was quite so successful and effective in combining the post-Christian narrative possibilities of the quasi-messianic, the sublime, and the secular pilgrimage. She went on to create other self-sacrificing reformers, apostolic if not fully messianic, notably her fictional alter ego the passionate and strong-willed Marcella Boyce in *Marcella* (1894) and its sequel *Sir George Tressady* (1896), who trains as a nurse and equips herself to engage with the social and economic problems of the day, but such activities were usually kept more or less separate from the issue of religion in crisis. There are versions or intuitions of the sublime in other novels. The Niagara Falls provide a stupendous and rather obscurely significant backdrop for the closing chapters of *Daphne*, though even they fail to lift the novel above mediocrity. The rare beauty of a summer evening among the Westmoreland hills elicits a renewed sense of hope and love from Fenwick's damaged soul at the end of *Fenwick's Career*, though this is something of a set piece apart from the rest of the novel. The pilgrim theme tends to be either ironic or problematic in many novels of doubt because the point of the pilgrimage has ceased to be self-evident. J. A. Froude's *The Nemesis of Faith* (1849), perhaps the best-known earlier novel of doubt and spiritual quest, had registered intellectual and psychological barriers to conventional Christian belief, which led to a kind of moral paralysis. But Froude's narrative could not move on from that point. It had not attempted to work out an effective post-Christian social ethics, to continue the secular pilgrimage on the far side of the slough of despond, finding it easier to consign the guilty and despairing protagonist to a monastery so he could end his days without having to make further decisions of his own.

Ward's *Elsmere* is bolder and more imaginatively resourceful than Froude's novel. It is also much longer. Her realist narrative, morally engaged, well populated, well observed, and carefully detailed, recalls the scope and ambition of George Eliot. But she also makes use of romance elements and dream-consciousness in the manner of Jean-

---

[31] See, for example, W. Stacey Chapman, *The Critical Method and the History of Testimony as Discoursed in 'Robert Elsmere'* (Melbourne: Samuel Mullen, 1888); Colonel [Robert] Ingersoll, *Repairing the Idols* (London: Progressive Publishing Co., 1888), reporting a *New York World* interview about *Robert Elsmere* with a leading American freethinker.

Mary Ward and the Problems of History   151

Paul, Bulwer Lytton, and the Brontës to create more space for religious or quasi-religious intuition. She makes Robert Elsmere start off as an exemplary and energetic young clergyman with a social conscience, whose parish work in Murewell bears some resemblance to that of Charles Kingsley in Eversley.[32] But he is soon confronted with the burden of more than a century of radical scepticism about traditional interpretations of the scriptures and the historical foundations of orthodox Christianity, culminating in the self-consciously scientific agnosticism of T. H. Huxley. Elsmere follows Ward's own path away from conventional belief in what seems at first a kind of negative pilgrimage. His growing interest in the nature of evidence in religious history and in the history of testimony, supported by the magnificent library and bloodless scepticism of Squire Wendover, takes him through the doubtful evidences of miracle and the supernatural, which had made Hume and Gibbon sneer into the more modern concerns articulated in *Essays and Reviews*. Wendover is partly modelled on Ward's own mentor Mark Pattison who had contributed to *Essays and Reviews*. Elsmere comes to share the sense of constantly developing and changing presentations of the truth of God—which another contributor, Rowland Williams, had commended in Baron Bunsen—and to feel increasingly uncomfortable with traditional theology. To the dismay and bewilderment of his devout but religiously conservative wife Catherine, loyal daughter of an old-fashioned evangelical clergyman, he feels his position as a beneficed clergyman of the Church of England is incompatible with his misgivings. The increasing strain on his marriage as religion drives Catherine and him further and further apart retains even the unbelieving modern reader's sympathy and interest. Narrow though Catherine may be, even in her distress she manifests a baffled love and generous humanity that prevent us from losing patience with her. In a sense, this tension even-handedly replays the corrosive religious differences between the author's parents, substituting the clash of rationalist theism with evangelicalism for the difference between Catholic and Protestant, itself a potentially tragic theme that Ward explored in her later novel, *Helbeck of Bannisdale* (1898). Elsmere resigns his living and despite indifferent health devotes himself to a

---

[32] Recorded in his widow's biography, F. E. Kingsley, *Charles Kingsley: His Letters and Memories of his Life*, 2 vols (London: Henry S. King, 1877).

152 *Mary Ward and the Problems of History*

more secular version of the Church's social mission in the East End of London.

A magnetic personality and an inspiring speaker, generous and self-sacrificing, endowed with natural gifts of intellect and infectious enthusiasm, Elsmere's gifts answer to the spiritual gifts or *charismata* of which Paul spoke in the New Testament and which Max Weber adapted for his own sociological purposes. He is one of the most 'charismatic' figures in Victorian fiction, represented as a much more compelling and successful version of that other unorthodox and self-sacrificing moral teacher Clym Yeobright in Hardy's *Return of the Native*. This may be one of the reasons why Hardy, progressive but glum, professed to see the doctrinal vagueness of what he called the 'Robert Elsmere school' as fair game for satire.[33] According to the gospel narrative Christ had the power to cast out devils and heal the sick, and passed it on to his disciples.[34] Seeley in *Ecce Homo* had rationalized such activity as the work of inspired individuals procuring good against the odds, working moral miracles by awakening good impulses in unlikely places.[35] Elsmere is presented as just such an inspired individual. The narrative stays just within the bounds of formal realism: Elsmere is not quite a miracle-worker but he is not very far removed from the romance figures who can lift evil spells. Despite his mental and spiritual turmoil he retains the gift of moral healing, metaphorically casting out devils in a manner that tacitly proposes a moral rather than miraculous reading of biblical exorcisms. He generously calms and helps his old enemy Henslowe, the corrupt and disgraced estate manager at Murewell, when they meet, so that 'the demon in Henslowe had been for the moment most strangely tamed after half an hour's talk'.[36] Little by little he emerges as a sub-messianic figure, set apart for special responsibility like the anointed figures of the Old Testament, subdued and hampered by still adverse circumstances and by his own indifferent health but contributing, if only a little, to the social and moral redemption of mankind in his own generation.

---

[33] Hardy to Frederick Harrison, 17 May 1888, *The Collected Letters of Thomas Hardy*, R. L. Purdy and M. Millgate (eds), 7 vols (Oxford: Clarendon Press, 1978–88), I, p. 176.

[34] Luke 8; 9:1.

[35] Seeley, *Ecce Homo*, chapter 20.

[36] Ward, *Robert Elsmere*, chapter 30, p. 367.

Mary Ward and the Problems of History   153

Near the end of the novel, exhausted and ill, the coherence of daylight certainties and realist narrative slips away from him as it would slip away from Hardy's Jude the Obscure in Christminster. He dreams he is on the brink of the river of death, described as 'that old familiar image', familiar from Bunyan. He sees old friends on the other side. But he feels no pang of separation for he knows he is about to join them.[37] His death has its own sublime mystery, which somehow gestures towards the portentous strangeness as well as the pain of Gethsemane and the crucifixion. Catherine and he have remained painfully divided in religious opinion, but perhaps there is a deeper spiritual reality, a vision of love that lies beyond opinion. Elsmere has taken a stand against literal belief in miracles, but a version of miracle, a trance or hallucination conveying a sense of the transcendent, comes to Catherine as Elsmere is dying. She has a kind of vision of the human Christ, the Son of man, who seems to beckon her. But she knows her life must be with Elsmere to the end. Perhaps that represents Christ for her. This intuition is immediately followed by her husband's sudden 'ecstasy of joy' as he relives his jubilant relief and thanksgiving when their child was born and her pain was over. After this shared moment of joy after pain, transcending all differences of dogma and conviction, he dies in her arms.[38] He and she have found their own version of Bunyan's Beulah, their own renewal of married fulfilment, their own good place.

There are other sublime moments in the novel that push beyond the limitations of realist convention. Wordsworth had articulated for post-romantic and even post-Christian readers the possibility of access to the numinous through nature, 'a sense sublime/Of something far more deeply interfused/Whose dwelling is the light of setting suns'.[39] His romantic and religious vision of 'nature's holy plan' attracted the derision of the post-Darwinian Hardy in *Tess of the d'Urbervilles*, but Mary Ward, like George Eliot before her, was more respectful. Her grandmother's home in Wordsworth's Lake District had been a special and happy place during her childhood, and the Lakeland fells provide an important point of origin in the first section

[37] Ward, *Robert Elsmere*, chapter 50, p. 565.
[38] Ward, *Robert Elsmere*, chapter 51, p. 576.
[39] William Wordsworth, 'Lines written a few miles above Tintern Abbey', lines 96–8, in William Wordsworth, *A Selection*, ed. Stephen Gill and Duncan Wu, Oxford Poetry Library (Oxford: Oxford University Press, 1994), p. 59.

154 *Mary Ward and the Problems of History*

of the novel, entitled 'Westmoreland'. A quotation from a Wordsworth sonnet sets the scene and helps to establish an atmosphere of religious possibility:

> It is a beauteous evening, calm and free,
> The holy time is quiet as a nun
> Breathless with adoration.[40]

The movement of nineteenth-century England from country to city, from simplicity to unmanageable complexity, from faith to doubt and whatever might lie beyond doubt, is recapitulated in the movement of the novel. Rural Westmoreland, where it begins, is where Robert and Catherine fall in love, and it is where the mercy and the love of God seem to be most apparent. They are manifest not just in Catherine's practical goodness among the poor but in a moment of special religious significance among the fells, without benefit of clergy, a kind of epiphany, what Wordsworth himself might have described as a 'spot of time'. Catherine retells a story she had heard from an old man who had been low in spirits, anxious about his ailing wife, when he had a kind of vision of Christ, a shining face appearing through the mist, giving him new hope and energy. Catherine is transfigured by the story she tells, and Robert is entranced by her telling of it, taken over by powerful feeling in which it would be difficult to disentangle religious sympathy and his growing love for Catherine.[41] Unfortunately religious certainty and uncomplicated personal happiness cannot last, any more than the traditional life of the pre-industrial countryside, and the action gradually moves to London and the contemporary problems of the East End.

Despite the apparently teleological ambition of the novel, its commitment to intellectual evolution and growth and its determinedly progressive assumption that in religion and society one must inexorably move away from the dead past towards a living future, there is a kind of inevitability in its hero's defeat and in the sense that all such heroes, in generation after generation, will suffer similar defeats. This is closer to Walter Benjamin's 'weak messianism' than the messianic passages of Isaiah. In a sense it anticipates Bishop Cauchon's despairing question in the epilogue of George Bernard Shaw's *St Joan* (1924): 'Must then a Christ perish in torment in every age to save those that

---

[40] Ward, *Robert Elsmere*, chapter 2, p. 30.
[41] Ward, *Robert Elsmere*, chapter 6, p. 88.

Mary Ward and the Problems of History 155

have no imagination?'[42] Perhaps the protest and the witness of messianic figures is what matters, not immediate practical success. Ward seems almost to have acknowledged as much in a subsequent, unfairly neglected novel, *The Case of Richard Meynell* (1911), set in a country parish a generation later when modernizing processes in religion have made further advances among thinking men but still animated and unified by a Wordsworthian sense of nature, the transcendent and the moral life of man. An epigraph from Wordsworth's *Ecclesiastical Sonnets* (1821) emphasizes both continuity and change:

> Truth fails not; but her outward forms that bear
> The longest date do melt like frosty rime.[43]

As a kind of base-line the narrative endorses and quotes Wordsworth's description in 'Tintern Abbey' of a good man's life with 'His little nameless unremembered acts/of kindness and of love.'[44] Meynell is not just a good man but another Elsmere figure, a gifted, indeed 'charismatic' clergyman, in love with Elsmere's daughter Mary. The son of an evangelical soldier, he may be partly modelled on that controversial and very liberal and progressive churchman W. H. Fremantle (1831–1916), grandson of a field marshal, evangelical in youth like Meynell, educated at Jowett's Balliol, eventually Dean of Ripon, author of *The Gospel of the Secular Life* (1882) and *The World as the Subject of Redemption* (1885). During his time in Oxford Fremantle had come under some of the same liberal influences as Ward herself, not just Jowett but A. P. Stanley, biographer and disciple of her grandfather Thomas Arnold. Meynell shares Fremantle's sense of the religious dignity and importance of enlightened citizenship and the common duties of ordinary secular life, and his Arnoldian vision of the inclusive nature of the National Church as the entire nation in its spiritual aspect. He unsuccessfully challenges religious orthodoxy in the name of progressive thought, with the result that, like Elsmere a generation earlier, he too finds himself in

---

[42] George Bernard Shaw, *Saint Joan* (London: Constable, 1924), p. 108.
[43] William Wordsworth, 'Mutability', lines 7–8, in *Ecclesiastical Sketches* (1822), *Sonnet Series and Itinerary Poems, 1820-1845*, ed. Geoffrey Jackson (Ithaca: Cornell University Press, 2004), p. 197.
[44] Mary Ward, *The Case of Richard Meynell* (London: Smith, Elder, 1911), chapter 10, p. 216.

156 *Mary Ward and the Problems of History*

the wilderness, though unlike Elsmere he tries to stay in the Church of England in order to reform it from within.

That difference in itself is evidence of Ward's keen sense of historical change within her own lifetime: she had lived to see liberal views make some headway inside and outside the Church of England. In Leo XIII's encyclical of 1893 *Providentissimus Deus* there had even been a limited acceptance on the part of the papacy of the need for modern critical methods of biblical study. Biblical criticism was now more widely accepted; new and controversial theological insights were being entertained not just in England and Germany but in Catholic France. The inclusive and socially and theologically liberal impulses within the Church of England, which can be traced back to Coleridge and Thomas Arnold, had been given some encouragement by A. P. Stanley and by the Christian Socialist Movement of the 1840s and 1850s associated with F. D. Maurice, Charles Kingsley, and Thomas Hughes before they were picked up by Fremantle and other Balliol men such as T. H. Green and Arnold Toynbee. Uncomfortable with the sometimes combative dogmatisms of the Church of England at both its evangelical and Anglo-Catholic extremes, moderates and liberals were sometimes collectively designated the 'Broad Church' party or movement, though many of them felt uncomfortable with the idea of representing yet another divisive church party when they were committed to an inclusive vision of the national church. The Broad Church vision, if there was such a thing, was written up by that most liberal and cultivated of clergymen, H. R. Haweis—musician, traveller, and popular lecturer H. R. Haweis—in his book *The Broad Church, or What is Coming* (1891). This included a Preface on *Robert Elsmere* suggesting that Elsmere and his creator belonged inside rather than outside the Church, a view increasingly shared by Mary Ward herself. An organized version of some of the Broad Church aspirations emerged with the foundation in 1898 of the Churchmen's Union for the Advancement of Religious Thought and the publication of its journal *The Modern Churchman* from 1911. Dean Fremantle was an early contributor. This initiative was not intended to be a new or breakaway movement so much as a way of bringing together clergymen of liberal outlook in theological matters. Richard Meynell belongs, or would like to belong, with just such a liberal grouping within rather than outside the Church of England.

Mary Ward and the Problems of History   157

There is a slightly confusing mingling in *The Case of Richard Meynell* of the real and the fictitious, of several generations of controversy, of English and continental concerns, and of Protestant and Catholic liberalisms and conservatisms. The actual problems of Rev. Charles Voysey (1828–1912), mentioned several times in the novel, provide one of the models for Meynell's difficulties, but Voysey had been driven out of the Church of England a generation earlier, in 1871, when his prosecution for heresy by the Archbishop of York had been upheld by the Judicial Committee of the Privy Council. The problems of the Catholic modernists such as George Tyrrell, who was expelled from the Jesuit order in 1906 and died in 1909, and Alfred Loisy, excommunicated in 1908, were of more recent date.

Unlike Elsmere, Meynell is a liturgical reformer, aware that the much-loved but time-worn Anglican prayer-book services were not only the product of a different age and a different mindset but incorporated some misreadings of scripture. George Eliot's description of Dinah Morris's informal open-air preaching in *Adam Bede* had tried to recover some of the quality of Christian faith and feeling in its earliest days, and liturgical reform was intended to produce the same effect. A Midlands clergyman writes to Meynell that, 'among our own people one seems to realize at last something of what the simplicity and sincerity of the first Christian feeling must have been! No "allowances" to make for scandalous mistranslations and misquotations...' He gives as an example a misappropriation of a passage in Job, the author of which, 'neither said what he was made to say in a famous passage, nor meant what he was supposed to mean'.[45] The passage begins, 'I know that my Redeemer liveth', familiar as the splendid soprano aria in Handel's *Messiah*. It was based on the resonant King James translation of an obscure and probably textually corrupt Old Testament passage, Job 19:25–7, which had been incorporated into the Anglican burial service. The very familiarity of both the burial service and Handel's music had encouraged generations of worshippers to take this as a prophetic reference to Christ the Redeemer and to the Christian hope of the resurrection, and long before that Jerome's Latin version had implied as much by using the term *redemptor*. But modern scholarship indicated that 'Redeemer' was a mistranslation and that some theologically less loaded term such as

---

[45] Ward, *The Case of Richard Meynell*, chapter 14, pp. 296–7.

158   *Mary Ward and the Problems of History*

'advocate' or 'vindicator' would be more accurate. Loisy's French translation of Job (1892) closely followed an earlier translation by the controversial Hebrew scholar Ernest Renan: both had used the phrase 'mon vengeur existe', 'my avenger (or vindicator) lives', and Loisy had attacked Jerome's tendentious conjectural reading of the text in his Introduction.[46] Meynell's modernizing project of prayer-book revision is smartly up-to-date: it had just been proposed by the American 'Ethical Culturalist' Dr Stanton Coit in his book *National Idealism and the Book of Common Prayer*, published in 1908 and garnished with an epigraph from the modernist George Tyrrell: 'The only infallible guardian of truth is the spirit of truthfulness.' But Coit was a much more uncompromising and iconoclastic humanist than either Meynell or Ward. He had indeed attacked *Robert Elsmere* as not radical enough, even 'likely to strengthen the position of ortho-doxy'.[47] His chapter on the burial service takes exception to much of the existing text but he seems more concerned with emotional uplift and literary value than philology or specifically religious meaning. Without apparent irony he selects and quotes suitably uplifting passages from Marcus Aurelius, William Cullen Bryant, Matthew Arnold, Shelley, and Walt Whitman, and suggests they should be adopted in a reconstructed burial service.[48] For all their reforming enthusiasm, Meynell and his associates were never as crass as this.

This incorporation (and sensible modification) of actual initiatives and the concerns of rebellious spirits in the churches over the past forty years is strategic, a way of suggesting that Meynell and those who join him in the stand he takes are representative of the growing momentum of liberal and radical religious thought and action, not just within the Church of England but across Europe. All these visionary rebels risk the ignominy and discomfort of exile from the Church they had hoped to serve and to reform. Catherine Elsmere sees that Meynell will soon be an exile and a wanderer, and he sees himself in the same terms, recalling the New Testament appropri-ation of the pilgrim idea as alienation, the condition of being

---

[46] Alfred Loisy, *Le Livre de Job, traduit de l'Hébreu* (Amiens: Rousseau-Leroy, 1892), pp. 124, 8; Ernest Renan, *Le Livre de Job traduit de l'Hébreu* (Paris: Lévy Frères, 1859), p. 82.

[47] William S. Peterson, *Victorian Heretic*, p. 174.

[48] Stanton Coit, *National Idealism and the Book of Common Prayer: An Essay in Reinterpretation and Revision* (London: Williams and Norgate, 1908), p. 439.

Mary Ward and the Problems of History 159

'strangers and pilgrims on the earth' (Heb. 11:13).[49] But this is linked as it is in Bunyan with a vision of progress, a process of widening and deepening consciousness in the life of man. The destination of individual pilgrimage in Ward, if not exactly Bunyan's celestial city or even an already transfigured earthly city, is often linked with brief intuitions of the sublime or some kind of transcendent meaning. *Marcella*, published in 1894, constructs around Marcella's personal quest for effective social action a social-problem novel, which revives the concerns of condition-of-England novels such as Disraeli's *Sybil* or Kingsley's *Alton Locke*. It notes the thorny personal question of 'the ethical relationship of the individual to the World's Fair and its vanities'.[50] The 'World's Fair' could be read in general terms, but for contemporary readers the capital letters might have suggested the Chicago World's Fair of 1893. They would have taken the hint that for all its marvels it might be a modern version of Bunyan's distracting and merely materialist Vanity Fair. The allusion signalled the problems as much as the achievements of economic progress and developing modernity, and the responsibility of the pilgrim soul to address them. Ward's nephew Aldous Huxley, born the year the novel was published and called after its hero Aldous Raeburn,[51] would ironically imagine a Brave New World in his own fiction, but for Ward the world of the future was not yet clearly in focus and there was much still to be done to reform the old one. The extent to which the work of reform is a religious quest is rather muted in this novel, but not completely excluded. The dying social reformer Hallin, based on Arnold Toynbee, Oxford historian and pioneer of the East End Settlement movement with which Ward was associated, knows he is approaching the last things, which are a mystery of the spirit. He realizes that the elaborate traditional detail supplied by Dante or Bunyan (or, he might have added, their various illustrators) is quite irrelevant. The final mystery is something dark and unknown to the mind, 'but to the heart it seems unveiled—with the heart, I see'.[52]

---

[49] Ward, *The Case of Richard Meynell*, chapter 21, p. 437; chapter 24, p. 517.
[50] Mary Ward, *Marcella*, Beth Sutton-Ramspeck and Nicole B. Meller (eds) (Peterborough, Ontario: Broadview, 2002), book 2, chapter 5, p. 203.
[51] Sutherland, *Mrs Humphry Ward*, p. 167.
[52] Ward, *Marcella* book 4, chapter 2, p. 495.

160 *Mary Ward and the Problems of History*

Sir George Tressady (1896), a sequel to *Marcella*, is less reticent and less agnostic. It combines the themes of class conflict and spiritual quest, drawing in part on the familiar model of Bunyan's *The Pilgrim's Progess*. Tressady is a wealthy mine-owner and politician who has rather lost his way in life and has had sharp differences with a particularly truculent trade unionist. Mary Ward is too subtle to labour the point, but this latter-day St George *manqué* might with more energy and determination have been able to slay a few modern dragons and deliver his society from injustice and class conflict. He fails to do so, but takes some steps in the right direction before he self-sacrificingly risks his life to try to save others in a pit disaster, working alongside his old adversary. Mortally injured in a roof-fall, in the hour of his death he encounters a sense of reconciliation, homecoming, and ultimate belonging that had previously eluded him. He has intuitions that his rather desultory life's journey might after all have been a kind of pilgrimage, that he might have been guided along his road as the children of Israel were guided in the desert by alternating flame and cloud: 'There was a momentary sense of ecstasy, of something ineffable. And with that sense came a rending of all barriers, a breaking of long tension, a flooding of the soul with joy.'[53] This sublime, highly charged dying moment conveys an intuitive sense of the numinous, passing beyond language altogether. It is characteristic of Ward's almost secular religion that it depends on experience rather than traditional dogma: the scene offers moral resolution, emotional certainty, and a peace that passes all understanding. But there is no theology, no trumpets, no Shining Ones, no elaborate vision of the Celestial City. That called for a different kind of religious imagination, of the kind to be explored in the next chapter. Modern versions of some of the more visionary aspects of biblical pilgrimage—given sharper visual focus by Dante, Bunyan, and Milton, and their illustrators—were part of the imaginative stock in trade of Rider Haggard.

---

[53] Mary Ward, *Sir George Tressady* (London: Smith, Elder, 1896), chapter 24, p. 571.

7

Rider Haggard: Adventures with the Numinous

Mary Ward, like George Eliot and Thomas Hardy, had attracted the more or less hostile interest of conservative churchmen such as Samuel Law Wilson. Wilson's wariness of new religious ideas, conveyed in his *Chapters in Present Day Theology* (1897) which takes a few side-swipes at *Robert Elsmere*, extended to the new comparative study of religion. But it did not occur to him to relate his concerns to the work of Henry Rider Haggard (1856–1925). Perhaps it should have done. The popular author of *King Solomon's Mines* (1885) and *She* (1887), and many other works, deserves to be taken more seriously as—among other things—a multicultural religious novelist. The best of his romances still captivate readers not just through vivid and violent narrative but through his capacity to imagine archetypally awe-inspiring scenes and situations, often with biblical resonances, often in exotic settings. While there were other more short-lived sensation fictions attempting to explore some of the same imaginative territory, such as Haggard's contemporary Marie Corelli's *The Sorrows of Satan* (1895), no one else did it so well. Part of the appeal was subliminal: Rider Haggard's readers did not always consciously realize the extent to which his quest narratives and intuitions of the sublime could represent an imaginative exploration of the things of the spirit and the nature of religious awareness, which owed much to the Old Testament.

Rider Haggard was enormously successful in his own day, perhaps the best-paid writer in the country between 1887 and 1894. In its first year alone *King Solomon's Mines* sold 31,000 copies in England, and ran through thirteen editions in the USA. *She* was instantly dramatized and ran in London and New York, with the famous dancer Loie

162   *Rider Haggard: Adventures with the Numinous*

Fuller in the title role in the New York production. A version of it was performed as a ballet of 'twelve tableaux and an apotheosis' in Budapest (without the author's permission) in 1898. Under the title of *La Colonne de Feu* some of it was filmed as a silent spectacular in 1899 by one of the pioneers of French cinema, Georges Méliès. Other film versions of *She* were to follow, and by 1916 Haggard had sold the film rights for five other novels.[1]

Yet even in his heyday Rider Haggard was not really taken seriously, except by a few discerning friends such as Andrew Lang and Rudyard Kipling. Perhaps he was just too popular, and wrote too much and too hastily. His work was soon a target for parody. *King Solomon's Wives* by 'Hyder Ragged' was published in 1887. *She* was facetiously flanked by would-be sequels called *He* and *It*. *Punch* engaged in rather cumbersome mockery of 'Rider Laggard', 'Reader Faghard', or 'Walker Weird, author of Hee-Hee and Solomon's Ewers.'[2] Bracketed with Kipling as a mere entertainer, he prompted condescending sneers from the self-consciously sophisticated, such as the young Cambridge don J. K. Stephen, Virginia Woolf's cousin, who in 1891 looked forward to a time when:

> The Rudyards cease from Kipling
> And the Haggards ride no more.[3]

Kipling is now taken seriously as a writer and artist, but not Rider Haggard: his work is still read and reread, but among literary critics it is more patronized than admired, if it is noticed at all. His varied life as writer, traveller, land reformer, and public figure has attracted biographers, but his once-popular novels, too easily dismissed as just boys' books, now seem to interest largely unsympathetic commentators

---

[1] See J. E. Scott, *A Bibliography of the Works of Sir Henry Rider Haggard 1856–1925* (Bishop's Stortford: Elkin Mathews, 1947), p. 224; Philip Waller, *Writers, Readers, & Reputations: Literary Life in Britain 1870–1918* (Oxford: Oxford University Press, 2006), p. 12.

[2] See, for example, 'Adam Slaughterman by Walker Weird, author of Hee-Hee and Solomon's Ewers', *Punch*, 27 August 1887; 'She-That-Ought-Not–To-Be-Played', *Punch*, 22 September 1888; parodies and adaptations are listed in Scott, *A Bibliography*, updated in Peter Berresford Ellis, *H. Rider Haggard: A Voice from the Infinite* (London: Routledge, 1978), pp. 279–80.

[3] [J. K. Stephen] 'To R.K.' (*Cambridge Review*, 1891) in *Lapsus Calami* (Cambridge: Macmillan & Bowes, 1896), p. 3.

Rider Haggard: Adventures with the Numinous   163

writing feminist critique or committed to illustrating the iniquities of imperialism.[4] These perspectives, while inadequate, are not in themselves unreasonable. In the matter of gender Haggard is in some respects of his time and partly complicit with the more or less conventional expectations of the popular market for which he wrote. But even if adventure in Rider Haggard is a mainly masculine pursuit, with lots of fighting along the way, and, even if his women seem to be there mainly to love and to be loved, his more regal heroines, such as the mysterious 'She', are also powerful and disconcerting. They include not just Helen of Troy and Cleopatra but characters explicitly modelled on them such as Mameena in *Child of Storm* (1913), described as a 'Zulu Helen', and the dark inscrutable Cleopatra figure Sorais in *Allan Quatermain* (1887), a sequel to *King Solomon's Mines*. It is not inappropriate to read his numerous African stories, at least, in the context of late-Victorian imperialism, since as a very young man he had spent six years in South Africa, starting in 1875 with an appointment on the staff of Sir Henry Bulwer, Lieutenant Governor and then Governor of Natal. But Haggard had enduring sympathy and respect for African peoples, particularly Zulus, and the ultimately tragic outlook of his African novels is hardly that of a naive and brutally triumphalist colonialist.

Nor is it entirely what one might expect from a writer of exclusively juvenile fiction. He had in fact already published history and fiction for adult readers before his first great success, *King Solomon's Mines*. This arose from a bet with his brother that he could write just as good a boys' book as Robert Louis Stevenson's *Treasure Island* (1883). The quest in Haggard's novel involves African diamonds rather than pirate gold ('more picturesque and easier to handle', he explained), and the setting is Matabeleland rather than the Spanish Main, but both books are animated by a boyish sense of exotic adventure. Haggard dashed off his story in six weeks, allegedly, and sent the manuscript to Stevenson's publisher Cassell who accepted it.[5]

---

[4] See for example Sandra Gilbert, 'Rider Haggard's Heart of Darkness' (1983), in Lyn Pykett, ed., *Reading Fin de Siècle Fictions* (Harlow: Longman, 1996); Laura Chrisman, *Rereading the Imperial Romance: British Imperialism and South African Resistance in Haggard, Schreiner and Plaatje* (Oxford: Clarendon Press, 2000); Wendy Katz, *Rider Haggard and the Fiction of Empire* (Cambridge: Cambridge University Press, 1987).

[5] Lilias Rider Haggard, *The Cloak that I Left: A Biography of the Author Henry Rider Haggard, KBE* (London: Hodder, 1951), pp. 121–3; Henry Rider Haggard, 'The Real King Solomon's Mines', *Cassell's Magazine* (July 1907), 146.

164   *Rider Haggard: Adventures with the Numinous*

But this early success in the juvenile market is not the whole story, or even the most interesting part of the story, of Haggard's popular appeal. He wrote rapidly, and sometimes carelessly, out of a vivid imagination, and his imagination was quickened by the spiritual ferment of his time, the anthropological discoveries and the travellers' tales from remote parts of a world that was still being explored. He was not much given to acknowledging or documenting sources, even in non-fictional work, and liked to give the impression that, like his action-hero Allan Quatermain ('who, after all, is only myself set in a variety of imagined situations') he was not a bookish man.[6] But whether from books or travel or conversation with others he readily picked up considerable quantities of cultural and historical information, and assimilated and transformed myths and legends from many cultures. He was particularly influenced by the ancient, archetypal narratives and solemn cadences of the Old Testament (King James version). We need not go as far as the eccentric American commentator Leo Michael who managed to see *She* as an allegory of the Church,[7] but the religious and mythopoeic dimension of Haggard's work, which commended it to C. S. Lewis, a literary critic with his own creative interest in religious myth, merits attention that it has seldom received.[8] Haggard is very different from the self-consciously intellectual Mary Ward, but the strange, compelling imaginative worlds of his fictions, and in particular the mysterious 'She' who helped Carl Jung to develop his concept of the *anima* or female principle in the male psyche,[9] represent another and different reimagining of the numinous, and more specifically of biblical materials. Haggard as much as Eliot or Hardy needs to be considered as an ultimately religious writer in the context of late nineteenth-century

---

[6] Henry Rider Haggard, *The Days of My Life*, ed. C. J. Longman, 2 vols (London: Longmans, 1926), II, pp. 85–6.

[7] Leo Michael, *She: An Allegory of the Church* (New York: Frank F. Lovell, 1889).

[8] See C. S. Lewis's brief and in other respects rather dismissive comments on *She* in 'The Mythopoeic Gift of Rider Haggard' (1960), collected in *Of This and Other Worlds* (London: Collins, 1982), pp. 128–32, and John Coates, '"The Spiritual Quest" in Rider Haggard's *She* and *Ayesha*', *Cahiers Victoriens et Édouardiens* (Montpellier) 57 (April 2003), 33–54.

[9] For 'She' and the Jungian unconscious, see C. J. Jung, 'The Relations between the Ego and the Unconscious', in *The Archetypes and the Collective Unconscious, Collected Works*, 20 vols, trans. R. F. C. Hull, (London: Routledge, 1953–79), VII, p. 190; IX (Part 1), pp. 28, 30, 71.

Rider Haggard: Adventures with the Numinous   165

uncertainties about dogma and the Bible, outside the Church and even inside it. It is particularly germane to Haggard's work that 'religion' in the popular English mind no longer meant just 'Christianity' in its mildly Protestant Anglican form. Colonial ventures in Africa and India had gradually brought wider perspectives. Western knowledge of Indian religions had been growing in the course of the nineteenth century in the wake of the pioneering researches of Sir William Jones (1746–94) and the long series of publications of the Asiatic Society of Bengal, founded in 1784. The great Sanskrit scholar Friedrich Max Müller, whose work was well known to Haggard's friend Kipling and his family,[10] was very critical of Jones' work and in 1878 published his own much more sophisticated and nuanced *Lectures on the Origins and Growth of Religion as Illustrated by the Religions of India*. The *Sacred Books of the East* (1879–97), a set of some fifty volumes of pioneering English translations under his general editorship, contributed substantially to the growing awareness in England of other religions outside the Judaeo-Christian tradition. Max Müller seems to have coined the term *religionswissenschaft* (or 'science of religion') to describe the comparative study that was now becoming possible of different religious traditions. He had published his own *Introduction to the Science of Religion* in 1873. Max Müller's great scholarly rival Andrew Lang, Haggard's friend and collaborator, developed alternative theories, drawing on many religious systems across the world, in *Myth, Ritual and Religion* (1887) and *The Making of Religion* (1898). The new subject of 'comparative religion', an expression that makes an early appearance in the subtitle of the first edition of J. G. Frazer's famous study *The Golden Bough: a Study in Comparative Religion* (1890), was soon recognized as a useful introduction to the nature of religion as a phenomenon. The Unitarian scholar Joseph Estlin Carpenter (1844–1927), an authority on Indian and Chinese religions, gave several series of lectures on the topic at the Unitarian Manchester

---

[10] I owe this suggestion to Robert Fraser. Kipling knew of the translations of Max Müller through his father, a member of the Indian Educational Service and professionally knowledgeable about Indian religion and customs (see Charles Allen, *Kipling Sahib: India and the Making of Rudyard Kipling* (London: Little, Brown, 2007), p. 358), and there are passing references to Max Müller in Kipling's early stories such as 'The Enlightenments of Pagett MP' in *Under the Deodars* (1888), 'The Bisara of Pooree', in *Plain Tales from the Hills* (1888), and 'In the Rukh', in *Many Inventions* (1893).

166   *Rider Haggard: Adventures with the Numinous*

College in Oxford from about 1901, eventually contributing a volume on the subject to the Home University Library in 1913.

Haggard, aware of African religions from his time in South Africa, was also alert to other religions. He makes imaginative use of Buddhism and ideas of reincarnation, particularly in *Ayesha* (1905), the sequel to *She*, which is set in central Asia. Like many of his contemporaries, he was also fascinated with the religion of ancient Egypt, described by his favourite novelist Bulwer Lytton as 'the mother-country of human wisdom'.[11] Napoleon's Egyptian campaigns (1798–1801) had stimulated European curiosity and Egyptian mysteries had been probed by French, German, and English archaeologists in the course of the nineteenth century. Egyptian inscriptions, many of them preserved in the British Museum, were now being painstakingly deciphered and collated. Baron Bunsen, notorious even at one remove through Rowland Williams' coat-trailing discussion of his work in *Essays and Reviews*, had written learnedly, enthusiastically, and at great length about *Egypt's Place in Universal History* (1848–60). Egyptian religion had become slightly less mysterious and all the more intriguing through Carl Richard Lepsius' German edition of the Egyptian *Book of the Dead* in 1842. The Unitarian Egyptologist Samuel Sharpe tried to take account of ancient Egyptian religion in his comparative study *Egyptian Mythology and Egyptian Christianity, with their influence on the opinions of modern Christendom* (1863). In *Isis Unveiled* (1877) the theosophist Madame Blavatsky had annexed some of the matter of Egypt for her own purposes, with considerable unacknowledged help from the writings of Bulwer Lytton.[12] The ex-Chartist autodidact Gerald Massey, on whom George Eliot had based aspects of Felix Holt, turned armchair Egyptologist in later life and from 1881 onwards published a series of books culminating in *Ancient Egypt, the Light of the World* (1907), which claimed Egyptian priority for most things and drew attention to parallels between aspects of the life of Christ and the story of Horus, child of the virgin Isis and the god Osiris.

The Egyptian Horus gave Haggard an acknowledged basis for the fictitious religion of the White Kendah in *The Ivory Child* (1916).

---

[11] Quoted in S. B. Liljegren, *Bulwer Lytton's Novels and Isis Unveiled*, Essays and Studies on English Language and Literature 18 (Upsala: Lundequistka Bokhandeln, 1957), p. 33.

[12] Liljegren identifies Egyptian material in Blavatsky's *Isis Unveiled* imported from *The Last Days of Pompeii, Zanoni, A Strange Story*, and *The Coming Race*.

Rider Haggard: Adventures with the Numinous   167

Ancient Egypt was the home of Kallikrates, ancestor and prototype of Leo Vincey in *She*, and provides a general reference point for describing the architecture and atmosphere of the legendary Kôr in the novel. The Egypt of the Ramessids (*c.*1290–1075 BCE), which Haggard represented as a half-magical early time when almost anything might happen, provides the setting for *The World's Desire* (1890), a quasi-Homeric fantasy about first love, Odysseus, Helen of Troy, and Israel in Egypt, written jointly with Andrew Lang. Egyptian, Hebrew, and Homeric religion all rub shoulders in the same narrative. Recent archaeological discoveries had confirmed very ancient links between Greece and Egypt, and the bold juxtaposition of Homer and Exodus is just about possible chronologically if one selects an early date for the fall of Troy and a late date for the Exodus.

Comparative religious perspectives could encourage a retreat from dogma and dogmatic intolerance, at least in some quarters. To the alarm of religious conservatives, Victorian freethinkers from Henry Hetherington to Charles Bradlaugh could now compare Christ with Krishna, and point to Christianity as just one religion among many. Winwood Reade's secularist classic *The Martyrdom of Man* (1872) loftily damned all religions with faint praise: 'the religion of the Africans, whether pagan or Moslem, is suited to their intellects, and is therefore a true religion; and the same may be said of Christianity among uneducated people.'[13] Haggard and Lang give pause for thought in *The World's Desire* by mentioning a 'great chapel by the sea' that is in fact a 'Temple of Aphrodite, the Queen of Love'.[14] In *Allan Quatermain* Sir Henry Curtis is solemnly married to Nyleptha before the altar in a 'private chapel' by the high priest, according to the religious rites of Zu-Vendis, even though Quatermain supplements this (and perhaps pacifies conservative readers) by reading the prayer-book marriage service.[15] The theologically liberal Bishop Colenso of Natal, notorious for challenging the factual detail of Old

---

[13] Edward Royle, *Victorian Infidels Infidels: The Origins of the British Secularist Movement 1791–1866* (Manchester: Manchester University Press, 1974), p. 113; Winwood Reade, *The Martyrdom of Man* (1872) (London: Watts, 1934), p. 422.

[14] H. Rider Haggard, *The World's Desire* (1890) (London: Macdonald, 1953), chapter 2, p. 26. There is no complete standard or scholarly edition of Rider Haggard's work, which has been much reprinted, so for ease of reference references are given to chapters as well as pages in the editions cited.

[15] H. Rider Haggard, *Allan Quatermain* (1887), World's Classics, ed. Dennis Butts (Oxford: Oxford University Press, 1995), chapter 19, pp. 226–9.

168   *Rider Haggard: Adventures with the Numinous*

Testament narratives (as discussed in Chapter 3), was adamant that God spoke to men in different ways, not just through the Christian scriptures, and that these must be recognized and respected. He was happy to provide non-Christian religious quotations from Cicero, and from Hindu and Sikh sources, to illustrate his point.[16] Henry Callaway, a culturally sensitive missionary priest in Colenso's diocese, anticipated the interests of both Max Müller and Rider Haggard by reporting in detail on African religion in *The Religious System of the Amazulu* (1868–70), used in Max Müller's *Introduction to the Science of Religion*.[17]

The new comparative perspectives tended to polarize attitudes. If Colenso and Callaway did not insist on the supreme, exclusive value and truth of their own tradition and their own scriptures others felt driven to take refuge in biblical literalism or some other dogmatic stance, often conflated with offensive Eurocentrism or Anglocentrism. Writing for a symposium on religion and morality in 1877, the lawyer and essayist Sir James Fitzjames Stephen rather loftily discussed the 'differences which distinguish Englishmen from Buddhists' to the advantage of the former, while in the same symposium the Tractarian Lord Selborne, a former Lord Chancellor, considered that 'the modern Hindoos and Chinese have long been civilised, but are certainly not moral'.[18] *Robert Elsmere* had helped to stimulate—or scare—late-Victorian England conservatives into recuperations of traditional Christian doctrine in the light of modern knowledge. Charles Gore and other Anglo-Catholic essayists produced a scholarly delayed response to *Essays and Reviews* in the neo-orthodox collection *Lux Mundi* (1889). Gore and John Nash also set out to reaffirm Anglican orthodoxy, or at least the High Church construction of it, by republishing William Law's anti-Latitudinarian *Defence of Church Principles* (1717–19) in 1893. But, a generation before the American psychologist and philosopher William James'

---

[16] J. W. Colenso, *The Pentateuch and Book of Joshua Critically Examined*, 7 vols (London: Longmans, 1862–79), I, pp. 154–6.

[17] Henry Callaway, *Unkulunkula; or the Tradition of Creation as existing among the Amazulu and other tribes of South Africa* (1868), incorporated into *The Religious System of the Amazulu*, 4 parts (Springvale, Natal: J. A. Blair,1868–70). For Callaway and Colenso, see ODNB and Norman Etherington, *Preachers, Peasants and Politics in South-east Africa, 1835–1880* (London: Royal Historical Society, 1978), p. 41.

[18] Sir James Stephen, Lord Selborne, et al., 'The influence upon morality of a decline in religious belief', *The Nineteenth Century* 1 (April 1877), 331, 333.

Rider Haggard: Adventures with the Numinous 169

Varieties of Religious Experience (1902), Max Müller spoke for and encouraged a growing tendency to think of religion not as doctrine but as experience, intuition, and feeling, what he described as 'a yearning after a higher and better life—a life in the light of God', or a faculty for the apprehension of the infinite.[19] Almost a century earlier Friedrich Schleiermacher had defined religion in similar terms as 'a sense and taste for the infinite'. This influential formulation, very familiar to Max Müller and the German Lutheran tradition in which he been brought up, comes from his *Religion: Speeches to its Cultured Despisers* (1799).[20] The book was finally translated into English in 1893 and reissued in Germany in 1899, its centenary year, edited by Rudolph Otto. It was very much in the spirit of Schleiermacher that Otto went on to write *Das Heilige* (1917), translated as *The Idea of the Holy* (1923). Otto's work, drawing on Eastern religions and on the work of Andrew Lang, gave currency to the all-encompassing term 'the numinous' as a way of describing that which gives rise to religious awareness.

Rider Haggard's interest in world religions was imaginative and personal rather than polemical or scientific: he was not an aggressive secularist and freethinker like Charles Bradlaugh, nor a professional scholar like Max Müller. Despite some early and rather uneasy dabbling with spiritualism he saw himself as a fairly traditional member of the Church of England: 'I believe in the simple and unadulterated doctrines of Christianity as these appear within the four corners of the New Testament and are preached by the Church to which I belong.'[21] But he was not a conventionally religious writer, even though religious publishing was now booming. Regardless of agnostics and secularists, the need for cheap Sunday School prizes and suitably edifying Christmas presents in the new era of mass literacy had created a flourishing popular market for missionary biographies such as W. G. Blaikie's *The Personal Life of David Livingstone* (1880). There was also a huge demand for more or less sentimental religious fictions such as the American Susan B. Warner's *The Wide, Wide World* (1850, but still in print in the 1920s) or

[19] F. Max Müller, *Introduction to the Science of Religion* (London: Longmans, 1873), pp. 263, 13.

[20] Friedrich Schleiermacher, *On Religion: Speeches to its Cultured Despisers*, trans. John Oman (London: Kegan Paul, 1893), Second Speech, 'The nature of Religion', p. 39.

[21] H. Rider Haggard, *The Days of My Life*, II, p. 236.

170   *Rider Haggard: Adventures with the Numinous*

Mrs O. F. Walton's *Christie's Old Organ*, published by the Religious Tract Society (1882; 39th impression 1900), both of which were bestsellers. But this was not the market Haggard sought to capture. He satirized the large-scale—and extremely lucrative—religious publishing of his day in his novel *Mr Meeson's Will* (1888) and made a point of not writing conventional missionary stories. There are one or two missionaries in the novels, such as Allan Quatermain's wholly admirable father in *Allan's Wife* (1889) and *Marie* (1912), and the saintly missionary and martyr Thomas Owen in the strange novella *The Wizard* (1896), but as a writer he usually kept his distance from the missionaries, even though reports of their activities had helped to create the popular appetite for African adventure, which he tried to satisfy. Unlike Eliot, Hardy, and Ward, he seldom wrote about clergymen at all, and when he did, as in the sketch of the coarse, ambitious, and obsessive Mr Plowden ('a large man of a somewhat lumbering make') in the early novel *The Witch's Head* (1885),[22] or the more detailed presentation of the misogynistic and mean-souled Mr Knight in *Love Eternal* (1918), he was often far from flattering.

Haggard was neither a dogmatic theologian nor a conventionally pious moralist in his writing, but he was a believer, steeped in the English Bible, endowed with a profoundly religious imagination. Supreme among his gifts and achievements was a knack of reimagining the numinous through adventure and romance. For him, romance was not just more or less far-fetched escapist storytelling, though it could work very well at that level, but a mode of access to deeper matters, what he called 'a vehicle of much that does not appear to the casual reader'.[23] His friend Rudyard Kipling, commenting on the manuscript of the late novel *Wisdom's Daughter* (1923), the last of the stories about 'She', exclaimed, 'You are a whale at parables and allegories and one thing reflecting another', an insight that prompted Haggard to respond gratefully: 'As usual you see the truth, which few others do.'[24] Parable is of course a biblical form. In an early, rather self-promoting essay 'About Fiction' Haggard is critical of contemporary novels—English, French, and American—preferring and

---

[22] H. Rider Haggard, *The Witch's Head* [1885] (London: Spencer Blackett, 1887), chapter 18, p. 116.

[23] H. Rider Haggard, diary entry, 30 March 1917, *The Private Diaries of Sir H. Rider Haggard 1914–1925*, ed. D. S. Higgins (London: Cassell, 1980), p. 101.

[24] Lilias Rider Haggard, *The Cloak that I Left: A Biography of the Author Henry Rider Haggard KBE* (London: Hodder, 1951), p. 272.

Rider Haggard: Adventures with the Numinous 171

implicitly allying himself with a tradition of ultimately timeless 'purely romantic fiction' going back to *Robinson Crusoe*.[25] Timeless or archetypal narratives could function like biblical parables and other Bible stories by pointing to meanings beyond the specifics of time and place. At the end of *King Solomon's Mines* Sir Henry Curtis' missing brother George describes how he has lived for two years in an oasis in the desert, 'like a second Robinson Crusoe'.[26] *Robinson Crusoe*, *King Solomon's Mines*, and the Book of Job are all fables of endurance: stories about resilience, survival, and reward against the odds.

Haggard was not in the business of simply retelling and amplifying Bible stories in the manner of the American romancer J. H. Ingraham in his immensely popular *Prince of the House of David* (1855) and *The Throne of David* (1860). He occasionally did so: the story of the Exodus from Egypt is elaborated and retold from an (imagined) Egyptian perspective in *The World's Desire*, but this is largely incidental to the main theme of the story. The Bible, particularly the more historical and heroic narratives of the Old Testament, was not so much a specific source as a useful resource for his purposes, a familiar reference point. It gave widely shared access to an otherwise largely unknown early world of divine mystery, and more or less righteous conflict and adventure, and its dignified language, as represented by the familiar cadences of the King James version, could readily be imitated to convey ceremonial courtesy and formality among ancient, mythical, or little-known peoples, to suggest awe and wonder, or to hint at other grave matters. These kinds of appropriation also served to reposition the much-challenged authority of the Bible in Victorian culture by emphasizing its imaginative power and the archetypal, universal status of some of its stories without leaning too hard on questions of divine inspiration or literal truth, which belonged somewhere else.

The Jewish historian Josephus, the chronicler Eusebius of Caesarea, and Eusebius' Latin translator St Jerome had all tried to make sense of mysterious and exotic names, places, and peoples in the Old Testament. In the fourth century Helena, mother of the Emperor Constantine, had visited the holy places and stimulated pilgrimages and

---

[25] Rider Haggard, 'About Fiction', *Contemporary Review* 51 (February 1887), pp. 172–80.

[26] H. Rider Haggard, *King Solomon's Mines* [1885] World's Classics edition ed. Dennis Butts (Oxford: Oxford University Press, 2006), chapter 20, p. 197.

172　　*Rider Haggard: Adventures with the Numinous*

religious tourism, so it became all the more important to try to identify scenes and places mentioned in the scriptures.[27] The process continued right down into Haggard's day, not just in travellers' guides such as Rev. W. M. Thomson's *The Land and the Book* (1879) and George Adam Smith's *The Historical Geography of the Holy Land* (1894) but in Rev. Professor George Rawlinson's archaeologically informed scholarly commentary (published 1858–60) on the early Greek historian Herodotus, which discussed his awareness of the geography of the Old Testament world. Haggard's imagination filled some of the gaps and spaces that still remained.

Mysterious, opulent, distant Ophir, which John Masefield invoked as a source of ivory, apes, and peacocks in his poem 'Cargoes' (1903), was identified in 1 Kings 9:28 as the place whence gold was brought to Solomon, but no one really knew exactly where it was. Josephus and Eusebius had suggested India, but perhaps it was in Africa, in gold-rich Matabeleland? The story of Solomon being visited by the Queen of Sheba, bearing gold, spices, and precious stones, had been elaborated in the Talmud and in the Koran from brief mention in the Old Testament (1 Kings 10:1–10, 13). But that still left unanswered questions. Where exactly was Sheba? Nineteenth-century suggestions ranged as far afield as Java.[28] Eusebius, following Josephus word for word, had suggested it was an Ethiopian city. Ethiopian legend, formalized in the fourteenth-century narrative *Kebra Nagast* ('Glory of the Kings'), had derived the nation's ruling dynasty from the supposed union of Solomon and the Queen of Sheba.[29]

Haggard was able to draw on ancient mystery, and mythic and biblical if not exactly historical underpinning, for his African yarns such as *King Solomon's Mines* and *Queen Sheba's Ring* (1910). It is

---

[27] See Lionel Casson, *Travel in the Ancient World* (Baltimore: Johns Hopkins University Press, 1974), pp. 304–7. For advice on the history of sacred geography I am very grateful to Keith Whitelam.

[28] Robert Tytler, *Illustrations of Ancient Geography and History . . . Derived from Recent Investigations in the Eastern Indian Archipelago* (London: J. M. Richardson, 1825).

[29] For Sheba and Ophir in patristic commentary see Paulus de Lagarde, ed., *Onomastica Sacra* (Göttingen, 1870), pp. 184, 296, 303–4. Lagarde includes the text of Jerome's *Onomastica* and Eusebius' *Onomasticon*, both also available in Migne, *Patrologia Latina* 23. For the enduring influence of the legend Solomon and Sheba on Ethiopian dynastic politics, see Edward Ullendorff, *The Ethiopians: An Introduction to Country and People* (1960) 2nd ed. (London: Oxford University Press, 1965), pp. 64, 143–4.

Rider Haggard: Adventures with the Numinous   173

tempting to link these exotic adventure stories with juvenile imperial adventure from the same period such as G. A. Henty's *With Clive in India* (1884) or *With Kitchener in the Soudan* (1903), or Charles Kingsley's vivid and violent historical novels *Westward Ho!* (1855) and the saga-like *Hereward the Wake* (1866) a little earlier. There are no boy heroes in Haggard as there are in Henty, and winning the empire or defeating a national enemy is not usually a primary consideration, but there are some connections. Vigorous action takes precedence in all three writers. Haggard's novel *Eric Brighteyes* (1891) is a sanitized and romanticized version of Icelandic saga, which follows *Hereward* in giving every chapter a title in the form of 'How [someone, usually the hero] did [something]', emphasizing action throughout. Haggard's phrase 'A slaughter grim and great' in *Allan Quatermain* (1885) unconsciously echoes Kingsley's phrase 'a murder grim and great' in *Hereward*.[30] But to see Rider Haggard simply as a writer of sagas ancient and modern is to miss part of the point. He looked not just to blood-and-thunder yarns but to the romance, both the magical romance of *The Arabian Nights* and the more modern romances of Bulwer Lytton, uncle of Sir Henry Bulwer, his official superior in Natal.

Something of his sense of his own writing comes from his favourite reading. Asked in 1887 to list the books that had meant most to him as a writer, he mentioned *The Arabian Nights* and *Robinson Crusoe* in passing but nominated Dickens' *A Tale of Two Cities* (1859), Bulwer Lytton's *The Coming Race* (1871)—a strange work of futuristic science fiction, set largely underground like some of his own tales—and the desolate and desolating book of Ecclesiastes, which subsequently provided him with the title of his novel *The Way of the Spirit* (1906).[31] One can understand how he might admire *A Tale of Two Cities* with its theme of heroic self-sacrifice, since heroic life and death more or

---

[30] 'A slaughter grim and great' is the title of chapter 7 of *Allan Quatermain* and is (virtually) repeated within the chapter on p. 89: 'It was a slaughter great and grim'. Compare Charles Kingsley, *Hereward the Wake* (1866) (London: Macmillan, 1890), chapter 19, 'How he cleared Bourne of Frenchmen', p. 177: 'And then began a murder grim and great.'

[31] Rider Haggard, 'Books which have influenced me', *British Weekly Extra* no.1 (London: British Weekly, 1887), pp. 66–7. *The Way of the Spirit*, replacing the earlier title *Renunciation*, comes from Eccles. 11:5 and the novel also carries an epigraph from Eccles. 11:9. According to Haggard, Kipling and he hunted out the new title together: Henry Rider Haggard, *The Days of My Life* I, p. 159.

174 *Rider Haggard: Adventures with the Numinous*

less define the action-packed adventure story as it developed with Robert Louis Stevenson and himself. Interest in the bleak affirmation of the ultimate vanity of things in Ecclesiastes, what Haggard called 'the world's yearning anguish and disillusionment', is more unexpected. But it has connections with recurring themes in his fictions such as the loneliness and difficulty of quite possibly hopeless romantic quest, and the tragic but inevitable passing of life and of earthly power and authority, whether of Allan Quatermain's faithful servant Hans (in *The Ivory Child*) or of Cetewayo and the Zulus (in *Finished*) or of landowning English country gentlemen (in *Colonel Quaritch, V.C., a Tale of Country Life* (1888/9)). Bulwer Lytton, now largely forgotten except for *The Last Days of Pompeii* (1834), takes us into different territory again, the religious or quasi-religious realm of romance and mystery at the heart of life, not just in his fantasy *The Coming Race* but in earlier novels such as *A Strange Story* (1862). There are times when Haggard's attempts to emulate Bulwer Lytton's portentousness verge on parody: *Love Eternal* (1918) begins, preposterously, 'More than thirty years ago two atoms of the eternal Energy sped forth from the heart of it which we call God, and incarnated themselves in the human shapes that were destined to hold them for a while...'[32]

The English novel, according to the classic account, had made its way in the course of the eighteenth century against the unreality and escapism of the older romance form. But, as it has already been argued, the exclusion of romance from the serious novel, was not maintained into the later nineteenth century, not even in the self-consciously realist fiction of George Eliot. Haggard himself tried to distinguish between novels and romances in his writings, the former mainly concerned with contemporary life in England and the latter mainly set in remote locations where strange things can be expected to happen. But the distinction constantly breaks down, as it always had done. 'Novels' such as *The Witch's Head*, set in England and South Africa, and *The Way of the Spirit*, set in England and Egypt, have mysterious, uncanny 'romance' elements, implied even in their

---

[32] H. Rider Haggard, *Love Eternal* (London: Cassell, 1918) p. 1. This actually seems closer to Thackeray's parody of Bulwer Lytton than to Bulwer Lytton himself: *George de Barnewell*, by Sir E. L. B. L. Bart., begins 'In the Morning of Life the Truthful wooed the Beautiful, and their offspring was Love. Like his Divine parents, He is eternal...' W. M. Thackeray, *Novels by Eminent Hands* in *Burlesques* (London: Smith, Elder, 1869), p. 3.

Rider Haggard: Adventures with the Numinous   175

titles. On the other hand, some of the tales identified as 'romances' engage quite closely with the probable and indeed the actual. *Child of Storm* features reported ghosts and supernatural elements but also incorporates the true story of the succession struggle in the 1850s between the great Cetewayo (or Cetywayo: Haggard uses different spellings in different works) and Umbelazi for the throne of Zululand, while *Finished* reconstructs the specific historical circumstances of the annexation of the Transvaal, in which Haggard himself had been involved: bizarrely, he makes his younger self a minor character in the opening pages of his own novel, since he had been there at the time. The same novel also deals with the defeat and mysterious death of Cetewayo in 1884.

Common to both Haggard's novels and his romances is a romantic imaginative texture that provides intermittent access to different kinds of religious or quasi-religious awareness, what might best be described as reconfigured religion.

This texture, this awareness, can be identified and approached through the rather elastic categories of the soul, the sublime, and pilgrimage. It is interesting that the category of 'weak messianism' proposed by Walter Benjamin, which has been applied to other 'secular' yet ultimately religious fictions of the period (see Chapter 1 and Chapter 6), is less useful in relation to Haggard's work. His imagination was not usually directly engaged by quasi-messianic heroic leaders and the great or would-be great men of the age who dream mighty dreams and promise to bring in a new world or redeem the old one. A passing reference to 'Sir Garnet [Wolseley] or one of those big swells' early in *King Solomon's Mines* rather puts the grandees in their place.[33] The great men of history who featured in his work were not usually enduringly successful or noticeably messianic. He wrote a non-fictional study of the vanquished Zulu leader Cetewayo (*c.*1826–84), *Cetywayo and His White Neighbours* (1882); Cetewayo's uncle, the great Shaka (*c.*1787–1828), appears in several of the novels; the heroic Boer leader Piet Retief (1780–1838) features in *Marie* (1912). But these were essentially military commanders rather than redeemer figures or model princes, and their lives ended in defeat. They have few fictional counterparts. His own heroes are usually more private figures embarked on a more individual kind of

---

[33] H. Rider Haggard, *King Solomon's Mines*, chapter 2, p. 13.

176   *Rider Haggard: Adventures with the Numinous*

quest, brave and resourceful, responsive to the challenges of mystery and difficulty but without the ambition to reform a society or save a country or a world. The noble Umbopa/Inkosi in *King Solomon's Mines*, rightful king of Kukuanaland, is the only possible exception that comes to mind. The conventionally heroic Sir Henry Curtis in the same novel, large and strong and brave in battle, a kind of Nordic warrior who has somehow escaped into the present from a saga, marries and becomes prince-consort to Queen Nyleptha in Zu-Vendis at the end of *Allan Quatermain*, signing up to play Prince Albert to her Victoria, but it is at this point that both narrator and reader rather lose interest, and we hear no more about him in his new public role. Curtis and Lord Ragnall in *The Ivory Child*, scholar, athlete, and general-purpose Admirable Crichton, only seem to aspire to the status of public hero: they are actually less effective, and less engaging, than the sceptical, restless, unassuming old hunter Allan Quatermain who accompanies them on their travels. Haggard's model for Quatermain and broadly similar adventurers, such as Horace Holly in *She*, is not the virtuous and socially responsible Prince Albert or Davidic kingship in the Old Testament so much as the wily individualist and restless adventurer Odysseus, whom he brought to life with the help of the Homeric translator Andrew Lang in *The World's Desire*.

The Odysseus figure has enjoyed a long and active literary afterlife, as a type of restless wanderer in Dante and Tennyson, and as a Jewish and a Caribbean protagonist in James Joyce's *Ulysses* and Derek Walcott's *Omeros*. Haggard's Odysseus-like Quatermain, who features in all in some eighteen novels or short stories, achieves backdated rather than postdated celebrity, in the first instance because having already described his death in the early novel *Allan Quatermain* Haggard had no other way of exploiting his popularity with the public than of inventing earlier adventures for him. This stratagem was fine as long as all could be contained within the more-or-less plausible chronology of a single lifetime.[34] But there were limits. Eventually, in the late *Allan and the Ice-Gods* (1927), Quatermain becomes not so much reincarnated as preincarnated, as Wi the Hunter and a resourceful tribal leader at the dawn of history. Earlier incarnations or versions of other familiar characters such as Captain Good and Lady Ragnall are also mysteriously present in the same

---

[34] The chronology has been charted by J. E. Scott in *A Bibliography of the Works of Sir Henry Rider Haggard*, pp. 8–18.

Rider Haggard: Adventures with the Numinous 177

novel. This is not just a new way of flogging an almost-dead horse for the literary market: it dramatizes Haggard's long-held intuition, which he discussed with Sir Oliver Lodge, physicist and President of the Society for Psychical Research, that 'the Personality which animates each of us is immeasurably ancient', that human identity is not, or need not be, coterminous with a single span of earthly life.[35]

This notion develops but goes well beyond the traditional Christian belief in some kind of continuing existence expressed in the credal formulation of the resurrection of the (fleshly) body (*carnis resurrectionem*) and everlasting life (*vitam aeternam*). There are various fictional presentations of continuing identity or the persistence of soul or spirit throughout his work. Quasi-Buddhist reincarnations of the same essential spirit, such as Quatermain, is one possibility. Personal immortality is another: there are seemingly ageless African characters such as the witch-figure Gagool in *King Solomon's Mines* and the wizard Zakuli in *Child of Storm*. The third possibility is linked with idealized love, which Haggard regarded as immortal: perhaps there is some kind of disembodied continuity of the soul and of human love beyond the grave, and the tumult and difficulty of the world and the flesh.

Sources for this principle of continuity, with or without human love to help it along, can perhaps be sought in his early reading of Bulwer Lytton. In Lytton's last novel, *Kenelm Chillingly* (1873), the principle of indestructible—if problematic—individual identity is almost facetiously affirmed. The over-reflective Kenelm, aged eight, has been reading Locke and, because of his strong intuition of his own distinctiveness, has come to distrust Locke's denial of innate ideas. The language of Kenelm's exchange with his mother closely resembles Haggard's earlier account of an episode in his own childhood:

> 'Mamma, are you not sometimes overpowered by the sense of your own identity?'
> Lady Chillingly ... said, 'The boy is growing troublesome, too wise for any woman; he must go to school.'[36]

---

[35] H. Rider Haggard, *The Days of My Life*, II, p. 165.
[36] E. Bulwer Lytton, *Kenelm Chillingley* (1873) I, chapter 6; the autobiographical account of his early life is included in the biography by his grandson, the Earl of Lytton, *The Life of Edward Bulwer, First Lord Lytton*, 2 vols (London: Macmillan, 1913), I, p. 36.

178 *Rider Haggard: Adventures with the Numinous*

Elsewhere in Bulwer Lytton the idea of personal immortality, or at least some kind of psychic continuity, is a recurring theme and many of the novels could be described as psychic journeys. In *Zanoni* (1842), the plot of which apparently came to the author in a dream, the dream of personal immortality is approached by inventing a protagonist supposed to have the elixir of life, who nevertheless surrenders his immortality at the guillotine to save his wife (an idea that Dickens may have adapted for *A Tale of Two Cities,* one of Rider Haggard's favourite novels). Twenty years later, in *A Strange Story,* the materialist Dr Fenwick eventually comes to an awareness of soul and an inner conviction that his human love will not die with death. In the science-fiction fantasy *The Coming Race* the American protagonist says farewell to the queenly Zee among the Vril-ya (to Rider Haggard's great disappointment) and returns to his own world, but with an intuition of a life beyond death where they might meet again.[37] An early idealistic love affair with a girl at Ealing, who was abruptly married to someone else but never forgotten, may well have contributed to Bulwer Lytton's fantasies of eternal love and psychic continuity.[38] Haggard was also bitterly disappointed in love early in life when his father abruptly sent him to South Africa and, in Haggard's absence, his beloved soon married someone else (very unhappily). Where Bulwer Lytton's eventual marriage was notoriously stormy and unhappy Haggard's was not, but for him too the early disappointment left its mark in the fiction in various doomed or impossible loves resolved or alleviated by a vision of enduring spiritual love. There is no marriageable woman in *King Solomon's Mines* except for the luckless Foulata, but in a sense the distant mountain ridge with the twin peaks known as Sheba's Breasts gives the expedition something of the atavistic quality of a male quest for an eternal or mythic female principle.

The most familiar example of life and love everlasting is in *She,* set in uncharted central Africa. Both Leo Vincey, apparently some kind of reincarnation of his remote ancestor the ancient Egyptian Kallikrates, and She herself seem to have a kind of immortality that

---

[37] E. Bulwer Lytton, *The Coming Race* [1871] (London, 2007), chapter 29; H. Rider Haggard, 'Books which have influenced me', p. 67. Bulwer Lytton's interest in psychic continuity is discussed in A. C. Christensen, *Edward Bulwer-Lytton: The Fiction of New Regions* (Athens, Georgia: University of Georgia Press, 1976), pp. 194–207.

[38] Recalled in the autobiographical section of Lytton, *Life,* I, pp. 60–5.

Rider Haggard: Adventures with the Numinous 179

transcends the limitations of the flesh and of time and place. But suddenly, at the climactic moment of being united (or reunited) with Vincey/Kallikrates, loved across more than two thousand years, She visibly ages, withers away, and dies, even while promising to come again and to be once more beautiful. Many years later, in the sequel *Ayesha*, Vincey and his faithful friend and guardian Horace Holly find her again, reincarnate in the remote wastes of central Asia.

Even before *She*, a version of the theme of immortal souls and lost or impossible love is found in the early African novel *Jess*: the strange intense heroine of the title has fallen deeply in love with the soldier turned farmer John Niels who is engaged to marry her sister Bessie. Boer treachery and a violent electrical storm leave John and Jess in imminent danger of drowning when their cart is trapped in the middle of a swollen river. The biblical claim that 'love is strong as death... Many waters cannot quench love, neither can the floods drown it' (Song of Songs 8: 6, 7), is dramatically enacted in the moment of extreme peril, as it had been in Eliot's *The Mill on the Floss*. Haggard picks up the implied biblical reference by claiming that 'Death is very strong', but that a woman's perfect love can be stronger still. Jess is sure that love is stronger than death, and will continue beyond it if she and John die together:

> It was perhaps as wild and pathetic a love scene as ever the old moon above has witnessed. There they clung, those two, in the actual shadow of death experiencing the fullest and acutest joy that our life has to offer.[39]

In the event they both survive, only for Jess to die later. After further adventures the novel ends with John happily married to Jess's sister Bessie, but still as close as ever in spirit to his lost love, sometimes reflecting that if there is an 'individual future' beyond death, as he believes there must be, he will see Jess again.[40] Haggard loyally dedicated the novel to his wife, as if to mark his own happy marriage, but the storm and stress of his narrative seems to recall something of the intensity and the pain of his earlier lost love, cruelly frustrated by circumstances.

---

[39] H. Rider Haggard, *Jess* (1887), new edition (London: Smith, Elder, 1900), chapter 24, pp. 245–7.

[40] H. Rider Haggard, *Jess*, chapter 35, p. 368.

180   *Rider Haggard: Adventures with the Numinous*

Haggard's recurring theme of enduring passion beyond the grave despite a hostile world may seem trite and hackneyed, and sometimes it is. But it can be rescued from threadbare romantic cliché by the pressure of personal experience behind it, and this encouraged him to invest it with effectively religious significance. This can work quite well in narratives invoking exotic settings or the remote past, which conveniently licenses melodrama and strangeness, and helps suspension of disbelief. The mysterious and controversial ruins of Great Zimbabwe, which might have had something to do with the city of Kôr in *She*, though Haggard denied it, had recently been discussed by the traveller J. Theodore Bent in his *Ruined Cities of Mashonaland* (1892, new edition 1895) and these inspired *Elissa* (1900), a novella about how the great city and the civilization associated with it might have come to an end. Assuming a very ancient date for Great Zimbabwe and attributing it to a Phoenician colonial presence there, assumptions that are now vigorously disputed, he invents a grandson of the biblical King Solomon, Prince Aziel, who visits the troubled city and falls in love with Elissa (the ominous name is Phoenician, borrowed from the Elissa, Elissar or Elishat, better known as Virgil's unhappy Dido, who was a princess of Tyre and the founder of Carthage) who loves him in return. Rather than marry the wicked King Ithobal she flings herself over a cliff. But as the city burns Aziel recalls that Issachar (whose name is borrowed from one of the sons of the patriarch Jacob and whose advisory, prophetic role is also borrowed from the Old Testament) has foretold both the destruction of the city, and hope for Elissa and himself in a life beyond the grave.

It is, however, more difficult to present 'love eternal' in a contemporary setting without a certain mawkishness. The rather unconvincing potboiler *Love Eternal* (1918) is set in the recent past and the present. It describes a difficult courtship in the teeth of unreasonable parental opposition. The couple eventually marry, but the marriage is short-lived as the war quickly separates them and kills the wife in a Zeppelin raid. Her husband, convinced she had somehow come to him when his own life was in danger, realizes that it must have been her spirit as she would have been dead already. *The Way of the Spirit*, published in 1906, had offered a more effective version of what Haggard described as 'faith in personal survival and reunion',[41]

---

[41]   H. Rider Haggard, *The Way of the Spirit* (London: Hutchinson, 1906), p. 10.

Rider Haggard: Adventures with the Numinous   181

helped by the rich religious traditions of Egypt. Rupert Ullershaw, successful as an army intelligence officer in Egypt, married but betrayed and unhappy in love, eventually meets the Egyptian Mea, loves her and pledges himself to her in spiritual marriage. While this is at one level a rather awkward plot device to free Mea from blame for breaking up an apparently loveless and failing marriage (which is rather improbably repaired towards the end of the novel) it allows Haggard to make an absolute distinction between spiritual and earthly love: Ullenshaw contracts the plague while helping plague victims and dies of it, but Mea is happy to share his death, knowing that after death their spiritual love will be complete and lasting.

The most familiar doomed love in Rider Haggard is perhaps the love of Foulata for Captain Good in *King Solomon's Mines*. The abrupt resolution of the situation when she is killed is usually read and condemned as a form of authorial *apartheid* opposing mixed-race unions, the coming together of black and white, and Allan Quatermain bluntly gives it as his opinion that such an 'entanglement' would not have been 'desirable'.[42] Criticism may, however, too easily attribute to the author the views of his character—represented as a resourceful but essentially simple man with a limited outlook that cannot take full account of all the wonders he experiences. The episode is really another example of the ultimately religious theme of love translated or carried forward into life everlasting, an instance of the unobtainable ideal calling for some kind of transcendent resolution. In this case it is articulated in the language of the astral sublime, which has literary and imaginative currency extending from the Psalmist to Immanuel Kant: as Foulata is dying, she says,

> [My heart] is so full of love that it could live ten thousand years, and yet be young. Say that if I live again, mayhap I shall see him in the Stars, and that—I will search them all, though perchance there must still be black and he will—still be white.[43]

The sublime is present even in Haggard's melodramatic first novel *Dawn* (1884) as a slightly clumsy way of registering emotional trauma and its eventual resolution. In recovery from a profound shock Angela has the kind of bizarre dream that the example of Jean Paul (Johann Paul Richter) and of the Brontës had admitted into the realist

---

[42] H. Rider Haggard, *King Solomon's Mines*, chapter 19, p. 174.
[43] H. Rider Haggard, *King Solomon's Mines*, chapter 17, p. 210.

182 Rider Haggard: Adventures with the Numinous

novel. She seems to find herself in a vast, dark, pillared hall that rather resembles the setting of John Martin's enormously successful if rather theatrical painting *Belshazzar's Feast* (1820), familiar to the Victorians as a mezzotint engraving. The dream changes to present an apocalyptic sea of blood, 'the sum of the scarlet wickedness of her age', and 'an ocean of molten crystal', but somehow Angela is joined by her beloved Arthur and together they rise above the tumult and confusions of earth and find glory. At the end of the novel reality begins to catch up with the vision: the real Arthur comes looking for his lost Angela and the awesome dying glory of a magnificent sunset, with a sudden beam of light suggesting a resurrection morning, provides the setting for their reunion.[44]

The sublime is handled with more restraint in later novels, but Haggard continued to share with John Martin an imaginative relish for the dramatic interplay of light and dark, elemental scenes of fire and flood, storms and savage mountain crags. A late diary entry describes a London fog:

> A darkness as of midnight hung over the city, but below it was clear— with all the flaring lights a scene from Dante's Inferno or from the Greek Hades or the Jewish Gehenna. It was amazing—even terrible to see.[45]

The rhetoric of ominous darkness and flaring light represents one of Haggard's most effective ways of invoking the transcendent and the numinous. There is no hard evidence that he was directly influenced by reading up on the Burkean or the Kantian sublime, but in a sense reading was not needed. His master Bulwer Lytton was a Kantian of sorts and alluded to the Kantian philosophy of Sir William Hamilton in his anti-materialist novel *A Strange Story*, but it was temperament and imagination, stimulated by first-hand observation, which had given Haggard a taste for the sublime. The term 'sublime' had in any case been common currency for well over a century; its literary and religious possibilities were familiar from the poetry of Milton and Wordsworth, and its visual dimension was well known from paintings, descriptions of mountain scenery, and the drawings of artists

---

[44] H. Rider Haggard, *Dawn* (1884) (London: Griffith Farran, n.d.), Book III, chapter 20 ('Angela's Vision'), pp. 335–7; Book III chapter 28 ('Sunset, Night, and Dawn'), p. 371.

[45] H. Rider Haggard, *Private Diaries*, ed. D. S. Higgins (London: Cassell, 1980), p. 246 (22 November 1922).

Rider Haggard: Adventures with the Numinous   183

such as John Martin, illustrator of Milton's *Paradise Lost* (1827), and Gustave Doré, illustrator of both *Paradise Lost* (1866) and Dante's *Inferno* (1860).

The dramatic South African landscape, awesome or 'sublime' rather than ideally beautiful, liable to be swept by violent storms, is a prominent feature of *Jess*. The novel engages with traumatic loss, both of the beloved and of colonial territory. It is set in the Transvaal in 1881, at a time of violent disruption when control of the province was passing from the English to the Boers. More than human agency seems to be invoked by means of the sublime to articulate the central conflict between trauma and stoic resilience. A gathering storm on the veldt is described in terms of nightmare as the clouds cluster beneath a 'ghastly-looking ringed moon'. 'The scene resembled that of some awful dream, or one of Doré's pictures come to life.' Haggard may well have been thinking of Doré's nightmarish Dante illustrations, such as the one for the moment in the *Inferno* when 'The stormy blast of hell/With restless fury drives the spirits on': Doré depicts dwarfed human figures standing on a lofty crag over an abyss, contemplating a great swirl of wind-driven spirits.[46]

The distinction between the sublime and the beautiful articulated by Burke and others applies in a sense to Jess and her more conventionally beautiful but shallower sister Bessie. Haggard's description of the savage landscape of precipitous mountains, deep gorges and rushing torrents swollen by violent storms functions both at a literal level as an exercise in the topographical sublime and as a sustained metaphor for transcendent forces, the passions of love and power that can be painful and dangerous. The personal and political themes of the novel intersect when the ruthless Frank Muller, a politically ambitious and well-connected Boer landowner, becomes besotted with Bessie and tries to murder Jess and Niel in order to possess her. To save her sister, Jess, already terminally ill, kills Muller and then dies herself. Her death, a kind of metaphor for the failed project of an English Transvaal, is followed by Niel's return 'home' to England, since the country has ceased to be a place for Englishmen.

---

[46] H. Rider Haggard, *Jess*, chapter 23, p. 236. The quotation is from H. F. Cary's 1805 translation of *Inferno* 5, 31–3, which was reprinted along with later editions of Doré's illustrations from 1889. Selections of the illustrations were available in publications such as *The Doré Gallery* (London: Cassell, 1870) and can be viewed at <http://www.doreillustrations.com/divinecomedy/> (accessed 10 November 2009).

184   *Rider Haggard: Adventures with the Numinous*

In *King Solomon's Mines* the possibility of inconceivable reward at the end of the quest is subliminally hinted at by natural glories. The daunting march into the waterless desert, which will have to be followed by climbing snow-covered mountains, is introduced by a set-piece sunset: 'the great fiery ball of the sun was sinking into the desert, sending glorious rays of many-coloured light flying all over the vast expanse'.[47] The technique is more developed in *Allan Quatermain* where the path to adventure takes in Mount Kenya. Very few Europeans had seen it at the time the novel was published. There was a report of a massive snow-covered mountain almost on the equator as early as 1849, but snow on the equator seemed inherently improbable and the report was not confirmed until 1883, followed by exploration in 1887 after the novel was published. Haggard offers a new-minted African version of the alpine sublime,as exploited by artists such as Turner, to introduce the sense of overwhelming awe and mystery that is deepened as the narrative proceeds:

> There it rose straight and sheer—a glittering white glory, its crest piercing the very blue of heaven. As I gazed at it...I felt my whole heart lifted up with an indescribable emotion, and for a moment great and wonderful thoughts seemed to break upon my mind, even as the arrows of the setting sun were breaking on Kenia's snows.[48]

'Glory' had been a sign and attribute of the transcendent since biblical times. The Hebrew term *kabod*, which is usually translated 'glory', had overtones of abundance, even heaviness, as well as radiance.[49] It indicated the visible splendour of God as it radiated from the cloud in the wilderness (Exodus 16:10). Divine guidance in the form of the pillar of cloud by day and the pillar of fire by night (13: 21–2) brought the Israelites to Mount Sinai, where the glory of God appeared as cloud and burning fire on the mountain top (Exodus 24.16–17). Artists were attracted by the melodrama of such vivid biblical imagery; the Irish painter Francis Danby depicted *The Israelites Led by the Pillar of Fire by Night* (c.1825).[50]

---

[47] H. Rider Haggard, *King Solomon's Mines*, chapter 5, p. 44.

[48] H. Rider Haggard, *Allan Quatermain*, chapter 4, pp. 51–2.

[49] Discussed in G. J. Botterweck and Helmer Ringgren, eds, *Theological Dictionary of the Old Testament*, English translation, 15 vols (Grand Rapids, MI: Eerdmans, 1977–2006), VII, pp. 22–38.

[50] This painting is now in Nottingham Castle Museum.

Rider Haggard: Adventures with the Numinous 185

Awesome pillars of fire are everywhere in Rider Haggard as an aspect of his version of the sublime and a manifestation of divine (or sometimes demonic) energies. There is also rather a lot of oppressive unilluminated darkness to throw them into relief. The nightmare journey in *Allan Quatermain* 'through the bowels of the earth, borne on the bosom of a Stygian river',[51] explicitly draws on Virgil's account of the underworld in the sixth book of Virgil's *Aeneid* (Curtis is always obligingly to hand to provide classical flourishes to supplement Quatermain's plain narrative). While this and Haggard's other underground scenes may owe something to the underground setting of Bulwer Lytton's *The Coming Race* the principle debt is to the hell of Dante and Milton, which developed from Virgil's underworld, and to the artists such as Martin and Doré who attempted to illustrate it. In the middle of all of this the adventurers find themselves rushing towards a huge jet of flame rising from the water, 'this pillar of fire, which gleamed fiercer than any furnace ever lit by man'.[52] They survive the experience and eventually find themselves witnessing the sun-worship of Zu-Vendis, with a ritual hymn to the sun that combines elements from the Song of Songs and the Psalms in a manner that comes across as strangely Blakean. The midday sun then flashes into the temple, 'a splendid living ray of light, cleaving the twilight like a sword of fire'.[53] The visual effect and the religious atmosphere recall the dramatic treatment of light in paintings of biblical scenes such as Martin's *Belshazzar's Feast* or his mezzotint *The Deluge* (1828), or Danby's *The Opening of the Sixth Seal* (1828).[54]

Haggard trades on the same associations in subsequent novels. The combination of the sublime and impossible dreams, reaching out to an eternal female principle, is developed most fully in *She* (1887). The imperious immortal figure of Ayesha or 'she who must be obeyed' helped Carl Jung to illustrate his concept of the 'anima' or idealized female spirit that he represents as an aspect of the male psyche and its aspirations.[55] But She can only be approached by yet another long and arduous journey. The mysterious caves and underground passages again contribute to the eerie atmosphere of the novel, and

---

[51] H. Rider Haggard, *Allan Quatermain*, chapter 10, p. 114.
[52] H. Rider Haggard, *Allan Quatermain*, chapter 10, p. 117.
[53] H. Rider Haggard, *Allan Quatermain*, chapter 14, p. 174.
[54] The latter is now in the National Gallery of Ireland.
[55] See C. G. Jung, *The Archetypes and the Collective Unconscious*, IX (Part 1), pp. 28, 30, 71, etc.

186   *Rider Haggard: Adventures with the Numinous*

several reviewers made the link with the nightmare world of Dante's Hell, particularly as interpreted by Doré's illustrations.[56] Haggard goes out of his way to suggest parallels with the Virgilian underworld that contributes to the imaginative construction of both Dante's *Inferno* and Milton's Hell in *Paradise Lost*. It also provides Edmund Burke with an example of the sublime and terrible conjunction of '*Vacuity, Darkness, Solitude* and *Silence*'. Virgil's visitors to Tartarus, the abode of the wicked in the underworld, move on through the ominous and silent dark, and so do Haggard's adventurers:

> On we went for many minutes in absolute silence, like lost souls in the depths of Tartarus, Ayesha's white and ghost-like form flitting in front of us...[57]

Even more than in his other novels, Haggard draws heavily on the Bible for the sometimes portentous rhetoric of this narrative. Ayesha speaks in the language of Ecclesiastes, which Haggard admired so much, when she says: 'there is no new thing under the sun'.[58] The visionary cities of the narrative come from Bunyan and Revelation. If the travellers never find a Celestial City they encounter its antitype: the apocalyptic fall of Babylon is echoed in 'Fallen is Imperial Kôr!—fallen!—fallen!—fallen!'[59] But the biblical language does more than just add a certain solemnity and ancient dignity. The mysterious pillar of fire that guided the children of Israel in the wilderness makes another appearance, this time an emblem of supernatural terror rather than of divine glory, in the revolving pillar of flame that Ayesha embraces and by which she is consumed.[60] Years later, both in the chronology of Haggard's career and in the lives of his fictional Holly and Vincey, in the sequel *Ayesha* there is yet another immensely long and difficult journey to find She once again, but a distant active volcano provides them with guidance. The reader only gradually

---

[56] *Pall Mall Gazette* (4 January 1887) and *Public Opinion* 51 (January 1887), both quoted in H. Rider Haggard, *She* (1887), ed. Andrew M. Stauffer (Peterborough, Ontario, 2006), pp. 281–3.

[57] *She*, chapter 25, p. 256; Burke, *Philosophical Enquiry*, Part II, section 6; Burke actually quotes the lines underlying Haggard's description, Virgil's 'ibant obscuri, sola sub nocte per umbras/perque domos Ditis vacuas', *Aeneid* VI.268–9 ('On they went dimly, beneath the lonely night amid the gloom, through the empty halls of Dis'[Loeb]).

[58] H. Rider Haggard, *She*, chapter 16, p. 173; Eccles. 1:9.

[59] H. Rider Haggard, *She*, chapter 18, p. 196; Rev. 18:2.

[60] H. Rider Haggard, *She*, chapter 26, p. 260; Exod. 13:21–2.

Rider Haggard: Adventures with the Numinous 187

realizes the full significance: in the daytime their beacon is manifest as a column of smoke, or pillar of cloud, arising from the mountain, and in the darkness it is still visible as a pillar of fire. While the explanation makes modern sense of the Exodus narrative it does not remove its aura of ancient mystery. It also links the modern adventure of the novel with the archetypal wilderness journey in Exodus and the pilgrim people who undertook it.

But to what extent can the recurring journey motif be seen as pilgrimage in any religious sense? Rider Haggard—not ironically embattled against institutional religion like Hardy, more reticent than Mary Ward or George Eliot about the Church and contemporary Christianity—would not have directly insisted on the claim himself. In a way he was too much of a traditional Protestant for that. Despite the example of Chaucer's *Canterbury Tales* and Bunyan's *The Pilgrim's Progress* there had always been a certain embarrassment about pilgrimage in Protestant England, which he may have shared. Some of Chaucer's less than saintly Canterbury pilgrims illustrated the very mixed motives for late-medieval pilgrimages to particular shrines, and the early Lutheran *Augsburg Confession* of 1530 was distinctly uneasy about them. Identifying them as 'childish and needless works', it lumped them in with holy days, particular fasts, the use of rosaries and so on as unacceptable substitutes for saving faith.[61] The English word 'pilgrim' comes from the Latin *peregrinus*, so the Wycliffite Bible, based on the Latin Vulgate, consistently renders *peregrinus* as 'pilgrim', but Tyndale's version (1530–7) and the King James version of 1611 use the word very sparingly, often substituting 'stranger' or 'sojourner', as if to repudiate pre-reformation pilgrimage and all its works and dubious rewards.[62] It is usually the bleakness and difficulty of Haggard's journeys rather than what lies at the end of them that bring them closest to the biblical models. Material and even spiritual rewards are often curiously secondary. *King Solomon's Mines*, dashed off in emulation of Robert Louis Stevenson, seems to be the exception, but the fabulous uncut diamonds at journey's end arguably owe more to the pirate gold in Stevenson's *Treasure Island*

---

[61] Philip Schaff, *The Creeds of Christendom*, 6th ed. [1931] 3 vols, (Grand Rapids, Michigan: Baker Books, 2007), III, p. 20.

[62] For example, Wycliffe translates Exod. 23:9 as 'Thou schalt not be diseseful to a pilgrim [. . .] ye weren pilgrims in the lond of Egypt' but in both Tyndale and the King James version this is 'thou shalt not oppress a stranger [. . .] seeing ye were strangers in the land of Egypt'.

188 *Rider Haggard: Adventures with the Numinous*

than to Haggard himself, and finding Henry Curtis' missing brother George is at least as important. More characteristic is the heroic journey of Ignosi's mother across mountains and the desert, which is explicitly compared with the Old Testament journey of Hagar in the wilderness and provides a kind of model or parallel for the journey of Allan Quatermain and his companions.[63]

Haggard's quest-narratives concern more or less obsessive travellers, not so much Canterbury pilgrims as sojourners and strangers without permanent rights of settlement or much commitment to home comforts. Transformations of the vision of the Celestial City developed by Bunyan may still be part of the imaginative hinterland, but Haggard's visionary cities are more likely to fall into ruins, if not ruined already, than to greet the travellers with the sound of trumpets and give them permanent homes. The often sombre encounters with the sublime do not deliver the New Jerusalem nor any secular equivalent. In *She* the quest or pilgrimage includes a kind of epiphany when the mythic She is encountered face to face, but the novel ends not with Beulah or the beatific vision but with defeat and a sense of loss. It has been a journey to Hell, or at least to the darker recesses of the psyche: two of the four members of the original party had died in the attempt and 'the other two had gone through adventures so strange and terrible that Death himself hath not a more fearful countenance'.[64]

The archaic 'hath' and the melodramatic language recall quasi-biblical legends such as the apocryphal 'Testament of Abraham' in which Death, wearing a fearful countenance, appears to Abraham in person. But behind the legends, behind the novel, there lurk the primal fears of the Psalmist for himself and for his people who 'perish at the rebuke of thy countenance' (Psalm 80:16). The psalm concludes, 'Turn us again, O Lord God of hosts, cause thy face to shine; and we shall be saved'. But that goes further than Haggard is prepared to go, at least in his fictions. His characters, or some of them, may be saved from immediate perils, and there are hints and intimations of some kind of life after death, but larger questions of salvation and salvation history are off the map. There is in fact a sense of religious pilgrimage in Rider Haggard, but of pilgrimage that is radically incomplete, journeys of the spirit to a destination that perhaps can

---

[63] H. Rider Haggard, *King Solomon's Mines*, chapter 19, p. 193n; Genesis 16.
[64] H. Rider Haggard, *She*, chapter 28, p. 278.

be fleetingly glimpsed in the dreams of romance, though surrounded in mystery. The New Testament appropriation of the Old Testament pilgrimage idea, the sense of always being 'strangers and pilgrims on the earth' (Hebrews 11:13), is not spelt out in his fiction, but it underpins it.

For all the improbabilities of Haggard's quest-narratives, their effect is not just a certain solemnity and awe, perhaps infused with the sublime, but a sense that their audacious but inconclusive dealings with unknown places, love, time, and eternity are imaginatively continuous with biblical visions of ancient peoples confronting their history, episodes in the larger pattern of human history, rich in religious significance that may never be fully understood.

8

Conclusion: Authority, the Novel, and God

Recurring challenges to the grand narrative of secularization and modernization suggest that rumours of the death of God may have been exaggerated. Max Weber's 'disenchantment of the world' has been countered by explorations such as Peter Berger's edited collection *The Desecularization of the World* (1999) and, more recently, the American jurist Steven D. Smith's *The Disenchantment of Secular Discourse* (2010). Jürgen Habermas has offered us 'Notes on a post-secular society' (2008) and other interventions, and has debated the possibilities of the post-secular with prominent Catholic theologians including the present Pope. In 2003 the German sociologist Detlef Pollack suggested secularization itself might be a modern myth.[1] Against this background it has become easier to read ostensibly secular or post-Christian narratives as in fact post-secular, or religious by other means. Eliot, Hardy, Ward, and Haggard can now be seen not as secular novelists so much as pioneers of the post-secular. It is tempting to enrol them in a special 'school' of novelists devoted to reimagining the scriptures in the secular world, continuing the age-old process of rereading the Bible. There might be other candidates for admission such as 'Mark Rutherford' (1831–1913), novelist and translator of Spinoza, like Eliot, once a member of Bunyan's church in Bedford, who found ways to modernize Bunyan's Doubting

---

[1] P. L. Berger, ed., *The Desecularization of the World: A Global Overview* (Grand Rapids, MI: Eerdmans, 1999); Jürgen Habermas, 'Notes on a post-secular society', signandsight.com (online magazine), 18 June 2008, <http://www.signandsight.com/features/1714.html> (accessed 18/10/2010); see also Jürgen Habermas et al., *An Awareness of What is Missing: Faith and Reason in a Post-Secular Age* (Cambridge: Polity Press, 2010); Detlef Pollack, *Säkularisierung—ein moderner Mythos?* (Tübingen: Mohr Siebeck, 2003).

Conclusion: Authority, the Novel, and God   191

Castle and the Valley of the Shadow of Death;[2] or the post-Calvinist George MacDonald (1824–1905), whose fairy tale 'The Golden Key' has been identified as a theological parable with a pilgrimage plot.[3] But this retrospective conceit of a 'school' overhomogenizes very different writers. They are best seen as symptoms rather than as a school. The Church of England had nurtured Eliot, Hardy, Ward, and Rider Haggard, though not Mark Rutherford or George MacDonald. But the results were different in each case. Eliot and Hardy had little involvement with public service but Ward toiled in the East End and in 1916 toured munitions factories and wartime battlefields to report on the war effort, while Rider Haggard served on official commissions to report on emigration, agriculture, and forestry. Rider Haggard never left the church of his baptism even if his dreams strayed well beyond it. He dedicated his novel *Love Eternal* (1918) to his friend Rev. Philip T. Bainbrigge of St Thomas's, Regent Street. But Hardy's *Jude* was burnt by a bishop, in the absence of Hardy himself, and Eliot's refusal to attend church caused a bitter 'Holy War' with her beloved father. Ward may have rejected traditional Anglican teaching but she gradually mellowed and was still close enough in spirit to the established Church to be unhappy about a Registry Office wedding for her daughter Janet and the allegedly godless historian G. M. Trevelyan. She deplored the fact that he had been brought up in the 'absence [of] any English Church tradition *whatever*'.[4]

Despite differences and dissent from the orthodoxies of the day, all four writers had in common a moral and imaginative attachment to the Bible and the writers associated with it, particularly Dante, Milton, Bunyan, and Wordsworth. But Kukuanaland is a long way from Christminster. Eliot and Ward shared the same wariness of miracle and the supernatural, and the same moral and sociological seriousness, but they belonged to different generations and they read, and wrote, different books. What they shared with Hardy and Haggard was a distrust of theological dogma and a moral as well as imaginative commitment to the present world, or the secular, as the arena of

---

[2] Discussed by Vincent Newey in 'Bunyan's Afterlives: Case Studies', in W. R. Owens and Stuart Sim, eds, *Reception, Appropriation, Recollection: Bunyan's Pilgrim's Progress* (Bern: Peter Lang, 2007), pp. 39–46.

[3] Cynthia Marshall, 'Reading "The Golden Key": Narrative Strategies of Parable', *Children's Literature Association Quarterly* 14 (1989), 22–5.

[4] John Sutherland, *Mrs Humphry Ward: Eminent Victorian, Pre-eminent Edwardian* (Oxford: Clarendon Press, 1990), p. 250.

192   Conclusion: Authority, the Novel, and God

moral and spiritual endeavour. Liberal Protestants such as Dean Fremantle, author of *The Gospel of the Secular Life* (1882) and a possible model for Ward's Richard Meynell, had no difficulty with that, any more than later theologians such as Jürgen Moltmann in *God for a Secular Society* (1997). Ward's grandfather, Dr Arnold, and the Germans had been there first: Fremantle had learnt much from the Doctor and from Richard Rothe's *Theologische Ethik* (1845–8), both acknowledged in the Preface to his Bampton Lectures on *The World as the Subject of Redemption* (1885). Rothe had anticipated the novelists by insisting that 'secular science' would by its own methods reach the ends aimed at by theology. Eliot, well versed in Comte and Herbert Spencer, and Ward, a disciple of T. H. Green, author of *Lectures on the Principles of Political Obligation* (published in 1895; originally delivered 1879–80), can be regarded as social scientists and moral essayists designing what Eliot called 'experiments in life' as their way of being secular theologians.[5] Hardy in particular, anti-Church but not necessarily anti-Christian, would have endorsed Rothe's anti-dogmatic verdict that:

> A great deal of that which we consider as a contradiction of Christian faith is only a contradiction of the ecclesiastical formulating and manipulation of it . . . One of the chief efforts of believers in the present day, must be to help to set Christ free from the Church.[6]

Has this work of religious liberation and modernization got anywhere? Has anything come out of the various 'experiments in life' conducted in the fictions of Eliot, Hardy, Ward, and Haggard? Novels such as *The Bell* (1958) by the philosopher and moralist Iris Murdoch, author of *The Sovereignty of Good* (1970), arguably continue the work. Respectful of the social embeddedness of nineteenth-century realist fiction but also interested in exploring romance forms in her own work, sensitive to the cultural transformations of religion, Murdoch has something in common with Eliot and Ward. They would have understood and in a sense shared her conclusion that, 'The mythology of religion does not necessarily vanish but finds a new and different place as religion is newly understood. As A. N. Wilson

---

[5] Eliot to Dr J. F. Payne, 25 January 1876, *The George Eliot Letters*, ed. G. S. Haight, 9 vols (Oxford: Clarendon, 1954–78), VI, 216–17.

[6] Richard Rothe, *Still Hours* [1878], trans. Jane T. Stoddart (London: Hodder and Stoughton, 1886), pp. 404, 408–9.

Conclusion: Authority, the Novel, and God 193

says, ... "Jesus has survived".[7] But the religion that continued to haunt Murdoch's imagination is different, less biblical and Anglican, more Russian. As her biographer and critic Peter Conradi shrewdly notes, 'She was not the heir—as she early and wrongly imagined—to George Eliot, but to Dostoevsky, with his fantastic realism, his hectically compressed time-schemes, his obsessions with sado-masochism and with incipient moral anarchy.'[8]

With or without the direct influence of Eliot and the others, the novel in English has continued to be a site of serious moral and religious exploration. The Australian writer Morris West, once in a religious order, responded to and in a sense sought to continue the modernizing project initiated by Pope John XXIII and the second Vatican Council, particularly in his bestselling Vatican Trilogy *The Shoes of the Fisherman* (1963), *The Clowns of God* (1981), and *Lazarus* (1990). Like Ward, he was 'troubled by the spectacle of misery and poverty, and injustice and oppression, and the million faces of despair'. Like Hardy, he wondered how a just God could permit such things: 'I wrestle daily with the mystery of how all this could have issued, as the Christian faith affirms it does, from the single creative act of an all-good and all-knowing Divinity.'[9] But West's God was a Catholic God, inherited from an Irish-Australian rather than an English family background, and the settings of his novels, his literary parish, extended well beyond the Anglican communion.

Religious seriousness in fiction has become to some extent a Catholic preserve, for a variety of reasons. Bloomsbury scoffers such as Lytton Strachey and Virginia Woolf mocked Mrs Humphrey Ward and Victorian high seriousness in its national and (post-) Anglican mode in a manner that discouraged successors in the same vein. Too much religion could not be tolerated or expected of novelists of the secular world, despite the earnest studies such as T. G. Selby's *Theology of Modern Fiction*. Any kind of theological restatement that emphasized the secular and played down dogma and the miraculous was in any case a perilous undertaking, vulnerable to sniper-fire or

---

[7] Iris Murdoch, *Metaphysics as a Guide to Morals* [1992] (London: Vintage, 2003), p. 510.

[8] Peter J. Conradi, *Iris Murdoch: A Life* (London: HarperCollins, 2001), p. 596. See also the most recent study, Miles Leeson, *Iris Murdoch: Philosophical Novelist* (London: Continuum, 2010).

[9] Morris West, *A View from the Ridge* (London: HarperCollins, 1996), p. 127.

194   *Conclusion: Authority, the Novel, and God*

kidnap from either side in the no-man's-land between dogmatic orthodoxy and completely secular humanism. W. H. Fremantle's almost agnostic reflections on 'Theology under its Changed Conditions' were fiercely attacked in Charles Gore's conservative polemic *The Clergy and the Creeds* (1887).[10] In 1915 the once-radical liberal Dissenter R. J. Campbell repudiated his own highly experimental New Theology, which Hardy had linked with *The Dynasts*, and ended up safely inside the Anglican fold as a Canon of Chichester. Theologians might try to point out from time to time that the secular was still a religious category and that the opposite of 'sacred' was 'profane' rather than 'secular', but this was a difficult message to get across.

It was not the only difficulty. The humanitarian disasters of the First World War, which so disheartened Hardy, to be followed by the unimaginable horrors of the Holocaust in the Second and an enhanced awareness of poverty and want worldwide, made it harder to believe in the progressive grand narrative of salvation history or growing good inside or outside the national church, though George Eliot's narrative tributes to human suffering and self-sacrifice retained their popularity. Rider Haggard was less optimistic about society than Eliot or Ward, and more deeply read in the gloomy timelessness of the Book of Ecclesiastes. His mythopoeic imagination appealed to C. S. Lewis, at least, among the new generation of religious novelists, but Lewis owed much more to George MacDonald than he did to Haggard. Graham Greene's early reading of Haggard inspired excitement and fear, and gave him a taste for uncomfortable adventure in remote places. He wondered if it was the sinister fascination of the African witch-figure Gagool in *King Solomon's Mines* that brought him to Liberia in 1942, and *Montezuma's Daughter* certainly lured him to Mexico and the writing of *The Power and the Glory*. But Greene's religious sense came from elsewhere, from Catholic tradition. That had relatively little to do with the language of the English Bible, which mattered so much to Haggard.[11]

---

[10] W. H. Fremantle, 'The New Reformation (III): Theology under its Changed Conditions', *Fortnightly Review* 47 (March 1887), 442–58; Charles Gore, *The Clergy and the Creeds* (London: Rivingtons, 1887), pp. 37–40.

[11] Norman Sherry, *The Life of Graham Greene, 1904–1939* (London: Penguin, 1989), pp. 17–19.

Conclusion: Authority, the Novel, and God 195

But Haggard, Eliot, Hardy, and Ward have had a more indirect influence. It is clearer to us than it was to their contemporaries or themselves that they stood in and helped to renew an ancient tradition of imaginative bible reading. Modern biblical research on biblical narrative has drawn attention to the traditions of Jewish storytelling that lie behind New Testament parables. The gapped and not fully coherent narrative of the Torah could be supplemented and made useful for teaching by providing commentary in the form of additional narrative material, often incorporating verses from other parts of scripture. The midrashic parable or *mashal*, derived from the ancient near eastern tradition of wisdom literature, was an illustrative fiction, often in the form 'it is like . . .', often a story about a king in which the king symbolized God. The Hebrew term *mashal*, with a root implying likeness or similarity, was translated into Greek in the Septuagint as *parabole* from which we get 'parable'.[12]

This method of religious teaching through story allows for continuities between the Bible and the novel, between sacred and more 'secular' scripture. It bypasses vexed questions of literal truth and authority by locating authority in the nature of the story itself rather than its empirical verifiability or disputably divine authorship. It chimes with the American theologian Paul van Buren's insight that 'this word ["God"] comes through the tradition primarily in the context of a story or a collection of stories, that it is set in the context of myth, legend, narrative, and song, and not in that of propositions'. He goes on to suggest that 'the believer associates his [moral] intention with a particular religious story', which provides psychological support for the intention whether or not it is empirically true.[13] This has affinities with John Caputo's adventurously postmodern and post-secular 'Theology of the Event', developed from a quite different perspective. Caputo emphasizes the operation of the sacred in terms of event and sees the restless, ever-unfolding quality of the 'event' as always provisional, resisting attempts to fix or name it or organize it

---

[12] Daniel Boyarin, 'History Becomes Parable: A Reading of the Midrashic *Mashal*', in Vincent L. Tollers and John Maier, eds, *Mappings of the Biblical Terrain: The Bible as Text, Bucknell Review* 33 (1990), 54–71; David Stern, *Parables in Midrash: Narrative and Exegesis in Rabbinic Literature* (Cambridge, MA: Harvard University Press, 1991), pp. 1–19, 44.

[13] Paul van Buren, *The Edges of Language: An Essay in the Logic of a Religion* (London: SCM Press, 1972), pp. 17, 35.

196   *Conclusion: Authority, the Novel, and God*

into system, a provocation and a promise forever drawing us into the future.[14] As Mary Ward could have told him, thinking of God in these terms, for instance in the work of creation, necessarily involves not propositions but narrative. So does the earlier 'process theology' of A. N. Whitehead, which Peter Hodgson has linked with the suffering God in George Eliot. Novelists too think in stories rather than propositions. Morris West long resisted invitations to write about his personal religious pilgrimage and insights on the grounds that it was all there in the novels.

Religious insight disclosed and conveyed through story takes us back not just to the Bible and biblical commentary but to early apocryphal writings. The canonical Hebrew scriptures were supplemented by other, later, narratives associated with particular figures, Adam and Abraham, Moses and Shem, the son of Noah. Collectively designated the Pseudepigrapha, they were known to and quoted by early Christian writers.[15] They often incorporated and adapted themes, phrases, and details from the Hebrew Bible and from each other. Early Christian writers, such as the author or authors of the *Didache*, amplified the Christian story in rather the same way, or partly rewrote it, drawing on existing religious writings, including material later identified as New Testament scripture but shaping, extending, and adapting them for their own purposes. Something similar could be said of Eliot's reworking of Christ's preaching in *Adam Bede*, Haggard's pillars of fire and cloud adapted from Exodus, Hardy's ironic appropriations of the miseries of the biblical Job in *Jude*, and Ward's version of the messianic in the charismatic figure of Robert Elsmere.

These novelists in a sense revived and revitalized an old habit of writing instead of inventing a new one. Arguably the tradition continues in William Golding's narrative explorations of evil in *Lord of the Flies* (1954) (the title is a translation of the biblical Beelzebub, a Philistine deity later associated with the forces of evil) and in *Darkness Visible* (1979), Milton's phrase to describe hell in *Paradise Lost*. More recently Salley Vickers, who has worked as a psychotherapist

---

[14] See John D. Caputo, *The Weakness of God: A Theology of the Event* (Bloomington, Indiana: Indiana University Press, 2006), and his talk 'Spectral Hermeneutics', in Jeffrey W. Robbins, ed., *After the Death of God* (New York: Columbia University Press, 2007), pp. 47–50.

[15] See J. H. Charlesworth, ed., *The Old Testament Pseudepigrapha*, 2 vols (London: Darton, Longman & Todd, 1983).

Conclusion: Authority, the Novel, and God   197

and has studied the mythologies of older worlds, has used contemporary fictional narrative to explore ultimate questions about life, death, and the buried self in a manner that might be called religious by other means. A perplexed psychiatrist in her novel *The Other Side of You* (2006) comes to a friend for help, only to be told ' "You know, I don't know if in the end a really great story isn't more help!" '[16] Across the Atlantic, E. L. Doctorow's ambitious novel for the millennium, *City of God* (2000), set in New York, starts as the Bible does with meditation on cosmic origins, the theme of the Genesis creation account, and an intimidated intuition of the astral sublime, takes us into a ghetto under Nazi occupation, and brings together a Christian priest and a Jewish rabbi as 'divinity detectives', seekers after various kinds of truth.

Doctorow's protagonist is an episcopal minister of religion who is at the end of his tether; the novel is about religion but, despite some throwaway references to Paul Tillich and St Augustine, the deliberately fragmented narrative is more concerned with various kinds of intense and problematic experience than with formal theology. So were *Scenes of Clerical Life* and *Jude the Obscure*. William James' *Varieties of Religious Experience* (1902) and Rudolf Otto's *The Idea of the Holy* (1917), particularly influenced by Schleiermacher, were too late for Eliot, and there is no evidence that Hardy or Haggard ever read them, but Ward was reading William James in 1910.[17] Religion as personal experience rather than dogma—spirituality (or *spiritualité*) in its modern sense of the religious dimension of the inner life, a particular mentality that could be classified and studied—had become one of the themes of the *fin de siècle* in England.[18] It is specifically addressed in Richard Le Gallienne's *The Religion of a Literary Man* (1893). Le Gallienne, a novelist and poet, went out of his way to bypass theology and theological controversy, airily dismissing quarrels about miracle and the inspiration of scripture as difficulties that had passed. Leaving scripture, particularly the Old Testament, to one

---

[16] Salley Vickers, *The Other Side of You* (London: Harper Perennial, 2007), p. 43.

[17] Janet Penrose Trevelyan, *The Life of Mrs Humphry Ward* (London: Constable, 1923), p. 257.

[18] See, for example, Annie Besant, *Emotion, Intellect and Spirituality. A Lecture* (London: Theosophical Publishing Co., 1898). The French historian André Vauchez claims *spiritualité* developed its modern meaning of 'relations personelles avec Dieu' only in the nineteenth century: André Vauchez, *La Spiritualité du Moyen Âge occidental* (Paris: Presses Universitaires de France, 1975), p. 5.

198   *Conclusion: Authority, the Novel, and God*

side, he laid great emphasis on what he called the 'spiritual sense' and identified some of its constituent elements as the sense of wonder and the sense of beauty.[19]

Needless to say, Le Gallienne got no thanks from theologians such as the staunchly orthodox Samuel Law Wilson.[20] But he was unconsciously recalling and renewing the tradition of basing religion on intuition and feeling rather than dogma, which stemmed from Schleiermacher, more influential in Germany than in England. This perception would be carried onwards in the research of William James and Rudolf Otto, and psychologists of religion such as Edward Ames of Chicago, to find its apotheosis in the contemporary cognitive science of religion, drawing on psychology and anthropology, associated with the work of Thomas Lawson, Harvey Whitehouse, and others.[21] The tradition could be traced back to Spinoza, or to Melanchthon at the dawn of the Reformation, insisting against the scholastic philosophers obsessed with theological technicalities such as the modalities of the Incarnation that 'to know Christ is to know his benefits'.[22] But even before them the psalmist, declaring, 'I will praise the Lord at all times', had urged his hearers to 'taste and see that the Lord is good: blessed is the man that trusteth in him' (Psalm 35:8). There is a popular seventeenth-century paraphrase by Nahum Tate and Nicholas Brady that emphasizes the narrative possibilities of the psalm by expanding the phrase 'at all times' into 'Through all the changing scenes of life,/In trouble and in joy'. It renders 'taste and see' as:

> O make but trial of his love;
> Experience will decide
> How blest are they, and only they,
> Who in his truth confide.[23]

---

[19] Richard Le Gallienne, *The Religion of a Literary Man* (London: Elkin Mathews and John Lane, 1893), pp. 12, 14, 85–7.

[20] S. Law Wilson, *Chapters in Present Day Theology* (London: Richard D. Dickinson, 1897), p. 63.

[21] See Edward S. Ames, *The Psychology of Religious Experience* (London: Constable, 1910), and Ilkka Pyysiräinen and Veikko Anttonen (eds), *Current Approaches in the Cognitive Science of Religion* (London: Continuum, 2002).

[22] Philipp Melanchthon, Introduction to *Loci Communes* (1521).

[23] Ps. 34:8; Nahum Tate and Nicholas Brady, *A New Version of the Psalms of David* (1696).

Conclusion: Authority, the Novel, and God 199

'Experience' is central in C. H. Dodd's *The Authority of Scripture* (1928). Much less cavalier about the Bible than Le Gallienne, well versed in the severities of the German critical tradition that had impressed itself upon Eliot and Ward, he took full account of Rudolf Otto's discussion of mystery, awe, and the numinous. He suggested that the Bible had the authority of narrated religious experience, not just isolated individual experiences but 'the whole of life religiously interpreted'. To explain the effect of this authority he drew an analogy with reading *King Lear* or—interestingly—*Tess of the d'Urbervilles*, which makes us sharers in an intense and profound experience of life.[24]

Despite the death of God, or the death of older ways of imagining God, Eliot, Haggard, and Ward, as well as Hardy, could lay claim to something of the same kind of authority for their fictions. Novelists may see ultimate questions through a glass, darkly, but they can see something. Perhaps the last word should be from a novel, from Doctorow's *City of God*: 'You're the Lord our Narrator, who made a text from nothing, at least that is our story of You.'[25]

[24] C. H. Dodd, *The Authority of the Bible* (London: Nisbet, 1928), pp. 38–42, 135, 296–7.
[25] E. L. Doctorow, *City of God* (2000) (London: Abacus, 2001), p. 47.

Bibliography

Note: patristic texts, except when available in translation, are indicated by volume number in Migne's *Patrologia Graeca* (PG) or *Patrologia Latina* (PL).

Abbot-Smith, G., *A Manual Greek Lexicon of the New Testament* (Edinburgh: T. & T. Clark, 1999).

Abrams, M. H., *Natural Supernaturalism: Tradition and Revolution in Romantic Literature* (London: Oxford University Press, 1971).

Allen, Charles, *Kipling Sahib: India and the Making of Rudyard Kipling* (London: Little, Brown, 2007).

Allen, Grant, *The Evolution of the Idea of God* (London: Grant Richards, 1897).

Almond, Philip C., *Adam and Eve in Seventeenth-Century Thought* (Cambridge: Cambridge University Press, 1999).

Altizer, Thomas J. J. *The Gospel of Christian Atheism* (London: Collins, 1967).

Ames, Edward S., *The Psychology of Religious Experience* (London: Constable, 1910).

Andrews, Samuel J., *Christianity and Anti-Christianity in their Final Conflict* (New York: G. P. Putnam's Sons, 1898).

Arnold, Matthew, 'A Word More About Spinoza', *Macmillan's Magazine* 9 (December 1863), 136–42.

Ashton, Rosemary, *George Eliot: A Life* (London: Hamish Hamilton, 1996).

Astruc, Jean, *Conjectures sur les mémoires originaux dont il paroit que Moyse s'est servi pour composer le Livre de la Genèse* (Bruxelles: Fricx, 1753).

Athanasius, *Oratio contra Gentes*, PG 25.

Augustine, *Confessions*, trans. R. S. Pine-Coffin (Harmondsworth: Penguin, 1961).

Augustine, *City of God*, trans. Henry Bettenson (Harmondsworth: Penguin, 1984).

Augustine, *De Genesi ad Litteram*, PL 34.

Augustine, *Quaestiones Evangelii*, PL 35.

Augustine, *Epistola ad Catholicos contra Donatistas*, PL 43.

Augustine, *Contra Epistolam Manichaei quam vocent fundamenti*, PL 42.

Austen, Jane, *Northanger Abbey* [1818], World's Classics (Oxford: Oxford University Press, 2003).

Awano, Shuji, *Paradox and Post-Christianity: Hardy's Engagements with Religious Tradition and the Bible* (Yokohama: Shumpûsha, 1999).

Bibliography 201

Babylonian Talmud, ed. I. Epstein, 18 vols (London: Soncino Press, 1936).

Bakhtin, M. M., *The Dialogic Imagination*, trans. Caryl Emerson and Michael Holquist (Austin: Texas, University of Texas Press, 1981).

Barr, James, *Biblical Words for Time* (London: SCM Press, 1962).

Barr, James, *Holy Scripture: Canon, Authority, Criticism* (Oxford: Clarendon, 1983).

Barr, James, 'Why the World was Created in 4004 BC: Archbishop Ussher and Biblical Chronology', *Bulletin of the John Rylands University Library of Manchester* 67 (1985), 575–608.

Barton, John, *People of the Book? The Authority of the Bible in Christianity* (1988), rev. ed. (London: SPCK, 1993).

Baumer, Franklin L., *Religion and the Rise of Scepticism* (New York: Harcourt, Brace, 1960).

Beer, Gillian, *Darwin's Plots: Evolutionary Narrative in Darwin, George Eliot and Nineteenth-century Fiction* (London: Routledge, 1983).

Beer, Gillian, *The Romance* (London: Methuen, 1970).

Beerbohm, Max, *The Poet's Corner* (London: Heinemann, 1904).

Belanger, Jacqueline, ed., *The Irish Novel in the Nineteenth Century* (Dublin: Four Courts Press, 2005).

Benjamin, Walter, *Illuminations*, trans. Harry Zohn (London: Fontana/ Collins, 1973).

Berger, Peter L., *The Social Reality of Religion* (London: Faber, 1969).

Berger, Peter L. ed., *The Desecularization of the World: A Global Overview* (Grand Rapids, Michigan: Eerdmans, 1999).

Bergonzi, Bernard, *A Victorian Wanderer. The Life of Thomas Arnold the Younger* (Oxford: Oxford University Press, 2003).

Berlinerblau, Jacques, *The Secular Bible. Why Nonbelievers Must Take Religion Seriously* (Cambridge: Cambridge University Press, 2005).

Besant, Annie, *Emotion, Intellect and Spirituality. A Lecture* (London: Theosophical Publishing Co., 1898).

Bickersteth, Edward, *The Revised Version of the New Testament* (London: Rivingtons, 1885).

Blumenberg, Hans, *The Legitimacy of the Modern Age* (1966), trans. Robert M. Wallace (Cambridge, MA: MIT Press, 1983).

Bonaparte, Felicia, *The Triptych and the Cross. The Central Myths of George Eliot's Poetic Imagination* (New York: New York University Press, 1979).

Bonhoeffer, Dietrich, *Letters and Papers from Prison* (Glasgow: Collins/ Fontana, 1959).

Botterweck, G. J. and Ringgren, Helmer, eds, *Theological Dictionary of the Old Testament*, English translation, 15 vols (Grand Rapids, MI: Eerdmans, 1977–2006).

Bowker, John, *The Targums and Rabbinic Literature* [1969] (Cambridge: Cambridge University Press, 1979).

202 *Bibliography*

Boyarin, Daniel, 'History Becomes Parable: A Reading of the Midrashic *Mashal*', in Vincent L. Tollers and John Maier, eds, *Mappings of the Biblical Terrain: The Bible as Text, Bucknell Review* 33 (1990), 54–71.

Boyarin, Daniel, 'Midrash in Parables', review of David Stern, *Parables in Midrash* [1991], *Association for Jewish Studies Review* 20:1 (1995), 123–38.

Bramhall, John, *The Catching of Leviathan, or The Great Whale. Demonstrating, out of Mr Hobs his own Works, That no man who is thoroughly an Hobbist, can be a good Christian, or a good Common-wealths man, or reconcile himself to himself* (London: John Crook, 1658).

Bramhall, John, *Works*, 2 vols (Oxford: J. H. Parker, 1842).

Bright, John, *Jeremiah* (The Anchor Bible) (Garden City, NY: Doubleday, 1965).

Brown, Bill, 'The Dark Wood of Postmodernity (Space, Faith, Allegory)', *PMLA* 120 (May 2005), 734–50.

Brown, Callum, *The Death of Christian Britain: Understanding Secularisation 1800–2000* (London: Routledge, 2001).

Browning, Gary, *Lyotard and the End of Grand Narratives* (Cardiff: University of Wales Press, 2000).

Bruce, Steve, *God Is Dead. Secularization in the West* (Oxford: Blackwell, 2002).

Bruns, Gerard, 'Midrash and Allegory: The Beginnings of Scriptural Interpretation', in Robert Alter and Frank Kermode, eds, *The Literary Guide to the Bible* (1987) (Cambridge, MA: Harvard University Press, 1990), 625–46.

Budd, Susan, *Sociologists and Religion* (London: Collier-Macmillan, 1973).

Bullen, J. B., *The Expressive Eye: Fiction and Perception in the Work of Thomas Hardy* (Oxford: Clarendon Press, 1986).

Bultmann, Rudolf, *Jesus Christ and Mythology* (New York: Scribner's, 1958).

Bultmann, Rudolf, *Kerygma and Myth*, ed. H. W. Bartsch [1953], 2nd ed. (London: SPCK, 1964).

Bunsen, C. C. J., *Hippolytus and his Age*, 4 vols (London: Longmans, 1852).

Bunsen, C. C. J., *Christianity and Mankind, their Beginnings and Prospects*, 7 vols (London: Longmans, 1854).

Bunyan, John, *The Pilgrim's Progress*, ed. W. R. Owens (Oxford: Oxford University Press, 2003).

Burchtaell, J. T., *Catholic Theories of Biblical Inspiration since 1810: a Review and Critique* (Cambridge: Cambridge University Press, 1969).

[Burgon, J. W.] 'New Testament Revision: the New Greek Text' *Quarterly Review* 152 (October 1881), 307–68.

[Burgon, J. W.] 'New Testament Revision: the New English Version', *Quarterly Review* 153 (January 1882), 1–63.

[Burgon, J. W.] 'New Testament Revision: Westcott and Hort's Textual Theory', *Quarterly Review* 153 (April 1882), 309–77.

Bibliography 203

Burke, Edmund, *A Philosophical Enquiry into the Origins our Ideas of the Sublime and the Beautiful*, ed. Adam Phillips, World's Classics (Oxford: Oxford University Press, 1990).

Burke, Peter, *Popular Culture in Early Modern Europe* (London: Temple Smith, 1978).

Burleigh, Michael, *Earthly Powers: Religion and Politics in Europe from the Enlightenment to the Great War* (London: Harper Perennial, 2006).

Burleigh, Michael, *Sacred Causes: Religion and Politics from the European Dictators to Al Quaeda* (London: Harper Perennial, 2007).

Burnet, Gilbert, *An Exposition of the Thirty-nine Articles of the Church of England* (1699), ed. J. R. Page (London: Scott, Webster and Geary, 1837).

Burney, Fanny, *Evelina* (Oxford: Oxford University Press, 1968).

Burrow, John, *Evolution and Society* (Cambridge: Cambridge University Press, 1966).

Bynum, Caroline Walker, *Jesus as Mother: Studies in the Spirituality of the High Middle Ages* (Berkeley: University of California Press, 1982).

Callaway, Henry, *The Religious System of the Amazulu*, 4 parts (Springvale, Natal: J. A. Blair, 1868–70).

Calvin, John, *Institutes of the Christian Religion*, ed. J. T. McNeill, trans. F. L. Battles, Library of Christian Classics (Philadelphia: Westminster Press, 1960).

Calvin, John, *The Second Epistle of Paul the Apostle to the Corinthians* [1548], trans. T. A. Smail (Edinburgh,: Oliver & Boyd, 1964).

Cameron, Nigel M. de S., *Biblical Higher Criticism and the Defense of Infallibilism in Nineteenth-century Britain* (Lewiston, New York and Queenston, Ontario: Edwin Mellen, 1987).

Caputo, John D., *The Weakness of God. A Theology of the Event* (Bloomington, Indiana: Indiana University Press, 2006).

Caputo, John D., 'Spectral Hermeneutics', in Jeffrey W. Robbins, ed., *After the Death of God* (New York: Columbia University Press, 2007).

Caputo, John D. and Gianni Vattimo, *After the Death of God* (New York: Columbia University Press, 2007).

Carlyle, Thomas, 'Jean Paul Richter', *Foreign Review and Continental Miscellany* 5 (1830), 1–52.

Carpenter, Mary Wilson, *George Eliot and the Landscape of Time: Narrative Form and Protestant Apocalyptic History* (Chapel Hill: North Carolina Press, 1986).

Carroll, Robert Todd, *The Common-Sense Philosophy of Religion of Bishop Edward Stillingfleet 1635–1699* (The Hague: Martinus Nijhoff, 1975).

Carruthers, Jo and Tate, Andrew, eds, *Spiritual Identities: Literature and the Post-Secular Imagination* (Bern: Peter Lang, 2010).

Carson, James C. L., *The New Translation of the Scriptures*, privately printed for the author [1881].

204 Bibliography

Cassian, John, 'De Spirituali Scientia', *Collationes*, PL 49.

Casson, Lionel, *Travel in the Ancient World* (Baltimore: Johns Hopkins University Press, 1974).

Cave, Alfred, *The Inspiration of the Old Testament Inductively Considered* (London: Congregational Union of England and Wales, 1888).

Certain Sermons Appointed by the Queen's Majesty [1574], ed. G. E. Corrie (Cambridge: Cambridge University Press, 1850).

Chadwick, Henry, *Lessing's Theological Writings* (London: A. & C. Black, 1956).

Chadwick, Owen, *The Victorian Church*, 2 vols, 2nd ed. (London: A. & C. Black, 1970–2).

Chadwick, Owen, *The Secularization of the European Mind in the Nineteenth Century* (Cambridge: Cambridge University Press, 1975).

Chadwick, Owen, *The Early Reformation on the Continent* (Oxford: Oxford University Press, 2001).

Chapman, E. M., *English Literature in Account with Religion 1800–1900* (London: Constable, 1910).

Chapman, W. Stacey, *The Critical Method and the History of Testimony as Discoursed in 'Robert Elsmere'* (Melbourne: Samuel Mullen, 1888).

Charlesworth, J. H., ed., *The Old Testament Pseudepigrapha*, 2 vols (London: Darton, Longman & Todd, 1983).

Chateaubriand, François René de, *The Beauties of Christianity*, trans. Frederic Shoberl, Pref. by Henry Kett, 3 vols (London: Henry Colburn, 1813).

Chesterton, G. K., *The Victorian Age in Literature* [1913] (London: Oxford University Press, 1966).

Chrisman, Laura, *Rereading the Imperial Romance: British Imperialism and South African Resistance in Haggard, Schreiner and Plaatje* (Oxford: Clarendon Press, 2000).

Christensen, Allan Conrad, *Edward Bulwer-Lytton: The Fiction of New Regions* (Athens, GA: University of Georgia Press, 1976).

Chrysostom, St John, *Homilies on St Matthew*, PG 7 (i).

Chrysostom, St John, *Homilies on the Epistle of Paul to the Philippians, Colossians and Thessalonians* (Oxford: J. H. Parker, 1843).

Chrysostom, St John, *Homilies on the Epistle of Paul to Timothy, Titus and Philemon*, trans. J. Tweed (Oxford: J.H. Parker, 1843).

Clement of Alexandria, *Stromata* (PG 9) in *Writings*, trans. W. Wilson, 2 vols (Edinburgh: T. & T. Clark, 1868–9).

Clement [of Rome], in J. B. Lightfoot, ed., *The Apostolic Fathers*, part 1, vol. 2 (London: Macmillan, 1890).

Coates, John, '"The Spiritual Quest" in Rider Haggard's *She* and *Ayesha*', *Cahiers Victoriens et Édouardiens* (Montpellier) 57 (April 2003), 33–54.

Cohen, Morton, *Rider Haggard. His Life and Works* (London: Hutchinson, 1960).

Bibliography 205

Coit, Stanton, *National Idealism and the Book of Common Prayer: An Essay in Reinterpretation and Revision* (London: Williams and Norgate, 1908).

Colenso, J. W., *The Pentateuch and Book of Joshua Critically Examined*, 7 vols (London: Longmans, 1862–79).

Coleridge, S. T., *Marginalia* II, Camden to Hutton, ed. George Whalley (London and Princeton: Routledge and Princeton University Press, 1984).

Collister, Peter, 'Mrs Humphry Ward's *Eleanor*: a late-Victorian portrait of Chateaubriand and Pauline de Beaumont', *Neophilologus* 65 (October 1981), 622–39.

Conradi, Peter J., *Iris Murdoch: A Life* (London: HarperCollins, 2001).

Cook, F. C., *The Revised Version of the First Three Gospels* (London: John Murray, 1882).

Cowling, Maurice, *Religion and Public Doctrine in Modern England*, 3 vols (Cambridge: Cambridge University Press, 1980–2001).

Cox, Harvey, *The Secular City: Secularization and Urbanization in Theological Perspective* (1965), rev. ed. (New York: Macmillan, 1966).

Crossley, Ceri, *French Historians and Romanticism: Thierry, Guizot, the Saint-Simonians, Quinet, Michelet* (London: Routledge, 1993).

d'Alembert, Jean Le Rond, *Preliminary Discourse to the Encyclopedia of Diderot* trans. Richard M. Schwab (Chicago: University of Chicago Press, 1995).

Daniell, David, *The Bible in English: its History and Influence* (New Haven and London: Yale University Press, 2003).

Day, Geoffrey, *From Fiction to the Novel* (London: Routledge, 1987).

de Bolla, Peter, *The Discourse of the Sublime: Readings in History, Aesthetics and the Subject* (Oxford: Blackwell, 1989).

de Grood, David H., *Haeckel's Theory of the Unity of Nature* (Boston: Christopher Publishing House, 1965).

de Nerval, Gérard, *Oeuvres complètes*, ed. Jean Guillaume and Charles Pichois, 3 vols (Paris: Gallimard, 1989).

de Wette, W. M. L., *Beiträge zur Einleitung in das Alte Testament*, 2 vols (Halle: Schimmelpfennig, 1806–7).

Defoe, Daniel, *A New Family Instructor* (1727), ed. W. R. Owens (Religious and Didactic Writings of Daniel Defoe vol. 3) (London: Pickering and Chatto, 2006).

Desmond, Adrian, *Huxley: Evolution's High Priest* (London: Michael Joseph, 1997).

Dickey, Laurence, *Hegel: Religion, Economics, and the Politics of Spirit 1770–1801* (Cambridge: Cambridge University Press, 1987).

Didache, trans. (as *The Teaching of the Twelve Apostles*) I. H. Hall and J. T. Napier, Ante-Nicene Fathers (Grand Rapids, MI: Eerdmans, 1994).

Doctorow, E. L., *City of God* (London: Abacus, 2001).

206   *Bibliography*

Dodd, C. H., *The Authority of the Bible* (London: Nisbet, 1928).

Donne, John, *Selected Poetry*, ed. John Carey, World's Classics (Oxford: Oxford University Press, 1996).

Doody, Margaret A., *The True Story of the Novel* (New Jersey: Rutgers University Press, 1996).

Dostoevsky, Fyodor, *The Brothers Karamazov* (1880), trans. David Magarshack (Harmondsworth: Penguin, 1958).

Drury, John, *The Parables in the Gospels: History and Allegory* (London: SPCK, 1985).

Duffy, Eamon, *The Stripping of the Altars: Traditional Religion in England 1400–1580* (New Haven and London: Yale University Press, 1992).

During, Simon, 'Towards the Postsecular', in 'Forum: Responses to Bill Brown', PMLA 120:3 (May 2005), 876–7.

Durkheim, Emile, *The Elementary Forms of Religious Life*, trans. Carol Cosman (Oxford: Oxford University Press, 2001).

Duthie, Enid L., *The Foreign Vision of Charlotte Brontë* (London: Macmillan, 1975).

Du Veil, C. M., *A Letter to the Honourable Richard Boyle, Esq. defending the Divine Authority of the Holy Scripture and that is alone is the Rule of Faith. In answer to Father Simon's Critical History of the Old Testament* (London: Thomas Malthus, 1683).

Eagleton, Terry, *Reason, Faith, and Revolution: Reflections on the God Debate* (New Haven: Yale University Press, 2009).

Ebeling, Gerhard von, *Word and Faith* (Philadelphia: Fortress Press, and London: SCM Press, 1963).

Ehrman, Bart D., *The Orthodox Corruption of Scripture. The Effect of Early Christological Controversies on the Text of the New Testament* (New York: Oxford University Press, 1993).

Eichhorn, J. G., *Einleitung ins Alte Testament* (1780–3), 2nd ed., 3 vols (Leipzig: Weidmans Erben, 1787).

Eliot, George, 'Contemporary Literature of England', *Westminster Review* 57 (January 1852), 247–88.

Eliot, George, *The George Eliot Letters*, ed. Gordon S. Haight, 9 vols (Oxford: Clarendon Press, 1954–78).

Eliot, George, 'Evangelical Teaching; Dr Cumming', *Westminster Review* 64 (October 1855), 436–62.

Eliot, George, 'Silly Novels by Lady Novelists', *Westminster Review* 66 (October 1856), 442–61.

Eliot, George, 'Contemporary Literature: Art and Belles Lettres', *Westminster Review* (April 1856), 625–50.

Eliot, George, 'Worldliness and Other-Worldliness: the Poet Young', *Westminster Review* 67 (January 1857), 1–42.

Bibliography 207

Eliot, George, *'Middlemarch' Notebooks: A Transcription*, ed. J. C. Pratt and V. A. Neufeldt (Berkeley: University of California Press, 1979).

Eliot, George, *Daniel Deronda*, ed. Graham Handley, World's Classics (Oxford: Oxford University Press, 1988).

Eliot, George, *Felix Holt, the Radical*, ed. Fred C. Thomson, World's Classics (Oxford: Oxford University Press, 1988).

Eliot, George, *Collected Poems*, ed. Lucien Jenkins (London: Skoob, 1989).

Eliot, George, *Selected Essays, Poems and Other Writings*, ed. A. S. Byatt (London: Penguin, 1990).

Eliot, George, *Romola*, ed. Andrew Brown, World's Classics (Oxford: Oxford University Press, 1994).

Eliot, George, *Adam Bede*, ed. Valentine Cunningham, World's Classics (Oxford: Oxford University Press, 1996).

Eliot, George, *The Mill on the Floss*, ed. Gordon S. Haight, World's Classics (Oxford: Oxford University Press, 1996).

Eliot, George, *Silas Marner*, ed. Terence Cave, World's Classics (Oxford: Oxford University Press, 1996).

Eliot, George, *Middlemarch*, ed. David Carroll, World's Classics (Oxford: Oxford University Press, 1997).

Ellis, Peter Berresford, *H. Rider Haggard. A Voice from the Infinite* (London: Routledge, 1978).

Ermarth, Elizabeth, *The English Novel in History 1840–1895* (London: Routledge, 1997).

Essays and Reviews (1860), 7th ed. (London: Longman. Green, 1861).

Etherington, Norman, *Preachers, Peasants and Politics in South-east Africa, 1835–1880* (London: Royal Historical Society, 1978).

Eusebius, *Church History*, trans. A. C. McGiffert (Edinburgh: T. & T. Clark, 1890).

Evans, Joan, *Chateaubriand: A Biography* (London: Macmillan, 1939).

Fackenheim, Emil L., *The Religious Dimension in Hegel's Thought* (Bloomington and London: Indiana University Press, 1967).

Fairbairn, A. M., *Religion in History and in Modern Life, together with an Essay on the Church and the Working Classes* [1894] (London: Hodder & Stoughton, 1903).

Fenn, Richard K., ed., *The Blackwell Companion to Sociology of Religion* (Oxford: Blackwell, 2001).

Ferguson, Niall, ed., *Virtual History: Alternatives and Counterfactuals* (London: Picador, 1997).

Feuer, Lewis Samuel, *Spinoza and the Rise of Liberalism* (Boston: Beacon Press, 1958).

Filleau de la Chaise, Jean, *An Excellent Discourse Proving the Divine Original and Authority of the Five Books of Moses ... To which is added a second part, or an examination of ... part of Père Simon's critical history of the Old*

208   *Bibliography*

Testament, wherein all his objections, with the weightiest of Spinoza's, against Moses's being the author of the first Five Books of the Bible are answered, trans. W[illiam] L[orimer] (London: T. Parkhurst, 1682).

Finegan, Jack, *Handbook of Biblical Chronology* (Princeton: Princeton University Press, 1964).

Fishbane, Michael, *Biblical Myth and Rabbinic Mythmaking* (Oxford: Oxford University Press, 2003).

Foote, G. W., *Bible Romances* (London: Freethought Publishing Co., 1882).

Foote, G. W., *The Grand Old Book. A Reply to the Right Hon. W.E. Gladstone's 'The Impregnable Rock of Holy Scripture'* (London: Progressive Publishing Co., 1891).

Forstman, H. Jackson, *Word and Spirit: Calvin's Doctrine of Biblical Authority* (Stanford: Stanford University Press, 1962).

Fraser, Robert, *Victorian Quest Romance: Stevenson, Haggard, Kipling and Conan Doyle* (Plymouth: Northcote House, 1998).

Frei, Hans, *The Eclipse of Biblical Narrative: A Study in Eighteenth and Nineteenth Century Hermeneutics* (New Haven and London: Yale University Press, 1974).

Fremantle, W. H., 'The New Reformation (III): Theology under its Changed Conditions', *Fortnightly Review* 47 (March 1887).

Froude, James Anthony, 'Spinoza', *Westminster Review* 64 (July 1855), 1–37.

Frye, Northrop, *The Secular Scripture: A Study of the Structure of Romance* (Cambridge, MA: Harvard University Press, 1976).

Frye, Northrop, *The Great Code: The Bible and Literature* (Orlando, Florida: Harcourt Brace, 1983).

Gaonkar, Dilip Parameshwar, ed., *Alternative Modernities* (Durham, NC: Duke University Press, 2001).

Garrett, Don, ed., *The Cambridge Companion to Spinoza* (Cambridge: Cambridge University Press, 1996).

Gibbon, Edward, *Decline and Fall of the Roman Empire* [1776–88], ed. David Womersley, 3 vols (London: Allen Lane, 1994).

Gibson, John, *Fiction and the Weave of Life* (Oxford: Oxford University Press, 2007).

Gladstone, William Ewart, *The Impregnable Rock of Holy Scripture* (London: W. Isbister, 1890).

Gladstone, William Ewart, 'Robert Elsmere: the Battle of Belief', *The Nineteenth Century* [1888], reprinted in *Later Gleanings* (London: John Murray, 1897).

Glossa Ordinaria Pars 22 in Canticum Canticorum, ed. Mary Dove, Corpus Christianorum, Continuatio Mediaevalis CLXX (Tournai: Brepols, 1997).

Goode, W., *Holy Scripture the Sole Authoritative Expositor of the Faith, and its Subjection to Church Authority the Proved Pathway to the Church of Rome* (Sermon on Acts 17:11, 12) (London: Hatchard, 1862).

Bibliography

Goodenough, Erwin R., *The Theology of Justin Martyr* (1923) (Amsterdam: Philo Press, 1968).

Gore, Charles, *The Clergy and the Creeds* (London: Rivingtons, 1887).

Gore, Charles, ed., *Lux Mundi* (London: John Murray, 1889).

Gorringe, T. J., *A Theology of the Built Environment* (Cambridge: Cambridge University Press, 2002).

Gosse, Edmund, *Father and Son: A Study of Two Temperaments* (London: Heinemann, 1907).

Goulder, M. D., *Midrash and Lection in Matthew* (London: SPCK, 1974).

Graham, Gordon, *The Re-enchantment of the World: Art versus Religion* (Oxford: Oxford University Press, 2007).

Graham, Kenneth, *English Criticism of the Novel 1865–1900* (Oxford: Clarendon Press, 1965).

Graver, Suzanne, *George Eliot and Community* (Berkeley: University of California Press, 1984).

Greeley, Andrew M., *The Persistence of Religion* (London: SCM Press, 1973).

Greene, Edward Burnaby, *Critical Essays* (1770) (New York: Garland Publishing, 1970).

Gregory of Nyssa, *Select Writings and Letters*, trans. W. Moore and H. A. Wilson, Nicene and Post-Nicene Fathers, 2nd ser. vol. 5, (Oxford: Parker, 1893).

Gregory, Andrew F. and Tuckett, Christopher M., eds, *Trajectories through the New Testament and the Apostolic Fathers* (Oxford: Oxford University Press, 2005).

Gregory, Andrew F. and Tuckett, Christopher M., eds, *The Reception of the New Testament in the Apostolic Fathers* (Oxford: Oxford University Press, 2005).

Habermas, Jurgen, 'Notes on a post-secular society', signandsight.com (online magazine), 18 June 2008, <http://www.signandsight.com/features/1714.html> (accessed 18 October 2010).

Habermas, Jurgen, et al., *An Awareness of What Is Missing: Faith and Reason in a Post-Secular Age* (Cambridge: Polity Press, 2010).

Haggard, Henry Rider, 'About Fiction', *Contemporary Review* 51 (February 1887), 172–80.

Haggard, Henry Rider, 'Books which have influenced me', *British Weekly Extra* no. 1 (London: British Weekly, 1887).

Haggard, Henry Rider, *The Witch's Head* [1885] (London: Spencer Blackett, 1887).

Haggard, Henry Rider, *Colonel Quaritch V.C.* (London: Longman, 1890).

Haggard, Henry Rider, *Eric Brighteyes* (London: Longmans, 1891).

Haggard, Henry Rider, *Dawn* [1884] (London: Griffith Farran, 1893).

Haggard, Henry Rider, *Mr Meeson's Will* [1888] (London: Longmans, 1894).

210 *Bibliography*

Haggard, Henry Rider, *Allan's Wife and other Tales* (London: Spencer Blackett, 1899).

Haggard, Henry Rider, *Black Heart and White Heart and other stories* (London: Longmans, 1900).

Haggard, Henry Rider, *Elissa*, included in *Black Heart and White Heart and other stories* (London: Longmans, 1900).

Haggard, Henry Rider, *Jess* [1887] (London: Smith, Elder, 1900).

Haggard, Henry Rider, *The Way of the* Spirit (London: Hutchinson, 1906).

Haggard, Henry Rider, 'The Real King Solomon's Mines', *Cassell's Magazine* (July 1907).

Haggard, Henry Rider, *Queen Sheba's Ring* [1910] (London: George Newnes, 1913).

Haggard, Henry Rider, *Finished* (London: Ward, Lock, 1917).

Haggard, Henry Rider, *Love Eternal* (London: Cassell, 1918).

Haggard, Henry Rider, *Child of Storm* [1913] (London: Cassell, 1925).

Haggard, Henry Rider, *The Days of My Life*, ed. C. J. Longman, 2 vols (London: Longmans, 1926).

Haggard, Henry Rider, *Nada the Lily* [1892] (London: Macdonald, 1949).

Haggard, Henry Rider, *The World's Desire* [1890] (London: Macdonald, 1953).

Haggard, Henry Rider, *Ayesha: the Return of She* [1905] (London: Macdonald, 1956).

Haggard, Henry Rider, *The Ivory Child* [1916] (London: Macdonald, 1958).

Haggard, Henry Rider, *Marie* [1912] (London: Macdonald, 1959).

Haggard, Henry Rider, *Allan and the Ice-Gods* [1927] (London: Hutchinson, 1971).

Haggard, Henry Rider, *The Private Diaries of Sir H. Rider Haggard 1914–1925*, ed. D. S. Higgins (London: Cassell, 1980).

Haggard, Henry Rider, *Allan Quatermain*, ed. Dennis Butts (Oxford: Oxford University Press, 1995).

Haggard, Henry Rider, *Diary of an African Journey (1914)*, ed. Stephen Coan (London: Hurst, 2001).

Haggard, Henry Rider, *King Solomon's Mines* [1885], ed. Dennis Butts (Oxford: Oxford University Press, 2006).

Haggard, Henry Rider, *She* [1887], ed. Andrew M. Stauffer (Peterborough, Ontario: Broadview, 2006).

Haggard, Lilias Rider, *The Cloak that I Left: A Biography of the Author Henry Rider Haggard KBE* (London: Hodder and Stoughton, 1951).

Haight, Gordon S., *George Eliot: A Biography* (Oxford: Clarendon, 1968).

Hammond, Mary, '"The Great Fiction Bore": Free Libraries and the Construction of a Reading Public in England 1880–1914', in *Libraries and Culture: a journal of library history* 37:2 (Spring 2002), 83–108.

Bibliography

Hammond, Mary, *Reading, Publishing and the Formation of Literary Taste in England 1880–1914* (Aldershot: Ashgate, 2006).

Hands, Timothy, *Thomas Hardy: Distracted Preacher?* (Basingstoke: Macmillan, 1989).

Hanson, R. P. C., *Origen's Doctrine of Tradition* (London: SPCK, 1954).

Hanson, R.P.C., *Allegory and Event. A Study of the Sources and Significance of Origen's Interpretation of Scripture* (London: SCM Press, 1959).

Hardy, Florence Emily, *The Early Life of Thomas Hardy 1840–1891* (London: Macmillan, 1928).

Hardy, Thomas, 'The Science of Fiction', *New Review* 4 (1891), 315–19.

Hardy, Thomas, *The Dynasts* (London: Macmillan, 1910).

Hardy, Thomas, *Thomas Hardy: Complete Poems*, ed. James Gibson (London: Macmillan, 1976).

Hardy, Thomas, *The Collected Letters of Thomas Hardy*, ed. R. L. Purdy and M. Millgate, 7 vols (Oxford: Clarendon Press, 1977–88).

Hardy, Thomas, *The Distracted Preacher and Other Tales* (Harmondsworth: Penguin, 1979).

Hardy, Thomas, *Jude the Obscure*, ed. Patricia Ingham, World's Classics (Oxford: Oxford University Press, 1985).

Hardy, Thomas, *The Literary Notebooks*, ed. Lennart A. Björk, 2 vols (London: Macmillan, 1985).

Hardy, Thomas, *The Woodlanders*, ed. Dale Kramer, World's Classics (Oxford: Oxford University Press, 1985).

Hardy, Thomas, *Tess of the d'Urbervilles*, ed. Juliet Grindle and Simon Gatrell, World's Classics (Oxford: Oxford University Press, 1988).

Hardy, Thomas, *The Return of the Native*, ed. Simon Gattrell, World's Classics (Oxford: Oxford University Press, 1990).

Hardy, Thomas, *Two on a Tower*, ed. Suleiman M. Ahmad, World's Classics (Oxford: Oxford University Press, 1993).

Hardy, Thomas, *'Studies, Specimens & c.'*, ed. Pamela Dalziel and Michael Millgate (Oxford: Clarendon Press, 1994).

Hart, William David, 'Slavoj Zizek and the Imperial/Colonial Model of Religion', *Nepantia: Views from the South* 3.3 (2002), 553–78.

Hays, Mary, *Memoirs of Emma Courtney*, World's Classics (Oxford: Oxford University Press, 1996).

Hebblethwaite, Peter, *The New Inquisition? Schillebeeckx and Küng* (Glasgow: Collins, 1980).

Hegel, G. W. F., *Faith and Knowledge* (1802), trans. Walter Cerf and H. S. Harris (Albany: State University of New York Press, 1977).

Hess, Andrew W., Jasper, David, and Jay, Elisabeth, eds, *The Oxford Handbook of English Literature and Theology* (Oxford: Oxford University Press, 2007).

212 *Bibliography*

Hessayon, Ariel and Keene, Nicholas, eds, *Scripture and Scholarship in Early Modern England* (London: Ashgate, 2006).

Hill, Christopher, *The English Bible and the Seventeenth-Century Revolution* (London: Allen Lane The Penguin Press, 1993).

Hippolytus, *Against the Heresy of Noetus, Writings* II (Dogmatical and Historical), trans. S. D. F. Salmond, Nicene Christian Library (Edinburgh: T. & T. Clark, 1869).

Hobbes, Thomas, *Leviathan* (1651), ed. Richard Tuck (Cambridge: Cambridge University Press, 1991).

Hodgson, Peter C., *The Formation of Historical Theology: A Study of Ferdinand Christian Baur* (New York: Harper& Row, 1966).

Hodgson, Peter C., *Theology in the Fiction of George Eliot* (London: SCM Press, 2001).

Holroyd, Michael, *Lytton Strachey: A Critical* Biography, 2 vols (London: Heinemann, 1967–8).

Holyoake, George Jacob, *The Origin and Nature of Secularism; Showing that where Freethought Commonly Ends Secularism Begins* (London: Watts & Co., 1896).

Hooker, Richard, *Of the Laws of Ecclesiastical Politie* [1593] in *Works*, ed. W. Speed Hill et al., 6 vols (Cambridge, MA: Belknap Press, 1977–93).

Hooker, Richard, *The Works of Richard Hooker*, arranged by J. Keble, 3 vols (Oxford and London: Rivingtons, 1836).

Howard, Thomas Albert, *Protestant Theology and the Making of the Modern German University* (Oxford: Oxford University Press, 2006).

Howorth, H. H., 'The canon of the Bible among the Later Reformers', *Journal of Theological Studies* 10 (1908–9), 183–232.

Hudson, Anne, *The Premature Reformation: Wycliffite Texts and Lollard History* (Oxford: Clarendon Press, 1988).

Huxley, T. H., *Essays upon Some Controverted Questions* (London: Macmillan, 1892).

Index librorum prohibitorum, 1557–1966, available online at <http://www.beaconforfreedom.org/about_database/index_librorum.html> (accessed 12 August 2009).

Ingersoll, Robert, *Repairing the* Idols (London: Progressive Publishing Co., 1888).

Irenaeus, *Against Heresies* in *Writings*, trans. Alexander Roberts and James Donaldson, Ante-Nicene Christian Library (Edinburgh: T. & T. Clark, 1868).

Isidore of Seville, *Quaestiones in Vetus Testamentum*, PL 83.

Ispirescu, Petre, *The Foundling Prince and Other Tales*, trans. Julia Collier-Harris and Rea Ipcar (Boston: Houghton-Mifflin, 1917).

Jackson, J. L., *The Character of Scriptural Inspiration. The Authority of Holy Scripture with the Church of England* (London: L. and G. Seeley, 1842).

Bibliography 213

Jacobson, Eric, *Metaphysics of the Profane: The Political Theology of Walter Benjamin and Gershom Scholem* (New York: Columbia University Press, 2003).

Jaeschke, Walter, *Reason in Religion: The Foundations of Hegel's Philosophy of Religion*, trans. J. Michael Stewart and Peter C. Hodgson (Berkeley: University of California Press, 1990).

James, William, *The Varieties of Religious Experience* [1902] (London and Glasgow: Collins/Fontana, 1971).

Jay, Elisabeth, *The Religion of the Heart: Anglican Evangelicalism and the Nineteenth-century Novel* (Oxford: Clarendon Press, 1979).

Jędrzewski, Jan, *Thomas Hardy and the Church* (Basingstoke: Macmillan, 1996).

Jeffrey, D. L., ed., *A Dictionary of Biblical Tradition in English Literature* (Grand Rapids, MI: Eerdmans, 1992).

Jenkins, Neil, 'Haydn's *The Creation*: on preparing a new English text', *Early Music Review* 111 (February 2006), 16–21.

Jeremias, Joachim, *The Parables of Jesus*, trans. S. H. Hooke, rev. ed. (London: SCM Press, 1963).

Jerome, *Commentaria in Isaiam Prophetam*, PL 24.

Jerome, *Letters* in *Letters and Select Works*, trans. W. H. Fremantle, Nicene and Post-Nicene Fathers (Grand Rapids, MI: W. B. Eerdmans, 1996).

Jewel, John, *An Apology for the Church of England* (1562), trans. Ann Bacon (1564), ed. J. E. Booty (Ithaca, NY: Cornell University Press, 1963).

Jodock, Darrell, ed., *Catholicism Contending with Modernity. Roman Catholic Modernism and Anti-Modernism in Historical Context* (Cambridge: Cambridge University Press, 2000).

Johnson, Lionel, *The Art of Thomas Hardy* (London: John Lane, 1895).

Jowett, Benjamin, 'On the Interpretation of Scripture', *Essays and Reviews* [1860], (London: Longman, 1861).

Joy, Morny, ed., *Paul Ricoeur and Narrative: Context and Contestation* (Calgary: University of Calgary Press, 1997).

Jung, C. G., *The Archetypes and the Collective Unconscious*, trans. R. F. C. Hull, *Collected Works*, 20 vols (London: Routledge, 1953–1979), IX (Part 1).

Jung, C. G., *Nietzsche's* Zarathustra: *Notes of the Seminar Given in 1934–1939*, ed. James L. Jarrett, 2 vols (London: Routledge, 1989).

Justin Martyr, *Writings* (in Migne PG 6) trans. Marcus Dods, George Reith, and B. P. Pratten, Ante-Nicene Christian Library (Edinburgh: T. & T. Clark, 1868).

Kant, Immanuel, *Critique of Judgement* (1790), trans. W. S. Pluhar (Indianapolis: Hackett, 1987).

214   *Bibliography*

Kant, Immanuel, *Observations on the Feeling of the Beautiful and Sublime* [1764], trans. John T. Goldthwait [1960] (Berkeley: University of California Press, 2003).

Katz, David S., *God's Last Words. Reading the English Bible from the Reformation to Fundamentalism* (New Haven: Yale University Press, 2004).

Katz, Wendy, *Rider Haggard and the Fiction of Empire* (Cambridge: Cambridge University Press, 1987).

Keble, John, *Primitive Tradition Recognised in Holy Scripture*, 2nd ed. (London: Rivingtons, 1837).

[Keble, John], 'On the mysticism attributed to the early Fathers of the Church', Tract 89 of *Tracts for the Times* (Oxford: Parker, 1841).

Kelly, J. N. D., *Early Christian Doctrines*, 5th ed. (London: Continuum, 2006).

Kelly, J. Thomas, *Thorns on the Tudor Rose: Monks, Rogues, Vagabonds, and Sturdy Beggars* (Jackson, MS: University Press of Mississippi, 1977).

[Kenrick, John], 'On the Mythological Interpretation of the Bible', *Monthly Repository and Review*, 2nd ser. 1:9 (September 1827), 633–40.

Ker, Ian, *John Henry Newman, a Biography* (Oxford: Oxford University Press, 1988).

Kermode, Frank, *The Sense of an Ending: Studies in the Theory of Fiction* (London: Oxford University Press, 1967).

Kierkegaard, S., *The Point of View on my Work as an Author*, ed. and trans. Howard V. Hong and Edna H. Hong (Princeton, NJ: Princeton University Press, 1998).

Killen, John, *A History of the Linen Hall Library 1788–1988* (Belfast: Linen Hall Library, 1990).

Kim, Andrew E., 'History of Christianity in Korea: From its Troubled Beginning to its Contemporary Success', <http://www.kimsoft.com/1997/xhist.htm> (accessed 10 July 2006).

Kingsley, Charles, *Hereward the* Wake [1866] (London: Macmillan, 1890).

Kingsley, F. E., *Charles Kingsley: His letters and Memories of His Life*, 2 vols (London: Henry S. King, 1873).

Kipling, Rudyard, *Rudyard Kipling to Rider Haggard: the Record of a Friendship*, ed. M. N. Cohen (London: Hutchinson, 1965).

Kittel, Gerhard and Friedrich, Gerhard, eds, *Theological Dictionary of the New Testament*, trans. and ed. G. W. Bromiley, 9 vols (Grand Rapids, MI: W. B. Eerdmans, 1964–74).

Kohlenbach, Margareta, *Walter Benjamin: Self-Reference and Religiosity* (Basingstoke: Palgrave, 2002).

Kugel, James L., *In Potiphar's House. The Interpretive Life of Biblical Texts*, 2nd ed. (Cambridge, MA: Harvard University Press, 1994).

Lacan, Jacques, *The Four Fundamental Concepts of Psycho-analysis* (1973), trans. Alan Sheridan (London: Penguin, 1979).

Bibliography

Lagarde, Paulus de, ed., *Onomastica Sacra* (Göttingen, 1870).

Landow, G. P., *Victorian Types, Victorian Shadows: Biblical Typology in Victorian Literature, Art and Thought* (Boston, MA: Routledge, 1980).

Lang, Andrew, *The Making of Religion* (1898), 2nd ed. (London: Longmans, Green, 1900).

Larsen, Timothy, *Crisis of Doubt: Honest Faith in Nineteenth-Century England* (Oxford: Oxford University Press, 2006).

Larsen, Timothy, *A People of One Book: The Bible and the Victorians* (Oxford: Oxford University Press, 2011).

Latour, Bruno, *We Have Never Been Modern* (1991), trans. Catherine Porter (Harlow: Longman, 1993).

Leavis, F. R., *The Great Tradition* (London: Chatto, 1948).

Le Gallienne, Richard, *The Religion of a Literary Man* (London: Elkin Mathews and John Lane, 1893).

Lennox, Charlotte, *The Female Quixote*, World's Classics (Oxford: Oxford University Press, 1998).

Lerner, Laurence, *The Truth-tellers: Jane Austen, George Eliot, D. H. Lawrence* (London: Chatto, 1967).

Lerner, Laurence and Holmstrom, John, eds, *Thomas Hardy and His Readers* (London: Bodley Head, 1968).

Lessing, G. E., *Werke*, ed. Julius Petersen and Waldemar von Olshausen, 25 vols (Berlin and Leipzig: Bong, 1925).

Levine, George, ed., *The Cambridge Companion to George Eliot* (Cambridge: Cambridge University Press, 2001).

Lewes, G. H., 'Spinoza: His Life and Writings', *Westminster Review* 39 (May 1843), 372–407.

Lewis, Charlton D. and Short, Charles, *A Latin Dictionary* (Oxford: Clarendon Press, 1969).

Lewis, C. S., *Of This and Other Worlds* (London: Collins, 1982).

Lightfoot, J. B. and Harmer, J. R., eds, *The Apostolic Fathers* (London: Macmillan, 1898).

Liljegren, S. B., *Bulwer Lytton's Novels and Isis Unveiled*, Essays and Studies on English Language and Literature 18 (Upsala: Lundequistka Bokhandeln, 1957).

Livingstone, David N., *Adam's Ancestors: Race, Religion and the Politics of Human Origins* (Baltimore: Johns Hopkins University Press, 2008).

Loisy, Alfred, *Le Livre de Job, traduit de l'Hébreu* (Amiens: Rousseau-Leroy, 1892).

Longinus, *On the Sublime*, ed. D. A. Russell (Oxford: Clarendon Press, 1964).

Löwith, Karl, *Meaning in History* [1949] (Chicago: University of Chicago Press, 1957).

Lowth, Robert, *Lectures on the Sacred Poetry of the Hebrews* [1753], trans G. Gregory, 2 vols (London: J. Johnson, 1787).

216   *Bibliography*

Lukács, Georg, *The Theory of the Novel* [1916], trans. Anna Bostock (London: Merlin Press, 1971).

Luther, Martin, *Works*, American Edition, vol. 51, trans. John W. Doberstein (Philadelphia: Michlenberg Press, 1959).

Lutton, Robert, *Lollardy and Orthodox Religion in Pre-Reformation England*, Royal Historical Society Studies in History (Woodbridge, Suffolk: Boydell Press, 2006).

Lyotard, Jean-François, *The Postmodern Condition: A Report on Knowledge* [1979] trans. Geoff Bennington and Brian Massumi (Manchester: Manchester University Press, 1984).

Lytton, Earl of, *The Life of Edward Bulwer, First Lord Lytton*, 2 vols (London: Macmillan, 1913).

Lytton, Edward Bulwer, *Kenelm Chillingley* (London: Routledge, 1878).

Lytton, Edward Bulwer, *The Coming Race* [1871] (London: Hesperus Press, 2007).

McClure, John A., *Partial Faiths: Postsecular Fiction in the Age of Pynchon and Morrison* (Athens, GA: University of Georgia Press, 2007).

McFarland, Thomas P., *Coleridge and the Pantheist Tradition* (Oxford: Clarendon Press, 1969).

McGrath, Alister, *The Twilight of Atheism: The Rise and Fall of Disbelief in the Modern World* (London: Rider, 2004).

MacIntyre, Alasdair, *Secularization and Moral Change* (Riddell Memorial Lectures, Newcastle) (London: Oxford University Press, 1967).

MacIntyre, Alasdair and Ricoeur, Paul, *The Religious Significance of Atheism* (New York: Columbia University Press, 1969).

Mackay, R. W., *The Tübingen School and its Antecedents: A Review of the History and Present Condition of Modern Theology* (London: Williams and Norgate, 1863).

McKeon, Michael, *The Origins of the English Novel 1600–1740* (Baltimore: Johns Hopkins University Press, 1987).

MacRae, Donald G., *Weber* (Glasgow: Collins/Fontana, 1974).

Magnus, Leonard A., trans., 'The Foundling Prince', in *Russian Folktales* (London: Kegan Paul, 1915).

[Manning, Henry and Marriott, Charles] *Testimony of Writers in the Later English Church to the Duty of Maintaining quod semper, quod ubique, quod ab omnibus traditum est* [1836], new ed. (London: Rivingtons, 1839).

Manzoni, Alessandro, *The Betrothed (I Promessi Sposi)* [1827], trans. Archibald Colquhoun (London: Dent, 1951).

Manzoni, Alessandro, *Lettere* I, *Tutte le opere* VII, ed. Cesare Arieti (Verona: Arnoldo Mondadori, 1970).

Marshall, Cynthia, 'Reading "The Golden Key": Narrative Strategies of Parable', *Children's Literature Association Quarterly* 14 (1989), 22–5.

Bibliography

Martin, David, *On Secularization: Towards a Revised General Theory* (Aldershot: Ashgate, 2005).

Martin, David, *The Religious and the Secular: Studies in Secularization* (London: Routledge & Kegan Paul, 1969).

Mascall, Eric L., *The Secularisation of Christianity: An Analysis and a Critique* (London: Darton, Longman & Todd, 1965).

Matter, E. Anne, *Voice of My Beloved: the Song of Songs in Western Medieval Christianity* (Philadelphia: University of Pennsylvania Press, 1990).

Maurois, André, *Chateaubriand*, trans. Vera Fraser (London: Jonathan Cape, 1938).

Melanchthon, Philipp, *Loci Communi*, trans. Lowell J. Satre in *Melanchthon and Buber* (London: SCM Press, 1969).

Metzger, Bruce M., *A Textual Commentary on the Greek New Testament*, corrected edition (London: United Bible Societies, 1975).

Metzger, Bruce M., *The Canon of the New Testament*, Oxford: Clarendon Press, 1987).

Meyer, Ludovicus, *Philosophia S. Scripturae Interpres* (Eleutheropoli [Amsterdam], [1666], trans. Jacqueline Lagrée and Pierre-François Moreau as *La Philosophie interprète de l'écriture sainte* (Paris: Intertextes éditeur, 1988).

Michael, Leo, *She. An Allegory of the Church* (New York: Frank F. Lovell, 1889).

Milbank, John, *Theology and Social Theory. Beyond Secular Reason* (1990), 2nd ed. (Oxford: Blackwell, 2006).

Milbank, John, Pickstock, Catherine, and Ward, Graham, eds, *Radical Orthodoxy: A New Theology* (London: Routledge, 1999).

Millgate, Michael, *Thomas Hardy: A Biography Revisited* (Oxford: Oxford University Press, 2004).

Mineka, Francis E., *The Dissidence of Dissent: The Monthly Repository, 1806–1838* (Chapel Hill: University of North Carolina Press, 1944).

Mishnah, trans. Herbert Danby (London: Oxford University Press, 1933).

Molendijk, Arie L. et al., eds, *Exploring the Postsecular: The Religious, the Political and the Urban* (Leiden: Brill, 2010).

Moltmann, Jürgen, *God for a Secular Society: The Public Relevance of Theology*, trans. Margaret Kohl (London: SCM Press, 1997).

Morley, John, *On Compromise* [1874] (London: Macmillan, 1901).

Morris, David B., *The Religious Sublime. Christian Poetry and Critical Tradition in 18th-Century England* (Lexington, KY: University Press of Kentucky, 1972).

Morris, Jeremy, 'The Strange Death of Christian Britain: Another Look at the Secularization Debate', *Historical Journal* 46 (2003), 963–76.

Morris, William, *The Revised and Arianized Version of the English New Testament: A Protest and a Testimony* (London: Elliot Stock, 1881).

218   *Bibliography*

Moynahan, Julian, '*The Mayor of Casterbridge* and the Old Testament First Book of Samuel', *PMLA* 71 (1956), 118–30.

Mullan, John, *Sentiment and Sociability: The Language of Feeling in the Eighteenth Century* (Oxford: Clarendon Press, 1988).

Müller, F. Max, *Introduction to the Science of Religion* (London: Longmans, 1873).

Murdoch, Iris, *Metaphysics as a Guide to Morals* [1992] (London: Vintage, 2003).

Nash, David, 'Reconnecting Religion with Social and Cultural History: Secularization's Failure as a Master Narrative', *Cultural and Social History* 1 (September 2004), 302–25.

Newey, Vincent, 'Dorothea's Awakening: the Recall of Bunyan in *Middlemarch*', *Notes and Queries* 31 (1984), 497–9.

Newman, F. W., *Phases of Faith* (1859), introd. U. C. Knoepflmacher [reprinting 6th, 1860, ed.] (Leicester: Leicester University Press, 1970).

Newman, J. H., *Discussions and Arguments on Various Subjects* (London: Longmans, 1890).

Newman, J. H., *The Via Media of the Anglican Church*, 2 vols (London: Longmans, 1891).

Newman, J. H., *Tract Ninety, or Remarks on Certain Passages in the Thirty-nine Articles* (1841) introd. A. W. Evans (London: Constable, 1933).

Newman, J. H., *Letters and Diaries*, vol. 8, ed. Gerard Tracey (Oxford: Clarendon Press, 1999).

Nietzsche, Friedrich, *The Portable Nietzsche* ed. and trans. Walter Kaufmann (London: Chatto & Windus, 1971).

Nietzsche, Friedrich, *Twilight of the Idols* [1889], trans. Duncan Large (Oxford: Oxford University Press, 1998).

Nietzsche, Friedrich, *The Gay Science* [1882], trans. Josefine Naukhoff (Cambridge: Cambridge University Press, 2001).

Nineham, Dennis, *Christianity Medieval and Modern. A Study in Religious Change* (London: SCM Press, 1993).

Nockles, Peter, *The Oxford Movement in Context: Anglican High Churchmanship, 1760–1857* (Cambridge: Cambridge University Press, 1994).

Norman, Edward, *Secularisation* (London: Continuum, 2002).

Norris, Richard A., *God and World in Early Christian Theology. A Study in Justin Martyr, Irenaeus, Tertullian and Origen* (London: A. & C. Black, 1966).

Origen, *In Matthaeum*, PG 13.

Origen, *Writings*, 2 vols, trans. Frederick Crombie, Ante-Nicene Christian Library (Edinburgh: T. & T. Clark, 1869–72).

Origen, *Philocalia*, trans. George Lewis (Edinburgh: T. & T. Clark, 1911), available online at <http://www.tertullian.org/fathers/origen_philocalia_02_text.htm>.

Bibliography

Origen, *The Song of Songs: Commentary and Homilies*, trans. R. P. Lawson (New York: Newman Press, 1956).

Otto, Rudolf, *The Idea of the Holy* (*Das Heilige*) [1917] trans. John W. Harvey, 2nd ed. (Oxford: Oxford University Press, 1950).

Owens, W. R. and Stuart Sim, eds, *Reception, Appropriation, Recollection: Bunyan's Pilgrim's Progress* (Bern: Peter Lang, 2007).

Paley, Morton D., *The Apocalyptic Sublime* (New Haven and London: Yale University Press, 1986).

Pareto, Vilfredo, *The Mind and Society* [1916, 2nd ed. 1923], trans. Andrew Bongiorno and Arthur Livingston, 4 vols (New York: Harcourt, Brace, 1935).

Patrides, C. A., 'Renaissance Estimates of the Year of Creation', *Huntington Library Quarterly* 26 (1963), 315–22.

Pattison, Mark, 'Tendencies of Religious Thought in England 1688–1750', in *Essays and Reviews* (1860) (London: Longman, Green, 1861).

Peterson, William S., *Victorian Heretic: Mrs Humphry Ward's Robert Elsmere* (Leicester: Leicester University Press, 1976).

Plum, Harry Grant, *The Teutonic Order and its Secularization. A Study in the Protestant Revolt* (University of Iowa Studies in Sociology, vol. 3, no. 2), (Iowa City, 1906).

Pocock, Tom, *Rider Haggard and the Lost Empire* (London: Weidenfeld and Nicolson, 1993).

Pollack, Detlef, *Säkularisierung—ein moderner Mythos?* (Tübingen: Mohr Siebeck, 2003).

Pollock, Sir Frederick, *Spinoza: His Life and Philosophy* (1880), 2nd ed. (London: Kegan Paul, 1899).

Preus, J. Samuel, *Spinoza and the Irrelevance of Biblical Authority* (Cambridge: Cambridge University Press, 2001).

Prickett, Stephen, *Words and 'The Word': Language, poetics and biblical interpretation* (Cambridge: Cambridge University Press, 1986).

Prickett, Stephen, 'Biblical prophecy and nineteenth-century historicism: the Joachimite third age in Matthew and Mary Augusta Ward', *Journal of Literature and Theology* 2 (September 1988), 219–36.

Priestley, Joseph, *Autobiography*, introd. Jack Lindsay (Bath: Adams & Dart, 1970).

Punter, David, *The Literature of Terror: A History of Gothic Fiction from 1765 to the Present Day* (London: Longman, 1980).

Pykett, Lyn, ed., *Reading Fin de Siècle Fictions* (Harlow: Longman, 1996).

Pyysiräinen, Ilkka and Anttonen, Veikko, eds, *Current Approaches in the Cognitive Science of Religion* (London: Continuum, 2002).

Qualls, Barry, *The Secular Pilgrims of Victorian Fiction* (Cambridge: Cambridge University Press, 1982).

Quasten, Johannes, *Patrology*, 3 vols (Utrecht: Spectrum, 1966).

220   *Bibliography*

Ratramnus, *De Corpore et Sanguine Domini*, PL 121.

Reade, Winwood, *The Martyrdom of Man* [1872] (London: Watts, 1934).

Readings, Bill, *Introducing Lyotard: Art and Politics* (London: Routledge, 1991).

Reardon, B. M. G., *Religious Thought in the Nineteenth Century* (Cambridge: Cambridge University Press, 1966).

Rees, Timothy, *Sermons and Hymns* (London and Oxford: Mowbray, 1946).

Reeve, Clara, *The Progress of Romance through Times, Countries, and Manners*, 2 vols [1785] (New York: Garland, 1970).

Reid, J. K. S., *The Authority of Scripture: A Study of the Reformation and Pre-Reformation Understanding of the Bible* (London: Methuen, 1957).

Reinke, Darrell R., 'From Allegory to Metaphor: More Notes on Luther's Hermeneutical Shift', *Harvard Theological Review* 66 (July 1973), 386–95.

Renan, Ernest, *Le Livre de Job traduit de l'Hébreu* (Paris: Lévy Frères, 1859).

Reventlow, Henning Graf, *The Authority of the Bible and the Rise of the Modern World* [1980], trans. John Bowden (London: S.C.M. Press, 1984).

Richter, Jean Paul, *Siebenkäs* [1796–7], trans. E. H. Noel (as *Flower, Fruit and Thorn Pieces*), 2 vols (London: William Smith, 1845).

Richter, Jean Paul, *Vorschule der Ästhetik* [1804], ed. Norbert Miller (Munich: Carl Hanser Verlag, 1974).

Richter, Melvin, *The Politics of Conscience: T.H. Green and His Age* [1964] (Lanham, MD: University Press of America, 1983).

Robertson, J. M., *A History of Freethought in the Nineteenth Century*, 2 vols (London: Watts & Co., 1929).

Robinson, John A. T., *Honest to God* (London: SCM Press, 1963).

Rogers, Frederick, *Labour, Life and Literature: Some Memories of Sixty Years* [1913], ed. David Rubinstein (Brighton: Harvester, 1973).

Rogers, G. A. J., ed. and introd., *Leviathan. Contemporary Responses to the Political Theory of Thomas Hobbes* (Bristol: Thoemmes, 1995).

Rogerson, J. W., *Myth in Old Testament Interpretation* (Berlin and New York: Walter de Gruyter, 1974).

Rogerson, J. W., *Old Testament Criticism in the Nineteenth Century: England and Germany* (London: SPCK, 1984).

Rose, Jonathan, *The Intellectual Life of the British Working Class* (New Haven: Yale University Press, 2011).

Rosman, Doreen, *Evangelicals and Culture* (London: Croom Helm, 1983).

Rothe, Richard, *Still Hours* [1878], trans. Jane T. Stoddart (London: Hodder and Stoughton, 1886).

Royle, Edward, *Victorian Infidels: The Origins of the British Secularist Movement 1791–1866* (Manchester; Manchester University Press, 1974).

Rudavsky, T. M., 'Galileo and Spinoza: Heroes, Heretics and Hermeneutics', *Journal of the History of Ideas* 62 (October 2001), 611–31.

Bibliography

221

Saler, Michael, 'Modernity and Enchantment: a Historiographic Review', *American Historical Review* 111 (June 2006), 692–716.

Schaff, Philip, *The Creeds of Christendom*, 6th ed. [1931], 3 vols (repr. Grand Rapids, MI: Baker Books, 2007).

Schiller, Friedrich, *Sämtliche Werke* I (Gedichte/Dramen 1) (Munich: Carl Hauser Verlag, 1958).

Schleiermacher, Friedrich, *On Religion: Speeches to its Cultured Despisers*, trans. John Oman (London: Kegan Paul, 1893).

Schneider, John R., *Philip Melanchthon's Rhetorical Construal of Biblical Authority: Oratio Sacra* (Lewiston, Queenston and Lampeter: Edwin Mellen, 1990).

Schniedewind, W. M., *How the Bible Became a Book* (Cambridge: Cambridge University Press, 2004).

Schwarz, Regina, ed., *Transcendence: Philosophy, Literature, and Theology Approach the Beyond* (New York and London: Routledge, 2004).

Scott, J. E., *A Bibliography of the Works of Sir Henry Rider Haggard 1856–1975* (Bishops Stortford: Elkin Mathews, 1947).

Scott, Thomas, *Introduction to the Study of the Bible, being the Preface to his Commentary on the Holy Scripture* (1839) (London: Hatchards, 1881).

Seeley, J. R., *Ecce Homo* (London: Macmillan, 1865).

Selby, T. G., *The Theology of Modern Fiction* (London: Charles H. Kelly, 1896).

Selden, John, *Table Talk* (London: E. Smith, 1689).

Semmel, Bernard, *The Governor Eyre Controversy* (London: McGibbon & Kee, 1962).

Shaw, George Bernard, *Saint Joan* (London: Constable, 1924).

Shaw, George Bernard, *Back to Methuselah. A Metabiological Pentateuch* (London, 1925).

Shaw, Philip, *The Sublime* (London: Routledge, 2006).

Sheehan, Jonathan, *The Enlightenment Bible* (Princeton: Princeton University Press, 2005).

Sherry, Norman, *The Life of Graham Greene, 1904–1939* (London: Penguin, 1989).

Sim, Stuart, *Jean-François Lyotard* (London: Prentice Hall/Harvester Wheatsheaf, 1996).

Simms, Karl, *Paul Ricoeur* (London: Routledge, 2003).

Simon, Richard, *Histoire critique du Vieux Testament* [1678] trans. N. S. (from a Latin version) as *Critical Enquiries into the Various Editions of the Bible* (London: Tho. Braddyll, 1684).

Smeed, J. W., *Jean Paul's 'Dream'* (London: Oxford University Press, 1966).

Smith, Anne, ed., *George Eliot: Centenary Essays and an Unpublished Fragment* (London: Vision Press, 1980).

Smith, Graeme, *A Short History of Secularism* (London: I. B. Tauris, 2008).

222 *Bibliography*

Smith, Steven D., *The Disenchantment of Secular Discourse* (Cambridge, MA: Harvard University Press, 2010).

Smith, Warren Sylvester, *The London Heretics 1870–1914* (London: Constable, 1967).

Smith, W. Robertson, *The Old Testament in the Jewish Church* (Edinburgh: A. & C. Black, 1881).

Smith, W. Robertson, *Lectures on the Religion of the Semites*, 1st ser. (1889) (London: A. & C. Black, 1914).

Somerville, Alexander, *The Autobiography of a Working Man* [1848] (London: Macgibbon & Kee, 1967).

Sommerville, C. John, *The Secularization of Early Modern England: From Religious Culture to Religious Faith* (New York: Oxford University Press, 1992).

Spinoza, B., *Tractatus Theologico-Politicus* (1670) trans. R. H. M. Elwes, Bohn series (London: G. Bell, 1883) as *A Theologico-Political Treatise* (repr. New York: Dover, 1951).

Spinoza, B., *Ethics*, trans. Edwin Curley (London: Penguin, 1996).

Stanley, A. P., *Life and Correspondence of Thomas Arnold, D.D.*, 2 vols (London: Fellowes, 1845).

Stanley, A. P., *Essays chiefly on Questions of Church and State* [1870], new ed. (London: John Murray, 1884).

Steiner, George, *Real Presences: Is There Anything In What We Say?* (London: Faber, 1989).

Stephen, Fitzjames, *Defence of the Rev. Rowland Williams, D.D. in the Arches' Court of Canterbury* (London: Smith, Elder, 1862).

Stephen, Sir James, et al., 'A Modern Symposium: The Influences upon Morality of a Decline in Religious Belief', *Nineteenth Century* I (April, May 1877), 331–58, 531–46.

Stephen, Leslie, *George Eliot* (London: Macmillan, 1902).

Stern, David, *Parables in Midrash: Narrative and Exegesis in Rabbinic Literature* (Cambridge, MA: Harvard University Press, 1991).

Stillingfleet, *Irenicum. A Weapon-Salve for the Churches Wounds* (London: Henry Mortlock, 1662).

Stillingfleet, Edward, *Origines Sacrae, or, A rational account of the grounds of Christian faith, as to the truth and divine authority of the Scriptures* [1662], 3rd ed. (London: Mortlock, 1666).

Stirrat, R. L., *Power and Religiosity in a Post-Colonial Setting: Sinhala Catholics in Contemporary Sri Lanka* (Cambridge: Cambridge University Press, 1992).

Stone, Wilfred, *Religion and Art of William Hale White* [1954] (New York: AMS Press, 1967).

Strauss, D. F., *Der Romantiker auf dem Throne der Cäseren, oder Julian der Abtrünnige* (Mannheim, 1847).

Bibliography 223

Sutherland, John, *Mrs Humphry Ward: Eminent Victorian, Pre-eminent Edwardian* (Oxford: Clarendon Press, 1990).

Sylvan, David and Majeski, Stephen, 'A Methodology for the Study of Historical Counterfactuals', *International Studies Quarterly* 42 (1998), 79–108.

Tate, Nahum and Brady, Nicholas, *A New Version of the Psalms of David* [1698], (Oxford: Oxford University Press, 1838).

Taylor, Charles, *Sources of the Self: The Making of the Modern Identity* (Cambridge: Cambridge University Press, 1989).

Taylor, Charles, *A Secular Age* (Cambridge, MA: Belknap Press of Harvard University Press, 2007).

Taylor, Jeremy, *A Dissuasion from Popery* [1664] in *Whole Works*, ed. C. P. Eden, vol. 6 (London: Longmans, 1849).

Temperley, Nicholas, *Haydn: 'The Creation'* (Cambridge: Cambridge University Press, 1991).

Tertullian, *Writings*, trans. Alexander Roberts and James Donaldson, Ante-Nicene Fathers (Grand Rapids, MI: William B. Eerdmans, 1997).

Thackeray, W. M., *Novels by Eminent Hands* in *Burlesques* (London: Smith, Elder, 1869).

Thirlwall, Connop, *The History of Greece* [1835–44], new ed., 8 vols (London: Longman, 1845–52).

Thurber, James, *The Middle-aged Man on the Flying Trapeze* (New York: Harper, 1935).

Tomalin, Claire, *Thomas Hardy: The Time-Torn Man* (London: Viking, 2006).

Trevelyan, Janet Penrose, *The Life of Mrs Humphry Ward* (London: Constable, 1923).

Trevor, Meriol, *The Arnolds: Thomas Arnold and His Family* (London: Bodley Head, 1973).

Trollope, Anthony, *The Letters of Anthony Trollope*, ed. N. John Hall, 2 vols (Stanford: Stanford University Press, 1983).

Tytler, Robert, *Illustrations of Ancient Geography and History...Derived from Recent Investigations in the Eastern Indian Archipelago* (London: J. M. Richardson, 1825).

Ullendorff, Edward, *The Ethiopians. An Introduction to Country and People* [1960] 2nd ed. (London: Oxford University Press, 1965).

Vahanian, Gabriel, *The Death of God* (New York: George Braziller, 1961).

van Buren, Paul M., *The Secular Meaning of the Gospel* (London: SCM Press, 1963).

van Buren, Paul M., *The Edges of Language: An Essay in the Logic of a Religion* (London: SCM Press, 1972).

Vance, Norman, *Irish Literature, a Social History* (Oxford: Blackwell, 1990).

224 *Bibliography*

Vance, Norman, 'Hardy's "The Darkling Thrush" and G. F. Watts's *Hope*', *Victorian Poetry* 33 (Summer 1995), 295–8.

Vance, Norman, *The Victorians and Ancient Rome* (Oxford: Blackwell, 1997).

Vargish, Thomas, *The Providential Aesthetic in Victorian Fiction* (Charlottesville: University Press of Virginia, 1985).

Vauchez, André, *La spiritualité du Moyen Age occidental* (Paris: Presses Universitaires de France, 1975).

Vaughan, C. J., *Authorised or Revised? Sermons* (London: Macmillan, 1882).

Vawter, Bruce, *Biblical Inspiration* (London: Hutchinson, 1972).

Vickers, Salley, *The Other Side of You* (London: Harper Perennial, 2007).

Virkar-Yates, Aakanksha, 'Baptism and Ascent in the Poetry of Gerard Manley Hopkins', unpublished D.Phil. thesis, University of Sussex, 2009.

Voegelin, Eric, *The New Science of Politics* (Chicago: University of Chicago Press, 1952).

Voegelin, Eric, *The Political Religions* [1938], trans. Virginia Ann Schildhauer, in *Modernity without Restraint* (*Collected Works* 5). (Columbia: University of Missouri Press, 2000).

Voysey, Charles, trans., *Fragments from Reimarus* (London and Edinburgh: Williams and Norgate, 1879).

Voysey, Charles, *Theism as a Science of Natural Theology and Natural Religion* (London and Edinburgh: Williams and Norgate, 1895).

Waller, Philip, *Writers, Readers and Reputations: Literary Life in Britain 1870–1918* (Oxford: Oxford University Press, 2006).

Walzer, R., *Galen on Jews and Christians* (London: Oxford University Press, 1949).

Ward, Graham, ed., *The Blackwell Companion to Postmodern Theology* (Oxford: Backwell, 2001).

Ward, Humphry and Roberts, William, *Romney: a Biographical and Critical Essay*, 2 vols (London: Agnew, 1904).

Ward, Mary, 'The Poem of the Cid', *Macmillan's Magazine* 24 (October 1871), 471–86.

Ward, Mary, 'Isidore of Seville's Histories of the Goths, Vandals and Suevi', in William Smith and Henry Wace, eds, *Dictionary of Christian Biography*, 4 vols (London: John Murray, 1877–1887).

[Ward, Mary], *Unbelief and Sin: A Protest* ([Oxford]: Printed for the Author, 1881).

Ward, Mary, 'Recent Fiction in England and France', *Macmillan's Magazine* 50 (1884), 250–60.

Ward, Mary, *Robert Elsmere*, ed. Rosemary Ashton (Oxford: Oxford University Press, 1987).

Ward, Mary, *The History of David Grieve* (London: Smith and Elder, 1892).

Ward, Mary, *Sir George Tressady* (London: Smith, Elder, 1896).

Bibliography

Ward, Mary, *Daphne, or Marriage à la Mode* (London: Cassell, 1909).

Ward, Mary, *The Case of Richard Meynell*, (London: Smith, Elder, 1911).

Ward, Mary, *A Writer's Recollections* (London: Collins, 1918).

Ward, Mary, *Marcella*, ed. Beth Sutton-Ramspeck and Nicole B. Meller (Peterborough, Ontario: Broadview, 2002).

Warfield, Benjamin Breckinridge, 'The Oracles of God' [1900] repr. in *The Inspiration and Authority of the Bible* (London: Marshall, Morgan and Scott, 1951), pp. 351–407.

Warner, Susan, *Say and Seal* (London: Richard Bentley, 1860).

Watt, Ian, *The Rise of the Novel* (London: Chatto & Windus, 1957).

Weber, Max, *The Theory of Social and Economic Organization*, trans. A. M. Henderson and Talcott Parsons (London: William Hodge, 1947).

Weber, Max, 'Science as a Vocation' [1919] in H. H. Gerth and C. Wright Mills, eds, *From Max Weber: Essays in Sociology* (London: Routledge, 1948).

Weber, Max, *The Protestant Ethic and the Spirit of Capitalism* [1905], trans. Talcott Parsons (London: Routledge, 1992).

Webster, James, 'The Creation, Haydn's Late Vocal Music, and the Musical Sublime', in Elaine Sisman, ed., *Haydn and his World* (Princeton, NJ: Princeton University Press, 1997), pp. 57–102.

Welch, Claude, *Protestant Thought in the Nineteenth Century*, 2 vols (New Haven and London: Yale University Press, 1972, 1985).

West, Morris, *A View from the Ridge* (London: HarperCollins, 1996).

Westcott, B. F., *The Epistle to the Hebrews: The Greek Text with Notes and Essays* [1889], 2nd ed. (London: Macmillan, 1892).

Whately, Richard, '*Emma*', *Quarterly Review* 14 (October 1815), 188–201.

Whately, Richard, '*Northanger Abbey* and *Persuasion*', *Quarterly Review* 24 (January 1821), 352–76.

Wilde, Oscar, 'The Decay of Lying: A Dialogue', *The Nineteenth Century* 25 (January 1889) 40.

Willey, Basil, *More Nineteenth-Century Studies* (Cambridge: Cambridge University Press, 1956).

Williams, Ioan, ed., *Novel and Romance 1700–1800: A Documentary Record* (London: Routledge, 1970).

Williams, Rowland, 'Bunsen's Biblical Researches', in *Essays and Reviews* [1860] (London: Longman, 1861).

Williamson, Eugene, 'Thomas Hardy and Friedrich Nietzsche: The Reasons', *Comparative Literature Studies* 15 (December 1978), 403–13.

Wilmot, A., *Monomotapa (Rhodesia): Its Monuments and its History from the Most Ancient Times to the Present Century*, with preface by H. Rider Haggard [London: T. Fisher Unwin, 1896] (repr. New York: Negro Universities Press, 1969).

Wilson, A. N., *God's Funeral* (London: John Murray, 1999).

226   *Bibliography*

Wilson, Bryan, *Religion in Secular Society* (London: C.A. Watts, 1966).

Wilson, H. B., 'Séances historiques de Genève. The National Church', in *Essays and Reviews* [1860] (London: Longman, 1861).

Wilson, Keith, ed., *Thomas Hardy Reappraised: Essays in Honour of Michael Millgate* (Toronto: University of Toronto Press, 2006).

Wilson, S. Law, *Chapters in Present Day Theology* (London: Richard D. Dickinson, 1897).

Wilson, S. Law, *The Theology of Modern Literature* (Edinburgh: T. & T. Clark, 1899).

Wilt, Judith, *Behind her Times: Transition England in the Novels of Mary Arnold Ward* (Charlottesville: University of Virginia Press, 2005).

Woolf, Virginia, *Letters of Virginia Woolf*, ed. Quentin Bell and Angelica Garnett, 3 vols (London: Hogarth Press, 1975–77).

Worden, Blair, 'The Question of Secularization', in Alan Houston and Steve Pincus, eds, *A Nation Transformed: England after the Restoration* (Cambridge: Cambridge University Press, 2001).

Wordsworth, Christopher, *Remarks on M. Bunsen's Work on St Hippolytus, particularly on the preface of his new edition* (London: Rivingtons, 1855).

[Wordsworth, Christopher] *On the Revised Version of the New Testament. An Address Read at the Lincoln Diocesan Conference October 21, 1881 by the Bishop of Lincoln* (Lincoln: Williamson, 1881).

Wordsworth, John, *The One Religion: Truth, Holiness, and Peace desired by the Nations, and Revealed by Jesus Christ* (Oxford: Parker, 1881).

Wordworth, William, *A Selection*, ed. Stephen Gill and Duncan Wu, Oxford Poetry Library (Oxford: Oxford University Press, 1994).

Wordsworth, William, 'Mutability', lines 7–8, in *Ecclesiastical Sketches* (1822), *Sonnet Series and Itinerary Poems, 1820–1845*, ed. Geoffrey Jackson (Ithaca, NY: Cornell University Press, 2004).

Wright, T. R., *The Religion of Humanity: The Impact of Comtean Positivism in Victorian Britain* (Cambridge: Cambridge University Press, 1986).

Wright, T. R., ed., *Thomas Hardy on Screen* (Cambridge: Cambridge University Press, 2005).

Wyclif, John, *De veritate sacrae scripturae* [1377–8], Latin text ed. Rudolf Buddensieg, 3 vols (London: Wyclif Society, 1905), trans. as *On the Truth of Holy Scripture* by Ian Christopher Levy (Kalamazoo, MI: Medieval Institute Publications, Western Michigan University, 2001).

Index

Aben Ezra 72
Abraham 29, 188
Addison, Joseph 28, 119–20
Aeschylus 133
'agnostic' 30, 117
Alembert, Jean Le Rond d' 11
allegorical reading 31, 53–6,
    63–4, 116
Ames, Edward 198
Apostles' Creed 30
Apostolic Fathers 49–50
Arabian Nights 173
Aristotle 130
Arnold, Matthew 110, 135–7, 139
Arnold, Thomas (of Rugby) 136, 143,
    155, 192
Arnold, Thomas (the younger) 56, 136
Arnold, William Delafield 136
Astruc, Jean 78
Athanasius, St 51
Augsburg Confession 60–1, 64, 187
Augustine, St 4–5, 28, 44, 52, 54, 57, 61,
    67, 96, 125
Austen, Jane 19–20, 24, 26, 111
authority, problems of scriptural 2, 29–61,
    69, 195, 199

Bacon, Francis 11, 35
Bale, John 54
Bamford, Samuel 141
Bangorian controversy 76
Barker, T. J. 32
Basil, St 44
Bauer, G. L. 40
Beattie, James 18, 22
Beer, Gillian 2, 24
Beerbohm, Max 136
Belgic Confession 63
Belsham, Thomas 80
Benjamin, Walter 29, 154
Bentley, Richard 76
Berger, Peter 190
Bergson, Henri 134
Bernard of Cluny 16

Bible, *see under individual books of Bible*
    and specific biblical characters
    and themes
  translations, English, *see* King James
    Bible; Revised Version; Tyndale,
    William; Wycliffite Bible
biblical chronology 36–40
biblical geography 38, 171–2
biblical manuscripts, see Codex
    Sinaiticus; Codex Vaticanus;
    textual issues
biblical narrative 28, 195
Blavatsky, Madame Helena
    Petrovna 166
Blumenberg, Hans 5
Bochart, Samuel 38, 73
Bonhoeffer, Dietrich 15
Book of Common Prayer 68, 115, 158
Bradlaugh, Charles 16, 167, 169
Bramhall, John 69
Broad Church 156
Brontë, Charlotte 21, 24
Brown, Callum 13
Buddhism 166, 168
Bunsen, C.C.J. von 82–3, 151, 166
Bunyan, John 4, 18, 29, 104–5, 122–4,
    153, 159–60, 186–7, 190–1
Burgon, J. W. 88–9
Burke, Edmund 28, 119, 145, 183, 186
Burleigh, Michael 5
Burnet, Gilbert 33
Burney, Fanny 19
Burton, Robert 110
Byron, George Gordon, Lord 144

Callaway, Henry 168
Calvin, John 63, 69–71, 112
Campbell, R. J. 136, 194
canon of scripture 48, 63, 74
Caputo, John 195–6
Carlyle, Thomas 21–3, 105, 107
Casaubon, Isaac 110
Cassian, John 54
Catholic modernism 157–8

228 *Index*

Catholic teaching 33
Catholic tradition 60, 194
Chadwick, Owen 8
charisma 29, 113, 128, 152, 155
Chateaubriand, François-René, vicomte de 24, 144–6
Chesterton, G. K. 114
Chrysostom, St John 44, 66–7
Clement of Alexandria 50, 52
Cleopatra 163
Clodd, Edward 118
Codex Sinaiticus 88–9
Codex Vaticanus 88–9
Coit, Dr Stanton 158
Colenso, J.W. 85–7, 167–8
Coleridge, Samuel Taylor 67, 77–8, 94, 107
Colet, John 40
Collins, Anthony 76
Collister, Peter 145
Comte, Auguste 4, 6, 11, 90, 95, 116, 125, 192
comparative religion 161, 165–7
Conradi, Peter 193
Copernicus 40
Corelli, Marie 161
counterfactual history 144–9
Cowper, William 99, 109
Cox, Harvey 14
Cranmer, Archbishop Thomas 64–5, 67
Creation accounts, *see* Genesis
Creation, The (Haydn) 122
Creighton, Mandell 140
Cumming, Dr John 97, 99

Dalziel, Pamela 114, 116
Danby, Francis 184, 185
Dante Alighieri 56, 159–60, 182–3, 186
Darwinism 3, 30, 90, 126, 134
David, King 130
'death of God' 1, 16, 22, 190, 199
de Wette, Wilhelm 79, 83, 86
Defoe, Daniel 18 *see also Robinson Crusoe*
deists 26, 76, 82, 84
Dickens, Charles 25, 173, 178
Didache 102, 196
Disraeli, Benjamin 25, 148, 159
Doctorow, E. L. 197, 199
Dodd, C. H. 199
Doddridge, Philip 131
Donne, John 65

Don Quixote 18–19
Doody, Margaret 20–1
Doré, Gustave 183, 186
Dostoevsky, Fyodor 2, 6, 16, 27, 125, 193
Duffy, Eamon 10
Durkheim, Emile 13

Ecclesiastes 173, 174, 186, 194
Egyptian religion 166
Eichhorn, J. G. 77–9, 81
Eliot, George vii, ix, 1–3, 20, 23, 25, 27, 60–1, 79–81, 90–113, 116, 190–9
   Adam Bede 100–3, 110, 125, 157, 190–9
   Daniel Deronda 110–3, 128
   Felix Holt the Radical 107–8, 112–13
   Middlemarch 6, 96, 108–10
   Mill on the Floss 104–5, 179
   Romola 106
   Scenes of Clerical Life 99–100
   Silas Marner 105–7
Encyclopédie 11
Enlightenment 11, 35
Erasmus, Desiderius 80, 85
eschatology 4–5
Essays and Reviews 36, 68, 82–6, 88, 137–8, 151, 166, 168
Ethiopian legend 172
Eusebius of Caesarea 37–8, 171–2
evangelicalism 11, 25, 27, 92, 97, 99, 151
evolution 3, 154 *see also* Darwinism
'evolutionary meliorism' 124
Exodus 55–6, 167, 171, 184, 186–7
Eyre, E. J., Governor of Jamaica 112
Ezekiel 41–2

Ferguson, Niall 144
Ferguson, Robert 72
Feuillet, Octave 142
Feuerbach, Ludwig 81, 95, 103
Flaubert, Gustave 26, 142
Foote, George W. 34
Forster, William 136
Frazer, J. G. 165
Freeman, E. A. 140, 192
Fremantle, Rev. W. H. 42–3, 155–6, 192, 194
French Confession 63
Froude, J. A. 23, 94, 150
Froude, R. H. 65
Frye, Northrop 20

Index

229

Gadarene swine 34
Galen 41
Galileo Galilei 40
Gaskell, Elizabeth 25, 141
Genesis 28, 30, 41–4, 120
geology 30, 36
German biblical critics, *see* Higher
Criticism
Gibbon, Edward 75, 85, 117, 138, 151
Gladstone, W. E. 27, 34–5, 59, 89
Glossa Ordinaria 55
Goethe, J. W. von 92, 94, 126
Golding, William 196
Good Samaritan 54
Gore, Charles 168, 194
Gosse, Edmund 25
Göttingen, University of 77, 81
Graham, Gordon 15
Great Zimbabwe, ruins of 180
Green, J. R. 140
Green, T. H. 140, 156, 192
Greene, Graham 194
Gregory of Nyssa 43
Griesbach, J. J. 80–1, 115
Guillaume de Palerne 111

Habermas, Jürgen vii, 190
Haggard, Henry Rider ix, 2, 23, 39, 60,
86, 160–89, 190–9
'About Fiction' 170
Allan and the Ice-Gods 176
Allan Quatermain 163, 176, 184–5
Allan's Wife 170
Ayesha 166, 186–7
Child of Storm 163, 165, 175
Dawn 181
Elissa 180
Eric Brighteyes 173
Colonel Quaritch, V.C. 174
Finished 174–5
The Ivory Child 166, 174, 176
Jess 179, 183
King Solomon's Mines 161–2, 172,
176, 178, 181, 184, 187–8
Love Eternal 170, 174, 180–1
Marie 170
Montezuma's Daughter 194
Mr Meeson's Will 170
Queen Sheba's Ring 172
She 161–2, 176, 178–9, 185, 188
The Way of the Spirit 173–4, 180
Wisdom's Daughter 170

The Witch's Head 170, 174
The Wizard 170
The World's Desire 167
Hardy, Thomas viii–ix, 2, 27, 34, 80, 90,
114–34, 152, 190–9
'The Grave by the Handpost' 131
novels
Far from the Madding Crowd 115,
127, 129
Jude the Obscure 114, 116,
122–5, 128
A Laodicean 115
Mayor of Casterbridge 124,
129, 132
Return of the Native 118,
127–9, 152
Tess of the d'Urbervilles 114, 118,
121, 124–6, 128, 153, 199
Two on a Tower 120, 127
Under the Greenwood Tree 115
The Woodlanders 124–5, 128
poetry
The Dynasts 121, 126, 132–4
'God's Funeral' 125
Human Shows 117, 130
Late Lyrics and Earlier 119,
123, 124n
Moments of Vision 132
'The Oxen' 127
Poems of the Past and the Present 117
Satires of Circumstance 117–18
Time's Laughingstocks 118
Haweis, H. R. 156
Hawthorne, Nathaniel 24
Hays, Mary 19
Hegel, G. W. F. 1, 4, 6, 82, 95
Heilsgeschichte, *see* salvation history
Helen of Troy 163, 167
Helvetic Confessions 62, 84
Hennell, Charles 80, 93
Henty, G. A. 173
Herrick, Robert 143–4
Hetherington, Henry 167
Heyne, C. G. 77–8, 81
Higher Criticism 78–82, 156
Hippolytus, St 50, 83
Hoadly, Benjamin 76
Hobbes, Thomas 69–71
Hodgson, Peter 97, 103, 196
Hogarth, William 142–3
Holyoake, G. J. 9, 16
Holland House circle 144, 148

230 *Index*

Homer 119–20, 167
Homilies, Books of 66–7
Hooker, Richard 67–8
Hopkins, Gerard Manley 54
Hort, F. J. A. 87
humanity, religion of 113, 118
Hume, David 8, 32, 138, 151
Hunter, Ian 8
Hutton, R. H. 116
Huxley, Aldous 159
Huxley, T. H. 30, 32, 34, 117–18,
126, 151

Ingraham, J. H. 171
Irenaeus, St 51, 53
Isaiah 49–50
Isidore of Seville, St 55, 139

James, G. P. R. 93
James, Henry 116
James, William 168–9, 197–8
Jane Eyre 123
Jay, Elisabeth 116
Jean Paul, *see* under Richter
Jeremiah 47
Jerome, St 43, 50–1, 157–8, 171
Jewel, John 65–6
Job, Book of 115, 124, 157, 171
'Johannine comma' 85, 88
Johnson, Lionel 118
Johnson, Samuel 97
Jones, Sir William 165
Josephus 171, 172
Jowett, Benjamin 84–5, 88, 140, 155
Jung, Carl 164, 185

Kant, Immanuel 28, 104, 119–20, 182
Keble, John 67, 82
Ken, Thomas 110
Kenrick, John 80
King James Bible ('Authorized
Version') 59, 68, 85, 88, 157, 164,
171, 187
Kingsley, Charles 25, 30, 61, 123, 149,
151, 156, 159, 173
Kipling, Rudyard 162, 170

Lamb, Lady Caroline 144, 146
Landow, George 130
Lang, Andrew 162, 165, 167, 169, 176
Larsen, Timothy vi, 90
Latour, Bruno 6

Law, William 168
Lawson, Thomas 198
Lecky, W. E. H. 35
Le Gallienne, Richard 197–8
Lennox, Charlotte 19, 21
Lessing, G. E. 77, 82, 86, 93
Lewes, G. H. 94, 96, 126
Lewis, C. S. 164, 194
libraries, lending 26
Lincoln, Abraham 112
literal reading 3, 34–6, 43
liturgical reform 157
Lodge, Sir Oliver 177
Loisy, Alfred 157–8
Lollards 57–9
Longinus 28, 119, 121
Löwith, Karl 4–5
Lowth, Robert 28
Lucretius 118, 121
Lukács, Georg vi, 90
Luther, Martin 60, 62, 103
Lux Mundi 168
Lydgate, John 108
Lyotard, Jean-François 6, 28
Lytton, Edward Bulwer 21–2, 93, 148,
151, 166, 173–4, 177–8, 182

McCabe, Joseph 117
MacDonald, George 191, 194
Magnificat 133
Marcion 49
Martin, John 4, 104, 121, 182–3, 185
Martineau, Harriet 96
Marx, Karl 4, 11
mashal 41, 195
Massey, Gerald 166
Max Müller, Friedrich 140, 165, 168–9
Mazzini, Guiseppe 111–12
Melanchthon, Phillip 39, 60, 80, 198
Messiah, The (Handel) 157
'messianism' 29, 101, 105, 113, 130–2,
150, 152, 154, 175
Methodism 11, 101
Milbank, John 7, 14n, 122
Mill (or Mills), John 76
Milton, John 4, 110, 119–22, 160, 182–3,
186, 196
miracle 3, 30, 32, 40, 138–9, 143, 152–3,
191, 197
Mishna 42, 45
missionaries 169–70
Modern Churchman, The 156

Index

modernity vi–vii, 2, 7, 15, 35
modernization 190, 192
Moltmann, Jürgen 15, 192
Morley, John 126
Moses 41, 43, 70, 72–3
Murdoch, Iris, 192
Murger, Henry 142

Nayler, James 70
Neal, Daniel 107
Neale, John Mason 16
Nerval, Gérard de 1, 23
Netter, Thomas 58
Newman, John Henry 25, 33, 42,
      58, 65
Newton, John 129
Nicene Creed 30
Nietzsche, Friedrich 2, 15, 113, 125–6
Norman, Edward 14
novel, rise of vi–vii, 3, 17–27,
      174 *see also* romance

Odysseus 167, 176
Ophir 172
oral tradition and scripture 45–8, 53
Origen 43, 53–4, 66, 116
Otto, Rudolph 169, 197–9
Oxford Movement 81 *see also* Keble,
      John; Newman, John Henry

Papal Index 25–6
parable 31, 54, 195 *see also mashal*
Pattison, Mark 84, 137–8, 151
Paul, St 117
Pererius 38, 73–4
pilgrim quest 4, 29, 66, 122–4, 150,
      158–60, 187–9
Plato 44
Plum, Henry 9–10
Pollack, Detlef 190
post-secular, the vii–viii, 7, 17,
      190, 195
pre-Adamitism 38, 73–4
Priestley, Joseph 80
proof-texts 44, 68
Protestantism 31–34, 56, 64 *see also*
      under reformation
Providentissimus Deus (papal
      encyclical) 156
Psalms 4, 56, 115, 119–20, 130, 185,
      188, 198
Punch 162

Qualls, Barry 4

Ratramnus 55
Reade, Winwood 167
Red Sea crossing (in Exodus) 86
Rees, Timothy 103–4
Reeve, Clara 19
Reformation 32, 56, 58, 60, 64
Reimarus, H. S. 76–7, 86, 141
reincarnation 177
Renan, Ernest 26, 139, 158
Revelation, Book of 124, 186
Revised Version (of English Bible) 36, 87
Richardson, Samuel 18, 22, 25
Richter, Johann Paul 22–4, 151
Ricoeur, Paul 97
Rimmer, Mary 114
risorgimento 146
Robinson Crusoe 171, 173
romance 18–24, 34, 111–12, 173–4
Romney, George 144, 147
Rose, Jonathan 123
Rossetti, Dante Gabriel 130
Rothe, Richard 192
Rousseau, Jean Jacques 22, 25
Ruskin, John, 98, 111
Rutherford, Mark 190–1

Sadducees 46
salvation history 4, 113, 194
Savonarola, Girolamo 106–7
Scaliger, Joseph Justus 37
Schiller, Friedrich 12, 106
Schleiermacher, Friedrich 79–81, 94,
      169, 197
Scott, Sir Walter 21, 24–5, 92, 99,
      107, 112
Scudéry, Madeleine de 18, 111
'Secret of England's Greatness, The'
      (the Bible) 32
secularism 7–17
secularization 4, 6–17, 190
Seeley, J. R. 139, 149, 152
Selby, Thomas G. 27, 97, 114, 149, 193
Selden, Thomas 69
Sergeant, John 72
Sermon on the Mount 102, 129
Shakespeare, William 22, 107, 111, 119
Sharpe, Samuel 166
Shaw, George Bernard vi, 154
Sheba 172
Simon, Richard 72, 75

232

Index

Simpson, James 70
Smith, Steven D. vi, 190
social mission 149
Somerville, Alexander 141
Sommerville, John 10
Solomon, King 172
Song of Songs 54–5, 179, 185
Sophocles 133
South Korea, religion in 15
Spencer, Herbert 3, 6, 11, 26, 97, 134, 192
Spinoza, Baruch 40–1, 72–3, 75, 94, 130, 190, 198
spirituality 197
Spurgeon, C. H. 106
Sri Lanka, religion in 15
Staël, Anne-Louise-Germaine Necker, Madame de 23
Stanley, A. P. 155–6
Stephen, James Fitzjames 2, 68, 168
Stephen, J. K. 162
Stephen, Leslie 96
Sterling, John 105
Sterne, Laurence 25–6
Stevenson, Robert Louis, 163, 187
Stillingfleet, Edward 70–1
story vi, 31, 195–6, 199
Strachey, Lytton, 135–6, 193
Strauss, David Friedrich 1, 79–80, 94, 139
Stubbs, William 140
sublime, the 28–9, 104, 119–22, 160–1, 181–6, 197

Taine, Hippolyte 140
Talmud 39, 42, 46, 54
Tate, Nahum 198
Taylor, Charles 28
Teilhard de Chardin 134
Temple, Frederick 82
Teresa, St, of Avila 109
Tertullian 51–2, 66, 103, 118, 120
textual issues 75–6, 80–1, 83–4, 157
Thirty-Nine Articles 32–4, 64, 68–9, 74, 84, 149
Thomas à Kempis 100, 104
Thurber, James 144
Tindal, Matthew 76–7, 82
Toland, John 75, 82
Tomalin, Claire 115
Torah 45–6
Toynbee, Arnold 156, 159

Treasure Island, see Stevenson, Robert Louis
Trench, R. C., Archbishop 96
Trent, Council of 62, 64, 74
Trevelyan, G. M. 146, 191
Trinity, doctrine of 48, 80, 83
Trollope, Anthony 20, 26
truth (in scripture) 35, 40
Turner, J. M. W. 104, 119
Tyndale, William 59, 187
Tyndall, John 30
Tyrrell, George 157–8

Ussher, Archbishop James 37–9, 50

van Buren, Paul 195
Vaughan Williams, Ralph 124
Venn, Henry 129
Vickers, Salley 196–7
Virgil 185–6
Voegelin, Eric 4–5
Voltaire, François-Marie Arouet 8, 11, 126
Voysey, Rev. Charles 157

Wain, John 121
Ward, Mary (Mrs Humphry Ward)
ix, 2, 21, 27, 30, 42, 55–6, 61, 79, 135–61, 191–2
The Case of Richard Meynell 138, 140, 142, 155, 157–9, 190–9
Daphne, or Marriage à la Mode 143, 148, 150
Eleanor 145
Eltham House 145, 147
Fenwick's Career 145, 147, 150
Helbeck of Bannisdale 151
The History of David Grieve 141
Marcella 150, 159
The Marriage of William Ashe 145–6
Robert Elsmere ix, 27, 30, 43, 135, 137–8, 140–1, 143–4, 149–54, 156, 158, 162, 168
Sir George Tressady 150, 160
Warner, Anna Bartlett 32
Warner, Susan Bogert 169
Watt, Ian 17–18
Weber, Max vi, 6, 12–13, 17, 29, 101, 152, 190
Wellhausen, Julius 46
Wesley, John 101

Index

West, Morris 193, 196
Westcott, B. F. 87
Westminster Confession of Faith 32, 68, 74, 84
Westminster Review 95, 97–8, 112
Whately, Richard 26–7
Whitehead, A. N. 103, 196
Whitehouse, Harvey 198
Wilde, Oscar 135, 142, 149
Williams, Rowland 68, 82, 151
Wilson, A. N. 192–3
Wilson, Bryan 7, 13
Wilson, H. B. 84
Wilson, Rev. S. L. 96, 114, 117, 149, 161, 198
Wilt, Judith 135

Wolfenbüttel fragments, *see* Reimarus
Women's National Anti-Suffrage League 144
Woolf, Virginia 147, 162, 193
Worden, Blair 10–11
Wordsworth, Christopher 83
Wordsworth, William 34, 99–101, 116, 119, 126, 153–5, 182
World's Fair (Chicago) 159
Würtemburg Confession 64
Wycliffe, John 56–9, 136
Wycliffite Bible 57, 59–60, 187

Young, Edward 22, 97, 100

Žižek, Slavoj 28